Dr. Alan R. Moritz and Forensic Pathology

Forensic science has become a mainstay of popular culture on television, in movies, books and podcasts. Dr. Alan R. Moritz (1899–1986) was a highly influential figure in the development of the field of forensic science as we know it today.

Dr. Alan R. Moritz and Forensic Pathology: Tales That Dead Men Tell, written by Dr. Moritz's journalist grandson Rob Moritz, recounts his life and career from personal papers and correspondence, interviews, newspaper accounts and other sources, including archived materials from Harvard Medical School, the Rockefeller Foundation, Case Western Reserve University and the University Hospitals of Cleveland. Chapters chronicle more than a half-century of groundbreaking research and high-profile investigations, including some of the 20th century's most infamous cases. This includes the assassination of President John F. Kennedy, the Sam Shepherd case, the Cocoanut Grove nightclub fire, the Attica prison riots and the Texas Tower sniper, as well as his contributions to the well-known Nutshell Studies of Unexplained Death. Dr. Moritz, the inspiration for the first on-screen forensic scientist, is credited with being one of the most prominent pioneers of the last century, helping to move forensic medicine from the political jurisdiction of untrained local coroners to a respected scientific discipline that fascinates the public.

The book also details Dr. Moritz's travels, during which he experienced some of society's darkest chapters. This includes an infamous lynching during the "Red Summer" of 1919, the rise of Nazi Germany and the degradation of apartheid in South Africa, all of which influenced and shaped his worldview. Highlights of Dr. Moritz's work, recounted in detail, include career stops at Case Western Reserve University in Cleveland and Harvard Medical School in Boston. Coverage details his most salient and well-known research—as well as insightful anecdotes and stories that demonstrate Dr. Moritz's character and the development and evolution of his scientific views over the years.

This book:

- Profiles the life of a well-known and impactful figure in the advancement of forensic pathology's public perception and practices in the United States.
- Provides background on Dr. Moritz's seminal work, the article "Classical Mistakes in Forensic Pathology."
- Is of interest to medical practitioners, history of science buffs and forensic practitioners interested in the early history and development of forensic pathology as a discipline.

Dr. Alan R. Moritz and Forensic Pathology fills in a missing chapter on the life, research and lasting legacy of Dr. Moritz, providing insight into the development of modern forensic pathology practice by examining the momentous contributions and character of one of its true pioneers.

Dr. Alan R. Moritz and Forensic Pathology

Tales That Dead Men Tell

Rob Moritz

CRC Press
Taylor & Francis Group
Boca Raton London New York

CRC Press is an imprint of the
Taylor & Francis Group, an **informa** business

Designed cover image: Center for the History of Medicine at Francis A. Countway Library, Harvard University

First edition published 2025

by CRC Press

2385 NW Executive Center Drive, Suite 320, Boca Raton FL 33431

and by CRC Press

4 Park Square, Milton Park, Abingdon, Oxon, OX14 4RN

CRC Press is an imprint of Taylor & Francis Group, LLC

ISBN: 9781032886121 (hbk)
ISBN: 9781032885988 (pbk)
ISBN: 9781003539186 (ebk)

DOI: 10.4324/9781003539186

Typeset in Sabon

by Deanta Global Publishing Services, Chennai, India

To my father, John Alan Moritz, who said, "Here, you're the journalist," each time he gave me a box of his father's papers. This labor of love is for you and the family.

And to my wife, Gwen. Thanks for being patient and impatient with me. Without your help and advice, this book would never have been completed.

Contents

The Author ix

Acknowledgments x

Introduction 1

Chapter 1   From Nebraska to the World   3

Chapter 2   College and Medical School   10

Chapter 3   Red Summer, 1919   15

Chapter 4   Cleveland   19

Chapter 5   Vienna   24

Chapter 6   Getting to Harvard   29

Chapter 7   Nazi Germany   46

Chapter 8   Harvard Years   51

Chapter 9   Burn Studies   70

Chapter 10   Cocoanut Grove   79

Chapter 11   "Death on a Silver Platter"   84

Chapter 12   Leaving Harvard   92

Chapter 13   Going Hollywood   102

Chapter 14   Back in Cleveland   115

Chapter 15   Family Mystery   122

Chapter 16   "Classical Mistakes"   126

Chapter 17   JFK   131

Chapter 18   The Moritz Formula   140

Chapter 19   Apartheid   145

Chapter 20   Of Myth and Legend   155

Chapter 21   Legacy   163

Appendix 1   167

Appendix 2   170

Appendix 3   171

Index   178

The Author

 **Rob Moritz** is a veteran journalist who reported on crime, government and politics for newspapers in Arkansas, Texas and Tennessee before teaching journalism at the University of Central Arkansas. The third of four sons born to a bauxite miner and a saint, he was born in Kingston, Jamaica, and spent much of his youth in the small South American country of Suriname and in Pittsburgh, Pennsylvania, before moving to Arkansas in high school. His wife, Gwen, is a journalist who spent much of her career as editor of *Arkansas Business*. They have two adult sons.

Acknowledgments

Special thanks to my honorary aunt Barbara Boardman Jones, who filled me in on family history and loaned me her copy of Joel Carlson's amazing book *No Neutral Ground*. Yes, I will return it. And to Bruce Goldfarb, author of *18 Tiny Deaths: The Untold Story of Frances Glessner Lee and the Invention of Modern Forensics*. Seeing my grandfather's picture on the dust cover and reading his book persuaded me that Dr. Moritz's story deserved a wider audience than just the family. Thanks also to my good friend Sonny Rhodes for helping in the editing and to Nathania Sawyer, friend and archivist, for scanning most of the pictures used in the book.

Introduction

I took a tumble from my bike and my left arm was really aching. Fortunately, a world-renowned medical doctor was visiting my parents' home near Little Rock, Arkansas.

"Granddad, could you take a look at my arm? I think it might be broken."

My grandmother laughed out loud. "He'd be able to tell better if you were dead."

Today forensic science is part of our popular culture—on television, movies, books, even podcasts. But there was a time when it was a new science, and the United States was behind the curve. My grandfather, Alan Moritz, was one of the pioneers who moved forensic medicine from the clumsy jurisdiction of untrained local coroners to a respected discipline that fascinates the public.

While I knew him very well as my grandfather—I was 25 when he died—only in the decades since his death have I developed a proper appreciation for his work. He has been referred to, melodramatically, as the Sherlock Holmes of forensic medicine, a comparison he would hate. My wife says he was more like Zelig, the Woody Allen character, because he cropped up as a witness to so many historic events—including some of the darkest chapters of the 20th century in the United States and elsewhere.

Alan Richards Moritz was born in Nebraska on Christmas Day 1899. Throughout his life, then, he was always the age of the year—19 in 1919, when he witnessed an infamous lynching in Omaha; 37 in 1937, when he was hired to establish the Department of Legal Medicine at Harvard Medical School; 86 when he died in 1986.

He and his brother John Richards Moritz (born 1905) were among the fortunate few young men from the Midwest who were able to attend college and medical school a century ago. John Moritz undertook a general medical practice, becoming the first year-round physician hired by Union Pacific Railroad in 1939 for its new resort at Sun Valley, Idaho, where the local hospital eventually carried the Moritz name. Dr. John Moritz treated Ernest Hemingway after he attempted suicide in April

DOI: 10.4324/9781003539186-1

1961 and was listed as an honorary pallbearer when the Nobel Prize laureate killed himself three months later.

Alan Moritz did something completely different. Originally planning a career in surgery, he was working in a pathology lab when he befriended a coroner in Cleveland, Ohio. Seeing the coroner was not sufficiently trained, he began assisting in autopsies and at least once kept a man from going to jail on murder charges. From that point, he was hooked on forensic pathology, and he made better training for local death investigators a lifelong mission. A timely recommendation led him to Harvard Medical School, which sent him to study in Europe—including Nazi Germany—as World War II loomed.

Alan Moritz produced more than 100 research papers, many of them groundbreaking for their scientific advances, as well as nine textbooks, some of which are still must-reads for students of forensic pathology. He conducted or participated in thousands of autopsies, including highly publicized cases like that of actor George Reeves, television's first Superman. Erle Stanley Gardner frequented Moritz's lectures at Harvard to glean ideas for his Perry Mason novels, and my grandfather was the inspiration for a character played by Bruce Bennett in the 1950 film noir *Mystery Street*. He was involved in one of the biggest crime stories of the mid-20th century, the Cleveland-area murder trial of Dr. Sam Sheppard. That high-profile case inspired the popular TV series and later Hollywood movie *The Fugitive*.

He was one of four prominent pathologists who were asked in the late 1960s to conduct an official review of the findings of the Warren Commission, which had investigated the assassination of President John Kennedy. He traveled to Apartheid-era South Africa to testify that government officials had tortured and killed a black dissident.

This biography is a tribute to Dr. Alan Moritz by a loving grandson who had begun a three-decade career in journalism shortly before he died. I have used all manner of sources, which are identified either in the text or in footnotes. I am able to quote Dr. Moritz directly on many topics thanks to letters he wrote, 11 pages of autobiographical notes he produced late in life and transcripts of three lengthy interviews he gave late in life. (One was conducted in Cleveland in 1980 by an interviewer identified only as "Bonnie.") I have tried to be factual and candid, as my journalistic training demands, but my affection for and pride in my granddad may creep in from time to time.

CHAPTER 1

From Nebraska to the World

Dr. Alan Moritz was months from his 70th birthday when, in the spring of 1969, he traveled to Pretoria to testify at an inquest into the death of a black dissident. James Lenkoe would never become a household name in the United States, but his death in police custody a few weeks earlier was pivotal in the hard-fought movement to abolish the racist policy of apartheid in South Africa.

And, in many ways, Lenkoe's death was the event for which my grandfather had been preparing for a half-century.

By 1969, his reputation was at its peak. He was past president of the American Academy of Forensic Science and had been instrumental in developing the certification system for medical examiners. The previous year he had been one of four medical luminaries who reviewed the autopsy evidence included in the Warren Commission's investigation of the Kennedy assassination at the request of US Attorney General Ramsey Clark.

But his preparation was more than just a résumé. Moritz had observed torture victims in Nazi-era Germany and knew the propensity of brutal regimes to dismiss inconvenient homicides as suicides. He had testified in an infamous electrocution case that is recognized as an early landmark in the human rights of Americans with disabilities.

Most pertinently, Moritz had conducted research on burns that is still unmatched well into the 21st century. A South African pathologist enlisted by the Lenkoe family's attorney thought a curious mark on James Lenkoe's toe looked suspiciously like a burn he had seen in a medical journal some years earlier. He located the article at a library. It had been written by Dr. Alan R. Moritz and published in 1947 in the *Journal of American Pathology*.

Dr. Moritz testified that Lenkoe had been tortured to death with electricity. The court concluded that he had hanged himself, a conclusion that Moritz found wholly inconsistent with the medical evidence. His

DOI: 10.4324/9781003539186-2

3

testimony did, however, help bring international attention to the travesty of apartheid. And while a flurry of news reports and even Congressional attention quickly faded back home, the American pathologist who spoke truth to power was not forgotten in South Africa.[1]

CHILDHOOD

The grueling 30-hour trip to Pretoria started in Cleveland with stops in New York and London, but it really commenced seven decades earlier in Hastings, Nebraska. That's where Alan Richards Moritz was born on Christmas Day in 1899.

His mother, Genevieve Richards Moritz, was born in Wisconsin to immigrants from Cornwall in southwestern England. His father, Richard Daniel Moritz, had emigrated to Nebraska from Germany as a child, and Alan grew up near his German-speaking grandparents, Carl (originally Karl) Frederick and Martha Maria Stahlhut Moritz.

Carl Moritz, born and raised in Germany, was a machinist directing the installation of modern machinery in paper factories in Denmark, Belgium and Germany. Martha made and sold house slippers. The couple had four sons and two daughters, all born in different places because Carl's work required frequent moves.

In 1867, their oldest child, Charles, had been apprenticed as a 12-year-old cabin boy on a German sailing ship. He worked on sailing vessels until he reached military age, which was 17. He did not want to spend 3 years in the Kaiser's army, so he wandered away from his ship when it was docked in New York City. He headed west, working for a while on a farm in Illinois. By 1880, he was married and farming cheap land that he had acquired from the railroad near Juniata, Nebraska.

Bertha, the second oldest, was 15 when she emigrated to the United States and took a job as a maid on the Illinois farm where Charles was working. She soon married and by 1880 was living on a farm in Ohio.

Son William was a journeyman locksmith who spent nearly a year in a Russian prison because he had lost his identification and travel papers. Upon his release, and fearing conscription into the German army, he obtained a 10-day passport to visit an imaginary cousin in England. From there, he stowed away on a freighter for Philadelphia.

With three children living in the United States and Charles sending letters urging his parents to do the same, Carl and Martha Moritz decided to make the leap. Carl cashed in a life insurance policy, and in early May 1880, Martha and her two youngest children, Robert Edward, 12, and Richard Daniel, 8, left Ruprechtsau, Germany. Their ship landed at Castle Garden, New York, and the three made their way to William's home in Philadelphia. Karl and Martha's second daughter, also named Martha, 16, stayed in Germany to keep house for her father, who continued working to further fund the relocation.

"My parents looked upon the separation of the family only as temporary for, with three less mouths to feed, Father hoped to accumulate wherewithal to follow us to America a few years later," Richard wrote years later in an autobiography distributed to the family.[2]

After visiting with William in Philadelphia, Martha and the two boys traveled to Nebraska and moved in with Charles, who had a farm about 6 miles outside of Juniata. The farm consisted of a two-room shack, a sod barn and a windlass well "on a bleak and barren prairie without a shrub or tree in sight as far as the eye could see," Richard wrote.

This was the punishing prairie life of Willa Cather's celebrated novels. (Decades later, in Red Cloud, the Moritz family would become friendly with her parents, Charles and Mary Virginia Cather, and their younger children.) During the cold winters, sunbaked cow dung was burned in the fireplace because wood was scarce. By the fall of 1880, when his mother and youngest brothers arrived, Charles Moritz had cows for milk and meat and a good corn harvest.

Young Robert and Richard worked on the farm in the spring, summer and fall and were paid $8 a month. During the winter months, they attended a country school. Finally, in 1885, Carl and daughter Martha arrived from Germany, and William arrived from Philadelphia and set up a machine shop in Hastings.

Robert and Richard both realized early that they didn't want to be farmers. After completing high school in Hastings, each enrolled in college. Robert started at Hastings College, transferred to the University of Chicago and would go on to earn a Ph.D. in mathematics at the University of Nebraska and another Ph.D. at the University of Strasbourg in France. He became a professor and head of the Department of Mathematics and Astronomy at the University of Washington in Seattle.

Richard first attended the University of Nebraska but after one year transferred to Peru (Nebraska) State Teachers College, where he was expelled for 2 weeks for organizing a football team. He eventually completed the coursework needed to become a schoolteacher. His first teaching job was in Prosser, Nebraska. He later earned a degree in education from Hastings College and worked as a school principal and administrator in several small school districts in Nebraska. He retired as dean of rural education service and summer school sessions at the University of Nebraska.

In 1895, while a school principal in Roseland, Nebraska, Richard Moritz met Genevieve Richards at a community event at the school. He described her as "a charming girl, who, after much persuasion, consented someday to share the not-too-promising prospects of a pedagogue."

Genevieve had been born in 1874 in Dodgeville, Wisconsin, to John Richards, a disabled miner and a store owner, and Amelia Richards, both immigrants from Cornwall. She was the fifth of seven children born before the Richardses moved to Nebraska in 1878. Four more siblings were born there. John Richards opened a store in Ayr, Nebraska, and later at Roseland in Adams County, to be close to the Kansas City and Omaha Railway, which was offering land to homesteaders. Eight of the Richards children eventually became schoolteachers in Adams County. Another daughter, Josephine, went on to teach art at Carnegie Tech in Pittsburgh, Pennsylvania.[3]

Richard and Genevieve married in December 1897, and Alan arrived 2 years later. John Richards Moritz, who would have a distinguished medical career of his own, was born in Blue Hill in 1905, and Amelia Genevieve was born in Red Cloud in 1909.

FIGURE 1.1   Alan Richards Moritz, age 3 in 1903, before his siblings John and Genevieve were born. (Moritz Family Collection)

As Richard predicted, teaching was not a lucrative profession. To help feed his young family, Richard relied on the skills he learned on the farm—raising vegetables, chickens and a cow or two. He was involved in several other money-making ventures later in life, including owning a drugstore in Beatrice, Nebraska, with his son-in-law.[4]

LIFE ON THE PRAIRIE

My grandfather would never forget the barren landscape of Nebraska or his happy childhood there. "It was extremely empty land, and the first houses and animal shelters were constructed of blocks of prairie grass and sod. The winters were cold and the summers were hot and life was difficult. However, life was good," Alan wrote years later.

> I do know that the prayer that preceded dinner on Thanksgiving and Christmas in the homes of my grandparents invariably thanked God for having brought them to this land of bounty and freedom. I know of the sense of pride that I have in my antecedents and the sense of obligation I have always felt to do as well with my life as they did with theirs.[5]

FIGURE 1.2   Genevieve and Richard Moritz, parents of Alan Moritz, in 1956. (Moritz Family Collection)

Some of those prayers would have been spoken in German, as Alan's paternal grandparents clung to the old language. Understanding German and speaking it serviceably would become vital to him in a few years.

Life on the Great Plains was dangerous, with fierce windstorms, bitterly cold winters, hot and dry summers and threatening wildlife—especially rattlesnakes. "As a child, my parents were very alert as to whether or not there was a snake around," Alan recalled later. "As early as I can remember anything, it's how excited everyone was if there was a snake."[6]

Undaunted, young Alan spent most of his time outdoors. He hunted and fished, and in 1912 he joined a 2-year-old organization called the Boy Scouts of America. He played tennis in high school, and he played clarinet in the Red Cloud school band. Musically inclined, he learned to play the piano well enough to earn extra money accompanying the action at silent movie theaters during high school and college.[7]

When Alan was about 12, his father determined that his eldest could benefit from a little responsibility. Richard rented a small vacant lot next to their home in Red Cloud for the boy to garden and raise chickens. His father helped Alan build a chicken coop, he said in 1980.

"I established a vegetable garden ... and sold vegetables to the neighbors and to my family," Alan said. "I had a couple dozen Leghorns, so I sold eggs to the neighbors and my family." He was allowed to keep his earnings.

On his 15th birthday, Alan received a set of carpentry tools—saw, wood planer, hammer, screwdrivers—and a wooden toolbox that his father had made to hold them. "Every tool had its place," he said.[8] And so it was that Alan, who would spend much of his working days conducting autopsies and researching injuries and death, spent his spare time gardening and woodworking. "I have an excellent garden site and a green thumb," he said years later.[9] His gardens were always colorful and immaculate, with lettuce, cucumbers, corn, tomatoes, broccoli, rhubarb, radishes, asparagus and brightly colored flowers. Late in life he also took up painting and completed several pieces, mostly of landscapes and Native Americans, that were framed and now hang in the homes of his son and grandchildren.[10]

His woodshop was a special place. "I have a shop well equipped with woodworking machinery and a good supply of walnut, cherry and oak boards that I have been saving for years," he said as he made plans for retirement. "I like woodworking and I like gardening, and until now I have had too little time for either of these interests. I expect soon to make up for lost time in these areas of activity."[11]

Alan finished high school in Red Cloud while his father was superintendent of schools there, and he enrolled at the University of Nebraska in Lincoln in the fall of 1916. While in college, he also helped scout venues for the Chautauqua Institution, an adult education movement based near Chautauqua Lake in New York. Chautauqua, which started in the 1870s, was very popular in rural areas of the country because it brought entertainment and culture—speakers, teachers, entertainers and musicians—to small towns and rural communities. His enthusiasm for Chautauqua events continued for the rest of his life.[12]

NOTES

1. Joel Carlson, *No Neutral Ground* (New York: Thomas Y. Crowell Company, 1973), 227–256; Alan R. Moritz, transcript of interview by someone identified only as "Bonnie," *Cleveland, Ohio,* 1980 (Moritz Family Collection).
2. Richard Daniel Moritz et al., *Moritz Family History and Genealogy* (Washington, DC: Moritz Family Collection, n.d.).
3. Ben J. Richards et al., *Richards Family History and Genealogy* (Washington, DC: Moritz Family Collection, n.d.).
4. Richard Daniel Moritz et al., *Moritz Family History and Genealogy* (Washington, DC: Moritz Family Collection, n.d.).
5. Alan R. Moritz, "Alan R. Moritz: Autobiographical Notes in Extension of Information Contained in Curriculum Vitae. Prepared at Request of Miss K., Archivist of the University Hospitals," Mid-1970s (Path015 Alan R. Moritz, MD, Papers, Stanley A. Ferguson Archives, University Hospitals of Cleveland).
6. Alan R. Moritz, transcript of interview by someone identified only as "Bonnie," *Cleveland, Ohio,* 1980 (Moritz Family Collection).
7. John A. Moritz, interview by Rob Moritz, August 15, 2020, Benton, Ark.
8. Alan R. Moritz, transcript of interview by someone identified only as "Bonnie," *Cleveland, Ohio,* 1980 (Moritz Family Collection).
9. "First Chief of Staff: Dr. Moritz' Interests Lead to World Authority in Pathology," *The Archway University Hospitals of Cleveland* 22, no. 11 (November 1970): 5, (Case Western Reserve Archives).
10. John A. Moritz, interview by Rob Moritz, August 15, 2020, Benton, Ark.
11. "First Chief of Staff: Dr. Moritz' Interests Lead to World Authority in Pathology," *The Archway University Hospitals of Cleveland* 22, no. 11 (November 1970): 5, (Case Western Reserve Archives).
12. John A. Moritz, interview by Rob Moritz, August 15, 2020, Benton, Ark.

CHAPTER 2

College and Medical School

Alan Moritz was 16 when he graduated from high school and enrolled in the pre-medicine program at the University of Nebraska at Lincoln. Becoming a physician was something he had thought about since he was 7 or 8, after a local physician made a house call to take care of his mother. The boy was impressed with Dr. Mitchell's knowledge and skill and with the help he delivered in a time of need.

Alan's mother was suffering from severe abdominal pain. His father was extremely worried, as was his grandmother, who had been summoned to the house. Unable to reach Dr. Mitchell by phone because the operator of the local telephone company had closed the switchboard for the night, Richard dispatched Alan to fetch Dr. Mitchell.

Dr. Mitchell was quickly able to make his mother comfortable, as well as to ease the concerns of both his father and grandmother. "Father was terrified and even my grandmother who lived nearby was worried," he said. "In retrospect, I suspect mother was having biliary colic"—a gallbladder attack.

After tending to Genevieve, Dr. Mitchell sat down at the kitchen table to have a cup of coffee. Alan was also in the kitchen but did not sit at the table with the grown-ups. The family physician soon turned to the young boy. "He asked me what I was going to do when I grew up. I said I could not think of anything more rewarding than to become a doctor like him."

Moritz completed his undergraduate pre-med requirements in 2 years. In the ordinary course, he would begin medical school in Omaha in the fall of 1918, but that timeline was derailed because of the war in Europe.

The Great War had been raging since 1914, and the United States joined with its allies in April 1916. So, while Moritz was in college, he saw many friends and acquaintances leaving for basic training and ultimately to fight overseas. The wave of patriotism and desire to defend the United States and its way of life was everywhere, and Moritz's generation responded.[1] "Any able-bodied male who was unmarried seemed

DOI: 10.4324/9781003539186-3

to be tainted with traitorism if he wasn't either in the armed services or planning to be," Moritz said.

Deferring military service for college when he was underage was one thing, but 18-year-old Moritz was "uncomfortable" postponing service by going directly from college to medical school. A sergeant in ROTC while in college, Moritz volunteered for the Army in the summer of 1918 and was accepted into officer's training at Camp Hancock in Georgia.[2] He was ordered to report to the West Door of Grant Memorial Hall at the University of Nebraska in Lincoln at 8:30 a.m. on October 21. "From and after the day and hour just named you will be a soldier in the military service of the United States," said the order of induction.[3]

Exactly 3 weeks after he was inducted, on November 11, "the war to end all wars" was over. "I promptly applied for and was granted discharge from the army and immediately applied for late admission to medical school," my grandfather said. Pvt. Moritz was officially discharged from the Army on Dec. 17, 8 days before his 19th birthday.

Despite missing the first 8 weeks of classes, including histology, embryology and biochemistry, he was allowed to enroll at the University of Nebraska Medical School in Omaha for the fall semester. Several medical school faculty members, including Dr. Charles Poynter, the anatomy professor who ran the admissions office, doubted Moritz could make up the lost time and complete his first year successfully.

"I felt sure I could do it and [Poynter] agreed to let me try." Moritz managed "to make up the biochemistry and gross anatomy creditably and to correct my other deficiencies by going to summer school."

Entering medical school deep into the semester "was one of several lucky breaks that have been very important in the course of my professional career," Moritz said in hindsight. His determination and academic accomplishment impressed the medical school faculty and especially Poynter, who "took a friendly interest [in me] that probably would not otherwise have been the case."

Poynter became his mentor and a major influence on Moritz's decision to go into the academic and research side of medicine rather than becoming a "general practitioner in some county seat town in Central Nebraska."[4]

Following the fall semester, Poynter offered Moritz a way to make up for missing the entire course in embryology. Poynter said six students had failed the course in the fall and would be taking it again in the summer, and he suggested that Moritz "coach" them. "You'll have to work like hell because you'll have to learn the day before what you are going to coach them on the next day," he recalled Poynter telling him. "So, I coached six in embryology. I must say that I did some getting ready for it during weekends and other odd times and got away with it." All six students passed the course, and Moritz received credit as well.

FIGURE 2.1   Alan Moritz, right, and his younger brother John would both have distinguished but very different medical careers. (Moritz Family Collection)

Near the end of his first year of medical school, Moritz considered transferring. He applied to and was accepted by Harvard Medical School in Boston, but he decided to stay at Nebraska after Poynter offered him an assistantship and a $250 stipend to teach an anatomy class in his second year.[5] At the end of his second year, Poynter asked Moritz if he wanted to step away from the medical school program for a year and assist him in research. Moritz would receive a master's degree after successfully completing the one-year assignment. "I was so flattered that I accepted immediately although I hadn't the foggiest idea of what was involved."

During that year, Moritz worked directly with Poynter. He spent time in the medical school library and learned how to properly conduct scientific research, such as "what it meant to plan controls for evaluating the significance of experimental observations."

He and Poynter conducted a great deal of research that year and during his remaining time in medical school.[6] In 1923, the year Moritz completed medical school, the two published "The Effects of Ultraviolet Light on Pond Snails" in the *Journal of Experimental Zoology*. It was the first of more than 100 scholarly articles Moritz would write or co-write for national and international research publications and medical journals during his career.[7]

More than 50 years after he completed medical school, Moritz cringed at the quality of his education. "I look back on medical education, beginning in 1918 and for me extending to 1923, [and] I marvel at how people thought they were prepared for the practice of medicine," he said in 1976. Many graduates at that time did not go on to residencies, internships or further hospital training. They either started working with another doctor or "simply went to a town where there was no doctor, set up an office, accumulated supplies, and started to practice medicine."

As for the courses themselves—he specifically mentioned biochemistry, anatomy and physiology—"I don't know how they could have been presented more poorly; it may have been the times." While some of the concerns he raised about his medical education were probably valid, he did admit during the 1976 interview that he skipped out on patient care as often as possible. "If there was ever a chance to do something in the laboratory rather than in the ward, I chose the former with a certain amount of skillful arranging."

"I even avoided participating in the delivery of a single baby," he said.[8]

NOTES

1. Alan R. Moritz, "Alan R. Moritz: Autobiography Notes in Extension of Information Contained in Curriculum Vitae. Prepared at Request of Miss K., Archivist of the University Hospitals," mid-1970s (Path015 Alan R. Moritz, MD, Papers, Stanley A. Ferguson Archives, University Hospitals of Cleveland).
2. Alan R. Moritz, transcript of interview by Eugenia Kucherenko, *University Hospitals, Cleveland, Ohio*, 1976 (Path015 Alan R. Moritz, MD, Papers, Stanley A. Ferguson Archives, University Hospitals of Cleveland).
3. United States Army, Order of Induction into Military of the United States, Alan R. Moritz, October 21, 1918 (Moritz Family Collection).
4. Alan R. Moritz, transcript of interview by someone identified only as "Bonnie," *Cleveland, Ohio*, 1980 (Moritz Family Collection).

5. Alan R. Moritz, "Alan R. Moritz: Autobiography Notes in Extension of Information Contained in Curriculum Vitae. Prepared at Request of Miss K., Archivist of the University Hospitals," mid-1970s (Path015 Alan R. Moritz, MD, Papers, Stanley A. Ferguson Archives, University Hospitals of Cleveland). .

6. Alan R. Moritz, Transcript of interview by someone identified only as "Bonnie," *Cleveland, Ohio*, 1980 (Moritz Family Collection).

7. "Biographical Materials On: Alan Richards Moritz," University Hospitals, Cleveland, Ohio (Path015 Alan R. Moritz, MD, Papers, Stanley A. Ferguson Archives, University Hospitals of Cleveland).

8. Alan R. Moritz, transcript of interview by Eugenia Kucherenko, *University Hospitals, Cleveland, Ohio,* 1976 (Path015 Alan R. Moritz, MD, Papers, Stanley A. Ferguson Archives, University Hospitals of Cleveland).

CHAPTER 3

Red Summer, 1919

In September 1919, during his second year of medical school in Omaha, Alan Moritz and several fellow students witnessed violence and racism at its worst, the murder of an innocent black man and the lynching of another black man who had been accused of raping a white woman. The episode haunted him. Late in life, while presenting a review at a book club meeting, he lost his train of thought and told the group about the lynching he witnessed in his youth.[1]

The summer and fall of 1919 would come to be known as the Red Summer. The Omaha race riot was one of more than 40 such incidents of racial violence across the country that left hundreds dead. Historians point to the return from Europe of American troops as a precipitating factor, especially as black soldiers expected their equal service to their country to be rewarded with equal opportunity. The Omaha riot seems also to have been motivated by local political rivalries in which African Americans were collateral damage.

"It impressed me a great deal how thin a veneer of civilization we have and how easily it can be stripped off, exposing the animal in man," Moritz said years later. "I think that kind of thing can happen anywhere if you get a mob going."

As many as 20,000 people are believed to have witnessed the lynching of accused rapist Will Brown on the evening of September 18, 1919, including 14-year-old Henry Fonda, the future Academy Award-winning actor who grew up in Omaha, then a city of almost 200,000. He, too, would find the murder unforgettable.[2]

Six decades later, Moritz would describe his movements and the scene in detail—although his memories did not always jibe with other historical accounts. He recalled that he and his classmates were on the medical school campus at 42nd and Farnam streets when they heard about "a riot downtown and a lot of shooting." With the curiosity and confidence of youth, the medical students boarded a streetcar at 42nd to head east on Farnam toward the courthouse, which had been built at 17th and Farnam in 1912. The streetcar was unable to go any

DOI: 10.4324/9781003539186-4

farther east than 24th because of the crowds. Moritz and his friends got off to walk the remaining few blocks.

On the streetcar with him was a black man whom Moritz recognized as maître d' of the dining room at the Blackstone Hotel at 36th and Farnam, then a fashionable new venue. "We got off, and he did too. And being a Negro, he probably was just going to cross the street at 24th and get a streetcar going north or south on 24th because the Negro residential area was a little north of the streetcar stop," Moritz recounted.

As they climbed off the streetcar, Moritz saw a group of white people walking north on 24th—people he identified as being from the "very tough area" of south Omaha. "We had no more than crossed the street, which would have taken this Negro to where he would wait for a streetcar going north on 24th, when someone pushed this Negro off into the street."

Moritz said he and his friends "watched as someone else shot [the maître d'] through the chest with a revolver." The black man fell in the street and "two or three other people came up and everybody took a shot at his body," Moritz said. "Well, this was our introduction to the riot. This all happened within 10 feet of where we were standing."

Moritz said he and his friends "just stopped to see what the devil was going on." The shooting death of the black maître d' who stepped off a streetcar on 24th Street is not mentioned in any contemporary news accounts of the Omaha riot, but it can't be dismissed because the deaths of African Americans were routinely underreported in accounts of Red Summer uprisings.

The medical students, undaunted by what they had just seen, continued walking toward the courthouse between 17th and 18th on Farnam, where Moritz saw "a thousand people milling around"—undoubtedly a gross underestimate of the crowd. They saw a group of men lift up a boy of 12 or 14 so he could see into a window on the first floor of the courthouse. Someone then threw a couple of bricks through the window, and the boy was handed a gasoline can that he then tossed into the courthouse. Someone else lit a wad of cloth and tossed it through the broken window.

While the boy was still peering through the broken window, "a great flash of fire came back and just surrounded this kid, who was still at a height," Moritz said. "His clothing caught on fire and some people took off their coats" to put out the flames on the boy, who was then carried away.

While that was happening, police officers "on a railing several stories up in the courthouse" began shooting into the crowd. People on the ground began returning fire.

"I heard a zing go by my head which was a ricocheted bullet that hit the [ground] then bounced up, so I promptly got out of there," Moritz said. Finally recognizing the danger of the mob even to privileged young white men, the group went across the street and watched the events from the veranda of a bank building.

They saw Edward P. Smith, a moral reformer who had been elected mayor the previous year, arrive on horseback with a group of police officers. The mayor, who tried to speak to the crowd and stop the rioting, was pulled from his horse and injured in the melee.[3]

From his vantage point about 30 yards away, my grandfather saw rioters disarm the police officers with the mayor, and "someone else stepped up and just cracked [the mayor] across the face a couple of times. Well, he sort of wilted and was dragged without being further damaged." Other historical accounts say a rope was placed around the mayor's neck and he was strung up for a time before someone cut him down.

Moritz said most in the crowd appeared to be from the south side of Omaha, and "a group of hoodlums that were there to make as much trouble as possible" had apparently organized the riot. He added that there was "great dissatisfaction on the part of this criminal group in south Omaha over the reform mayor that had been elected and they were out to do him as much damage as possible." Tom Dennison, a political opponent of Mayor Smith, would be blamed for inciting the riot in an effort to discredit the mayor.

When firefighters arrived to deal with the arson on the first floor of the courthouse, the crowd "simply took over the fire trucks, put up ladders to a ledge that let them now get over the police and access the jail," Moritz said.

Rioters eventually forced the rape suspect, Will Brown, down the ladder to the roof of a fire truck. There, Moritz said, they

> stripped his clothes off and mutilated him in a fashion you might imagine—shot him and got him off the fire truck and down on the pavement, where they tied a rope around his neck and dragged him over to one of the stanchions that hold the streetcar wires. They threw the rope over a wire and pulled him up on the stanchion.

Moritz said Brown was shot "hundreds of times" before his body was lowered to the ground. My grandfather described seeing dozens of men and women grab the rope and drag Brown's body around the courthouse.

Moritz and the other medical students then headed back to their quarters, so they may have been gone when Brown's body was set on fire. Members of the white mob proudly posed for photos with the charred corpse—including men in overalls, men in suits and ties, and at least one smiling woman.

Henry Fonda observed the mob from his father's business, which overlooked the courthouse square. "It was the most horrendous sight I'd ever seen," he said in a 1975 BBC interview. "My hands were wet, there were tears in my eyes. All I could think of was that young black man dangling at the end of a rope."[4]

NOTES

1. Unless noted, information for this chapter is from Alan R. Moritz, transcript of interview by someone identified only as "Bonnie," *Cleveland, Ohio,* 1980 (Moritz Family Collection).
2. "A Horrible Lynching", *NebraskaStudies.org*, accessed July 9, 2024, https://www.nebraskastudies.org/en/1900-1924/racial -tensions/a-horrible-lynching/; Orville D. Menard, "Lest We Forget: The Lynching of Will Brown, Omaha's 1919 Race Riot," *HistoryofNebraska.gov.*, accessed July 9, 2024, https://history .nebraska.gov/lest-we-forget-the-lynching-of-will-brown-omahas -1919-race-riot/.
3. Orville D. Menard, "Lest We Forget: The Lynching of Will Brown, Omaha's 1919 Race Riot," *HistoryofNebraska.gov.*, accessed July 9, 2024, https://history.nebraska.gov/lest-we-forget-the-lynching -of-will-brown-omahas-1919-race-riot/.
4. Bayete Ross Smith, "How A White Mob Lynched a Black Man, Destroyed a City – And Got Away With It," *The Guardian*, July 9, 2021, America's Black Holocaust Museum, accessed July 9, 2024, https://www.abhmuseum.org/how-a-white-mob-lynched-a-black -man-destroyed-a-city-and-got-away-with-it/.

CHAPTER 4

Cleveland

On the advice of Dr. Poynter, Moritz applied for and was accepted into an internship at Lakeside Hospital in Cleveland, Ohio. "I still intended to prepare for clinical practice, but not for general practice," he said. "We decided, Dr. Poynter and I, that I would apply for a rotating internship at Lakeside with the intention of preparing for residency training on Dr. [George Washington] Crile's surgical service the following year." Crile, by then a renowned surgeon, had less than 20 years earlier become the first to successfully use a blood transfusion during surgery.[1]

During the 1923–1924 academic year, he interned in three separate disciplines at Lakeside Hospital. The first rotation with chronic illnesses was under the supervision of Dr. Charles Franklin Hoover in Ward H, which held about 25 patients. The building was near railroad tracks and would shake when a train carrying coal or some other ore sped by. Black soot would settle on the bedside tables if the windows were left open.

The work and living conditions were difficult, as was the harsh and gloomy winter on the shore of Lake Erie. Moritz initially had reservations about his decision.

He said:

> The grime, the interminable moaning of the fog horn, the rats so frequently encountered in the morgue and the laboratory buildings behind the hospital; the many gray, sunless weeks that passed between November and March; and the ward filled largely with chronically ill patients for whom little could be done combined to make me wonder if I hadn't made a mistake in leaving the spotless new University Hospital and the good air and sunny days that I had left behind in Nebraska.

He was not, however, lonely. Quick friendships developed with his colleagues, about half from the Western Reserve Medical School. "We ate together at the same time in the same dining room, which was immediately adjacent to a large reading/game room which had a piano, pool table, many comfortable chairs and a well-filled bookcase," Moritz

DOI: 10.4324/9781003539186-5

FIGURE 4.1   Lakeside Hospital in Cleveland, Ohio, where Dr. Alan Moritz began his medical career as an intern in 1923 and where he met his future wife, Velma Boardman, a head nurse. (Courtesy of the Stanley Ferguson Archives of University Hospitals of Cleveland)

recalled. Besides the interns, others at Lakeside included a purchasing agent, bookkeeper, plant engineer and dietitians.

The kitchen was open to the staff in the evenings, and they had free access to coffee, eggs, sandwiches and cereal. The evening meals were vital because the interns were otherwise provided only board and laundry, and their monthly stipends started at $20 with an annual increase to a maximum of $50.

CRILE AND KARSNER

His second rotation was in surgery under Dr. Crile, something he very much looked forward to. But it didn't take long for Moritz to question surgery as a career path—and to realize that Crile was as much a showman as a skilled surgeon.

"There was no question that the surgeon frequently saved life and restored disturbed function," he said. "There was also no question ... that a good deal of unjustified surgery was undertaken, sometimes with fatal or disabling results." While Crile was at the top of his field at that time, some things he did unsettled Moritz.

> It wasn't unusual for him to remove a dozen thyroids in a day. His cases were worked up at his clinic rather than at the hospital, and the hospital chart rarely contained the kind of information that would justify the diagnosis that brought the patient to the operating room.

Crile took pride in the speed with which he could perform a thyroidectomy—"and the bigger the audience of visiting surgeons the more rapidly he worked," Moritz said. If there was an exceptionally large group watching, "we knew he would spend the afternoon" performing surgeries.

The last rotation of that year was in pathology, which Moritz thoroughly enjoyed and eventually made his life's work. "To be sure, there was little opportunity to feel that you were helping sick people, but there was virtually unlimited opportunity to learn more about the causes and courses of disease," he said. Notably, he was "intrigued by certain problems in the metabolism of calcium."

So at the end of the academic year, Moritz faced a decision. "By now, I was not only less certain that I wanted to learn surgery under Dr. Crile, but I was sure that I would like to learn more pathology before I had any clinical training." He discussed his dilemma with Crile, "who had no objection to my taking a year of pathology before joining his team at the Clinic."

After discussing his reservations about surgery as a specialty and his desire to continue working in pathology with Dr. Howard Karsner, head of the pathology department at Western Reserve, Moritz was named a Hannah Research Fellow in the department. This essentially ended his chance to enter surgical training under Crile. As a research fellow in the pathology department from 1924 to 1926, he worked closely with Dr. Otto Saphir, a pathologist from Vienna, and Dr. Harry Goldblatt, who had recently returned from a 2-year Beit Fellowship conducting research in physiology and nutrition at the University of London. Karsner and Goldblatt would be major influences on Moritz's future as a pathologist.

One of the highlights of his 2 years in the Western Reserve pathology department was assisting Goldblatt in a study of the roles of vitamins A and D in the production of rickets and xerophthalmia in rabbits. In June 1925, he and Goldblatt co-authored a research article in the *Journal of Experimental Medicine* called "Experimental Rickets in Rabbits."

"That was probably the most useful educational experience I've ever had, from the standpoint of what I was shooting at, the two years of very close association with Goldblatt," he said.

Karsner, on the other hand, could be intimidating and overly critical of young residents and young doctors. Decades later, Moritz would recall giving a lecture about a liver that didn't meet with Karsner's approval.

"This was the liver of a person who had had [their] gallbladder removed some years before. And the duct taking bile from the gallbladder down into the duodenum was as big around my thumb. And I said, in demonstrating it, that this was a good example of the adaptation of an organ or structure to altered function. There no longer being a gallbladder, this duct had enlarged almost to gallbladder size and was serving the function of the gallbladder no longer there."

FIGURE 4.2   Dr. Alan Moritz, front right, with his mentor, Dr. Howard Karsner, center, and colleague Dr. Harry Goldblatt, front left, and other staff from the Western Reserve Department of Pathology. (Courtesy of the Stanley Ferguson Archives of University Hospitals of Cleveland)

At that point in the lecture, Karsner said, "Oh, bunk."

"Well, there were about 80 people in the auditorium, and I had a certain amount of prestige to maintain if I could," Moritz said. Moritz didn't immediately respond to Karsner's heckling. But after the lecture, he hunted up an issue of the *New England Journal of Medicine* "that had a very good article in it which included a review of the common duct's adaptation to the removal of the gallbladder." The article showed that the "dilated common duct did discharge its bile in reference to the digestive cycle just as the gallbladder used to."

Moritz took the article to Karsner's office and handed it to him without comment. About 30 minutes later, Karsner apologized.

And a week later, while Moritz was presenting another lecture to the same group of residents, Karsner apologized publicly. "The residents

FIGURE 4.3 Western Reserve University Institute of Pathology building, which opened in 1931. (Courtesy of the Stanley Ferguson Archives of University Hospitals of Cleveland)

gasped because this was certainly out of character," Moritz said. "As cruel as he was to students, he also was fair to students."

Karsner died in 1970 at the age of 91, and *The American Journal of Pathology* published a tribute to him in January 1971. The article was written by Alan Moritz.[2]

NOTES

1. Unless noted, information for this chapter is from Alan R. Moritz, transcript of interview by someone identified only as "Bonnie," *Cleveland, Ohio,* 1980 (Moritz Family Collection).
2. Alan R. Moritz, "Howard T. Karsner, MD 1879–1970," *The American Journal of Pathology* 62, no. 1 (January 1971): 3–5, (Case Western Reserve Archives)

CHAPTER 5

Vienna

By 1926, Moritz had met his future wife, Velma Boardman, a head nurse at Lakeside Hospital in Cleveland, and he was enjoying working in the pathology department at Western Reserve as a research fellow and instructor. The young pathologist, however, also knew that he needed more specialized training if wanted to further his career as a professor and researcher and to hone his lab skills. One popular way to do that was to study at a prominent institute in Europe. In fact, the two pathologists he most admired and worked closest with, Karsner and Goldblatt, had both studied abroad early in their careers and encouraged him to do the same.[1]

While marriage appeared to be on the horizon, Moritz heeded the advice of his mentors. He decided to spend a year studying under Dr. Jakob Erdheim at Vienna's city hospital. After borrowing $2,000 from his parents, he left Western Reserve in the summer of 1926, taking a train to New York and then a ship to France. He spent time in Hamburg, Berlin and Dresden before arriving in Vienna on July 25.

Erdheim was best known for his research on pituitary tumors, the parathyroid gland, bone disorders and the cartilage system. He also was an expert in calcium metabolism, one of the subjects Moritz had researched with Goldblatt.[2]

Moritz "spent the next year in Vienna doing research that was not experimental, but research of a kind that could best be done under a professor as Erdheim of Vienna, who contributed a great deal to the knowledge of the disease, in part by his vast experience and in part by his superb intellect," he recalled.

The two semesters in Vienna were most challenging academically and emotionally, Moritz revealed in letters to his family back in Nebraska. Most days he worked from dawn until dusk at the city hospital, conducting autopsies in the morning and attending Erdheim's lectures—in German, naturally—in the afternoon and evening. When away from the hospital, he didn't know anyone, rarely spoke English and longed for his loved ones in Nebraska and Cleveland.

DOI: 10.4324/9781003539186-6

FIGURE 5.1   Velma Boardman, the young nurse who would marry Alan Moritz in 1927. (Moritz Family Collection)

Moritz had grown up with what he thought was a solid foundation in the German language. His Wisconsin-born mother did not speak German, so it was not spoken in their home, but he regularly conversed with his paternal grandparents in German, and he took a German course in college. In Vienna, he became acutely aware of his linguistic limitations. He constantly worried about his ability to speak the language well enough to not embarrass himself and to understand it well enough to grasp the important points in Erdheim's lectures. All his classwork was in German.

"I had to write my protocols in German," he remembered, and that included a final research paper that was 140 pages long. He received periodic lessons from his landlord's wife to improve his reading and comprehension. The landlord and his wife, the parents of his Western Reserve colleague Dr. Otto Saphir, lived on the second floor of a six-story building in an area of Vienna known as Prater. Moritz lived in a small apartment on the top floor. He walked to a nearby trolley stop and rode a trolley to the hospital. During the bitter and windy winter, he moved to an apartment closer to the hospital.

Moritz promptly determined that Erdheim's reputation as one of the leading pathologists in the world was well deserved. "That certainly was my introduction to real hard work, because Erdheim was a workaholic fellow," he said years later. The professor, in fact, rarely left the hospital because he lived in the same building as his laboratory.

"Professor Erdheim is a tall, enthusiastic bachelor, very eccentric, but very cordial and an excellent teacher," Moritz wrote in an August 1926 letter to his parents. A typical schedule for Monday, Wednesday and Friday had Moritz getting to work by 8 a.m. and conducting autopsies and collecting specimens that were to be used in lectures by Erdheim. After a lunch break, he then attended a 2 p.m. lecture on microscopic pathology by Erdheim. That lecture would continue until 7:30 or 8 p.m., with perhaps a 30-minute break. "Then dinner and my German lesson from 8:30 to 9:30 or 9 or 10, depending on how much time I spent on dinner." Bedtime was 11 p.m.

"Never before have I ever worked as diligently as I did that year," he said years later.

While gathering and preparing specimens for the morning lectures, Moritz was given some discretion on which specimens he collected, but his work was always critiqued by Erdheim. From a letter to his parents in October 1926:

> Friday evening I took my first series of findings to the Professor, all written up in German and I certainly had sweat blood over them. He was very nice—said he was surprised and very pleased and generally said nice things. That cheered me up a lot because it's an awfully tough job. I haven't had any training whatsoever in Histopathology and least of all Bone pathology and then to be given a specimen from a rare disease that is a controversial point among those that have seen it and make a detailed and analytical study of it and write the findings in German is an undertaking. You don't have any idea how limited you are in a language until you try to write descriptions and analytical composition. I've almost worn out my dictionary and grammar too. I hope it gets easier—it's too hard work for my liking.

In another letter, he said what he was "seeing and doing are beyond my most optimistic expectations" and that Erdheim

> has been fine to me and every day he assigns me enough work to keep me busy for a week if I would do it all. Things that have always been just names to me are now realities and if I can only remember a part of what I am seeing and hearing I will be delighted—and wise.

When he was not working, Moritz was lonely for his family and also for his girlfriend. Velma is only mentioned a few times in his letters to his parents, including one where he tells them that she mailed him a Christmas gift. On the weekends, when not catching up on work at the hospital, Moritz loved to walk Vienna's historic Ringstrasse, where he could see the Imperial Palace, various museums and the Vienna Opera. The Prater, a large park where the 1837 World Exhibition was held, was also a favorite.

The letters he received from his family were most important to him during that year. Not only were they from loved ones, but they were in English. "Every once in a while I feel as tho I would blow up," he wrote. "I can express so little of what I think to anyone because of my limited German and to go four or five days without speaking English raises my mental pressure to the breaking point." He enjoyed some relief when Dr. Karsner and his wife traveled from Cleveland to Vienna for a visit.

Professor Erdheim, however, enjoyed no activity other than work, and he expected similar devotion from his students. When Moritz tried to escape the building before 9 p.m., Erdheim would come out of his laboratory and ask, "Mr. Moritz, are you ill?" Frequently, however, Erdheim did invite the young pathologist into the laboratory to look over his work. "I never left his laboratory without new insight into the complexities of pathology."[3]

Despite his complaints of overwork, Moritz documented some pleasure trips. He went kayaking in the Danube, rode a bicycle and hiked in the nearby countryside. He also learned to ski. During one ski trip, he and some co-workers went to the Rax Alps, "which is a high mountainous plateau about 5,000 feet above Vienna." In a letter to his parents, dated January 17, 1927, he described his adventure. "This is a Monday morning and I'm so stiff from yesterday skiing that it's hard to settle down to work," he wrote.

His letters also included observations about post-World War I Europe. In one, he discussed his new appreciation for the people of Austria and the surrounding region, many of whom he described as "poor." He reasoned that the city's struggling economy, and that of Austria as a whole, was caused by sanctions leveled against the country at the end of World War I.

From a July 1926 letter to his family:

> The streets are quiet and the stores not busy. One sees many beggars, many prostitutes and many people that appear to be actually hungry. I feel awfully sorry for Austria. She is a head without a body. Italy took her harbors and her cash [;] Cheskoslovenska and Hungary [her] farmlands [;] and Austria is left with a small area of semi arable land with a city of 2,000,000 people with no outlet. The tolls exacted by

> her neighbors even to ship goods thru them are so enormous that the industry here is stifled. That is obviously due to the dishonesty and dishonor of Italy and to the Versailles treaty.

Despite the economic hardships suffered by the city and its residents, Moritz said the people of Vienna are "quite wonderful—happy, hospitable and certainly most kind to strangers." He said that a

> policeman will walk a block or a street conductor will get off his car to give you directions. I never saw anything like it. They thank you, apologize and bless you on every occasion. Needless to say I am in love with this city already and I know I'll enjoy the year.

In mid-June 1927, he left Vienna and spent several days in Rome, Paris and London before boarding a ship for the journey back to Cleveland. He left one thing behind. His 140-page research paper, on the effects of neurosyphilis on bone joints, was published in *Virchows Archiv,* the official journal of the European Society of Pathology, in 1928. "I wonder if as many as 100 people have ever been sufficiently interested in the subject to read it," he said years later.

NOTES

1. Unless noted, information for this chapter is from 34 letters Alan R. Moritz wrote and sent to friends and family in the United States while studying in Vienna in 1926–1927 (Moritz Family Collection); Alan R. Moritz, transcript of interview by someone identified only as "Bonnie," *Cleveland, Ohio,* 1980 (Moritz Family Collection).
2. J. M. Pascual et al., "Jakob Erdheim (1874–1937): Father of Hypophyseal-Duct Tumors (Craniopharyngiomas)," *Virchows Archiv* 467 (2015): 459–469, accessed July 17, 2024, https://doi-org .ucark.idm.oclc.org/10.1007/s00428-015-1798-4 ; Alan R. Moritz, transcript of interview by someone identified only as "Bonnie," *Cleveland, Ohio,* 1980 (Moritz Family Collection).
3. "Focus on Alan R. Moritz, M.D.," *Roche Medical Image,* April 1967, 15.

CHAPTER 6

Getting to Harvard

When Dr. Moritz returned to Cleveland in the fall of 1927 following his year in Vienna, he went to work as a resident in pathology at Lakeside Hospital, where he also was the chief pathologist. The education he received from Erdheim proved invaluable for his new job because the only other person in Lakeside Hospital's lab was an immunologist. Moritz had to do the biochemistry and microbiology work, along with some immunology and the necessary autopsies.[1]

In December, the month he turned 28, Alan Moritz married Velma Boardman.

Lakeside Hospital in downtown Cleveland was spitting distance from the Cuyahoga County morgue, which had been built in 1896. The morgue, run by an elected coroner, was located between two saloons, which were popular hangouts for politicians and the powerful because they were just a couple of blocks away from city hall and the courthouse.

To Oliver Schroeder, a law professor at Western Reserve University who would work with Moritz to create the school's Law-Medicine Center in the early 1950s, the Cuyahoga County morgue in the early 20th century epitomized the inadequate and highly politicized coroner system that existed across the United States. Politicians and businesspeople often stopped by the morgue, before or after visiting one of the saloons, to talk to the coroner. The morgue itself was understaffed and ill-equipped—it had a typewriter but no microscope—to handle death investigations.[2]

For years, the coroner, a physician with little training in pathology or death investigations, had regularly sought help on difficult cases from the pathologist at Lakeside Hospital. When Moritz was named the hospital's pathologist, the coroner continued to seek input. When the morgue received a case that "he thought might get in the newspapers, which always meant trouble, he called me," Moritz said. Karsner, the head of pathology, had "no respect" for the coroner, Moritz said, and was not a fan of offering assistance. Moritz, however, embraced the opportunity, not only because he found the work interesting, but because he worried that, without his help, errors would occur and justice might be denied.[3]

DOI: 10.4324/9781003539186-7

Moritz's unofficial role advising the coroner—and seeing first-hand that the coroner was often in over his head—played a major role in his being hired as the first director of the Department of Legal Medicine at Harvard Medical School. The experience would also spark a lifelong mission to reform coroners' offices across the country.

One of the first cases in which the coroner enlisted Moritz's help involved a police officer who was accused of beating a man to death in the jail. The dead man's face "was pretty badly bumped—he had broken teeth and a lump on his scalp," Moritz recalled years later. "Without any further ado, the coroner had decided that he was a victim of assault" because the dead man, who had been drunk when he arrived at the jail, had no visible injuries when booked on charges of disorderly conduct and resisting arrest.

While the coroner's conclusion appeared reasonable—police had said the man had struggled while being arrested and the only person who had access to him in jail was a police officer—Moritz decided to conduct an autopsy just to be sure. What he discovered refuted the coroner's initial findings and ultimately kept an innocent police officer from being charged with homicide.

The man "had a congenital weakening of one of the larger arteries in his skull nourishing his brain, and looking back into his history he had trouble before," Moritz said.

> He had had several attacks of very severe headaches and vomiting and loss of consciousness because this artery was deceased, and every once in a while would weaken enough to let blood escape from it and increase the intra-cranial pressure. And when that happens, there's very likely to be compulsive seizures.

The seizures, Moritz said, would have caused the man to fall face down on the floor and might have resembled epilepsy. Moritz also discovered during the autopsy that the bleeding in the man's head had been going on for some time—much longer than the 8 hours he had been in jail. Moritz also learned that the deceased had been experiencing seizures on and off for weeks. "The result of this [was] my diagnosis ... that this man had died of natural causes and that his injuries could be most plausibly explained by the convulsive seizures he'd have after falling."[4]

Lakeside Hospital closed in 1929, and Moritz moved into the new Institute of Pathology on the Western Reserve campus in downtown Cleveland, but his interest in diagnosing the cause of deaths continued. His work with the coroner plus additional research resulted in the publication of an article in 1934 in *The Transactions of the American Therapeutic Society* titled "The Pathogenesis of Sudden Death." For the article, Moritz sampled more than 2,500 autopsies performed or studied by Western Reserve's Institute of Pathology and University Hospital in Cleveland over 10 years. The cases included deaths caused by brain injuries, lung obstructions and circulatory failure. Moritz's research found that the most common cause of sudden death was a "sudden change in a pathological lesion" and that in many cases, the person would have lived longer if the lesion had been discovered sooner.[5]

CORONER STUDY

While Moritz was learning first-hand that unqualified coroners often made errors that led to miscarriages of justice, the Rockefeller Foundation in New York and the National Research Council (NRC) in Washington, DC, were coming to a similar conclusion after a lengthy study.

In the early 1920s, the Rockefeller Foundation, which was already successfully reforming medical education, and the NRC began pushing the need for a state-of-the-art academic program that combined medicine and law to train medical examiners in the art and science of death investigations. Their interest was based on reports that mistakes by elected coroners, most uneducated and untrained, were becoming more common and leading to killers getting away with murder and innocent people going to jail. There were also reports that elected coroners were too cozy with local law enforcement and elected officials, as well as with local funeral homes.

Harvard Medical School in Boston had had a legal medicine program of sorts since 1907. It was run by Dr. George Burgess Magrath, a Harvard-educated pathologist who lectured third-year Harvard medical students and served as a Suffolk County medical examiner. But Magrath's courses in legal medicine were unique to Harvard because Massachusetts was one of just a few states where the coroner system had been replaced with a medical examiner system. Electing coroners with no medical training requirement was standard throughout most of the United States and remains common in many jurisdictions in the 21st century.[6]

In 1928, the Rockefeller Foundation and the NRC called for major changes to the coroner system. Their report, which compared coroner systems in Chicago, San Francisco and New Orleans with the medical examiner systems in Boston and New York, was a "scathing criticism of the coroner's office," according to Jeffrey Jentzen, who in 2009 published "Death Investigation in America: Coroner's, Medical Examiners, and the Pursuit of Medical Certainty." The Rockefeller/NRC study, as expected, found most coroners were not physicians. Autopsies were the exception rather than the rule and when done were often improperly documented and performed in unsanitary conditions. "Inquests frequently did not follow the required legal procedures, often used

quasi-professional witnesses, and in many cases reached unrealistic conclusions," Jentzen wrote.[7]

The study, Jentzen continued, "pointed to European forensic institutes as models for future development" and made several recommendations, including abolishing the office of coroner and requiring medical
examiners to be scientifically trained pathologists. It also recommended
that medical examiners be civil servants and that their office staff include
competent pathologists.

> The unanimous opinion of the committee was that there is, in this field,
> a splendid opportunity for pioneer work in this nation in the gradual
> elevation of standards of practice in the office of coroner and medical
> examiner and in many other ways of performing services in the inter-
> est of the Commonwealth and affecting the police departments and
> judiciary through practical aid, courses of instruction and research.[8]

After the report was released, the American Medical Association called
for the adoption of a medical examiner system and the creation of
forensic institutes in the United States "modeled on the European system of university-based facilities staffed by professors with specialized
training in pathology, with access to a wide range of experts in the various fields of criminology." A second report, which focused on how to
reform death investigations, was released in 1932 and again advocated
for trained medical examiners.[9]

THE BENEFACTRESS

Frances Glessner Lee, the matronly heir to the International Harvester
fortune, was troubled by the findings in the Rockefeller/NRC studies,
according to Jentzen. Her brother, George Glessner, and Dr. Magrath
were close friends, having been undergraduates at Harvard together.
When Magrath was Suffolk County medical examiner, George Glessner
sometimes accompanied him on calls to death scenes. Like millions of
true-crime fans in subsequent decades, Lee was fascinated by their dis-
cussions of those cases, but she was special in that her inherited fortune
allowed her to insert herself into a field for which she had remarkable
aptitude but no formal training.[10]

As Magrath, one of only a handful of professors who lectured on
legal medicine, grew older, he sometimes wondered aloud what would
happen after he retired. When Lee asked what could be done to make
sure the instruction continued, Magrath suggested a separate academic
program at Harvard devoted to legal medicine.[11]

Lee, then in her late 50s, proposed to officials at Harvard and the Rockefeller Foundation the creation of the Department of Legal Medicine at Harvard Medical School. She saw Harvard as the perfect location for such an academic program and offered a gift of $250,000—the equivalent of almost $6 million in 2024—to fund the new department. She envisioned a department that would not only train young pathologists and physicians to be medical examiners, but also educate law enforcement officers in scientific crime detection. The department would also assist police and medical examiners in Massachusetts and the region by offering autopsies and other death investigation services.[12]

In early 1936, Lee's $250,000 donation, which would be known as the George Burgess Magrath Endowment of Legal Medicine, was accepted. The Rockefeller Foundation would eventually provide more than $100,000 in additional funding to support the academic department at Harvard Medical School. "It was the only medical school in America that was really giving the attention that law medicine deserved," Moritz said years later.[13]

THE SEARCH

On Monday, April 13, 1936, at 11 a.m., Harvard University's Committee to Consider the Future of Legal Medicine met for the first time, according to minutes of the meeting in the Harvard archives. Chaired by Dr. S.B. Wolbach, head of pathology at Harvard Medical School, the panel's charge was to develop and implement a plan to establish a Department of Legal Medicine in the school of medicine.

During the meeting, the panel discussed the purpose and goals of the new department and divided them into three categories: medical sciences, which included pathology, toxicology, chemistry, bacteriology and immunology to determine the cause of death; applied sciences related to the detection of a crime; and the law as it applies to medical sciences and applied sciences.[14]

In October of that year, Dr. Sidney Burwell, dean of Harvard Medical School, sought advice from legendary FBI Director J. Edgar Hoover on what he thought the new department might need in order to become a state-of-the-art program. "We believe that by the development of this field important contributions can be made not only to scientific knowledge but also directly to the welfare of the community," he wrote in a letter to Hoover. "Accordingly I am writing to express the hope that you will at some convenient time, be willing to give me the benefit of your opinions to possible directions of development of this Department of Legal Medicine."

Burwell told Hoover the department had already received a $250,000 endowment. There is no indication in the Moritz archive at Harvard that Hoover responded to Burwell's letter.[15]

GROWING REPUTATION

While the word was getting out that Harvard was making plans for a new Department of Legal Medicine, Moritz was getting restless in Ohio. He liked his job and he had developed ties to Cleveland, both profession- ally and personally. It was where he had done his residency after medi- cal school, and he had been allowed a 1-year sabbatical to study under Erdheim in Vienna. Cleveland was where he met his wife and where the couple's three children—John and twins Richard and Anne—had been born in 1930 and 1933.

Moritz aspired to someday become chairman of Western Reserve's Institute of Pathology, but he realized that would not happen soon. "I could do the arithmetic and I knew when Karsner was going to leave. It seemed perfectly obvious to me that his successor would be Goldblatt," Moritz said. Goldblatt had been there longer than Moritz and had more experience as a pathologist.[16]

Meanwhile, the Harvard search committee realized that it would be difficult to find a candidate who met every qualification on its wish list. A 2-year Rockefeller fellowship to study well-established forensic medi- cine programs in Europe and North Africa was included in the job offer to prepare the candidate for the job of creating, essentially from scratch, the new Department of Legal Medicine. Letters were sent to leading pathologists across the country seeking names of potential candidates for the position. Karsner received the letter and recommended Moritz.[17]

Karsner's recommendation carried weight because he had lectured at Harvard early in his career and was well known and respected by the Rockefeller Foundation. Plus, the Rockefeller Foundation and Harvard officials were already aware of Moritz and his growing repu- tation. Medical journal articles he had written during the past decade documented his interest in forensic pathology and in finding the causes of unexplained deaths, as well as his concern that coroners lacked the proper training to conduct death investigations.[18]

When Harvard approached Moritz about the position in early 1937, he liked the "glamour about a Harvard professorship," and that the medical school was the only one in the United States trying to develop a world-class legal-medicine program. He thought he was the best can- didate for the position. But Moritz also worried whether taking the job was the right career move.[19]

He wrote to Dean Burwell in May 1937,

I have some accomplishment and a large investment of time and work in the field of Pathology and I would be gambling with my future to leave the field of General Pathology, to give up a good position in a good medical school, to spend two years studying abroad and then be faced with the insecure tenure of an Associate Professorship, an income considerably less than my present one and no assurance of a budget adequate to build up a department.[20]

He also expressed concerns about uprooting his family and moving from Cleveland to Boston.

Less than a month later, in June 1937, Moritz was offered the job as a professor of pathology and director of the new Department of Legal Medicine at Harvard. His initial annual salary was $7,000 and he received a promise that the department would be appropriately equipped and funded. To alleviate his concerns about possibly losing his credentials as a pathologist, Harvard managed to get Moritz named pathologist-in-chief at Peter Bent Brigham Hospital, which was not far from Harvard Medical School. "So, I kept being a fairly respectable academic pathologist while I was working in this special field," he said years later.[21]

TWO YEARS IN EUROPE

Alan and Velma Moritz and their three young children boarded the S.S. City of Norfolk in Baltimore in early October 1937 and sailed for Europe. They settled first in Glasgow, Scotland, and later in Edinburgh. And while he traveled to the various European institutes, Harvard and the Rockefeller Foundation worked on two fronts to prepare the new department. The first was to make sure that Moritz's various concerns were met and that the proper facilities were in place when he returned. The second was to develop relationships with federal, state and local law enforcement to make sure they were aware of the benefits that the new department could offer when it was up and running.[22]

Even before Moritz and his family left for Europe, he and Dean Burwell traveled to Washington to tour the FBI crime laboratory and meet with FBI Assistant Director Hugh Clegg and Ivan W. Conrad, who worked in the lab. Conrad later became director of the FBI lab. The meeting was arranged by J. Edgar Hoover, but there's no indication that Moritz and Burwell met with Hoover personally.[23]

The FBI is "clearly interested in the prospects of an active and developing Department of Legal Medicine in Harvard Medical School and assured us of their desire to cooperate," Burwell wrote in a letter to Frances Glessner Lee.[24]

FIGURE 6.1   Alan and Velma Moritz's children, John and twins Anne and Richard, about 1936, shortly before the family left Cleveland for 2 years in Scotland. (Moritz Family Collection)

SCOTLAND

At first, Moritz wanted to move the family to Austria so that he could work closely with a pathologist he knew there. That plan, however, fell through after the pathologist's professorship was stripped because he was anti-Nazi. And so it was the rising Nazi fervor in Austria and neighboring Germany, along with the looming threat of war, that persuaded Moritz to move his family to Scotland and use the University of Glasgow as a home base. The university had a respected institute of legal medicine and its director, Dr. John L. Glaister Jr., was a renowned professor of forensic medicine.[25]

Moritz thought his family could live safely in Glasgow while he traveled to "old universities where departments or institutions of legal or forensic medicine had been in existence for many years," he recalled more than 30 years later. It didn't take long, however, for Moritz to conclude that Glasgow was a mistake. "The end of my first month finds me definitely of the opinion that a protracted stay here would be a waste of time," he wrote in a letter to Burwell. The main problem, he said, was that there had not been any forensic medicine cases since he arrived.

> I have been in Glasgow for a month and I have learned nothing that I
> could not have learned sitting in my own laboratory at home. In the
> month that I have been here there have been no specimen of any kind
> examined and no autopsies performed, at least none so far as I know.[26]

While frustrated with his situation at the University of Glasgow, Moritz
also observed that each institute he visited in Europe was organized
differently and that coming up with a design and vision for the one at
Harvard would be more challenging than he had anticipated.

"My greatest problem to date has been to arrive at some more or
less definite idea as to what a department of legal medicine at Harvard
University should be," he said in a letter to Lee in January 1938.

> It seems this specialty is the chameleon of medicine and that not only
> its superficial aspects but also its functions vary from place to place
> depending on local circumstances. Some of the medical aspects of sci-
> entific criminal investigation are common to all of the departments
> that I know anything about but otherwise, the variation is great.

Moritz went on to say he needed to be very careful in how he spent his
time in Europe. He "did not want to give an inordinate amount of time
to something that will prove to be valueless and by the same token I do
not want to slight some phase of the work that I will need later."[27]

Moritz also realized that if the new department was to have any
success, it would need cases to work on. In a December 7, 1937, letter
to Burwell, he expressed concerns. "I knew last summer that we had
no promise of jurisdiction over local legal medicine and we agreed that
some sort of a connection between the existing agencies would be desir-
able in the future," he said, adding he "had a very hazy idea about the
organization and functions of a department of legal medicine."

Moritz was also keenly interested in the preparations being made
at Harvard for when he returned, including those political in nature. In
the same letter, he told Burwell that he was worried about who would
replace Dr. Timothy Leary, the Suffolk County medical examiner, who
was expected to retire soon. A good relationship with local medical
examiners was vital for the department, and Leary—not the infamous
promoter of LSD—was not considered a friend. He had applied for the
position of director of the new department but did not receive an interview. He subsequently questioned the motives of the department and of
Moritz, whom he considered an outsider, so Moritz stressed the importance of Leary's successor being on better terms with the department.

"If his successor is appointed without the consideration of our
needs it may be seven years or more before a similar opportunity pres-
ents itself," he said. Moritz then suggested Burwell use his professional

reputation and political skills, as well as Harvard's influence, to get Moritz named director of the medical examiner's office of the southern division of Suffolk County when he returned from Europe. The appointment would benefit both Harvard and law enforcement, he told Burwell.

"If this entering wedge could be made we could look forward to absorbing the medical police laboratory work and the autopsies for the state workmen's compensation board in the future," Moritz said.

> These services would ensure us of a well rounded supply of pabulum which would provide the stimulus for investigative work, the case material for the teaching of graduate and undergraduate students and make possible an organization which by precept should raise the general standards of the practice of legal medicine.[28]

By March 1938, Moritz's concerns about his work in Glasgow were lifted when he was offered a position at the University of Edinburgh working with Dr. Sydney Smith, a Regius Professor of forensic medicine. He accepted the job almost immediately and told Burwell it was a much better fit. His plans included traveling to London to see the new Metropolitan Police Laboratory and to the Institute of Forensic Medicine in Vienna. He was also preparing a teaching demonstration for the recruits at the Edinburgh Police College. A trip to Bonn, Germany, to present papers to the International Congress for Forensic Medicine was also scheduled.[29]

For Moritz, the move to Edinburgh was a success for his work and for his family. They moved into a spacious house with a walled garden, and they had a live-in governess and a cook so Velma could travel with him on some of his trips to the continent. The couple traveled together to France and several Scandinavian countries and spent several weeks in Cairo, Egypt. Many of the locations had highly respected pathology and legal medicine programs, as well as renowned art galleries, architecture and cuisine.[30]

Velma Moritz also traveled to France and Italy to see various museums and art galleries with Dr. Moritz's aunt, Josephine Richards. Richards was an art instructor at Margaret Morrison Carnegie School for Women in Pittsburgh, which at the time was part of Carnegie Tech. (In 1967, Carnegie Tech merged with Mellon Institute to become Carnegie Mellon University.) Richards "came over and spent the better part of the summer and she and Velma went to places that were of most interest to my aunt and also Velma," he said. "This aunt had been to Europe many times, knew the museums, knew the buildings that ought to be seen and they did [see them] in France and Italy."[31]

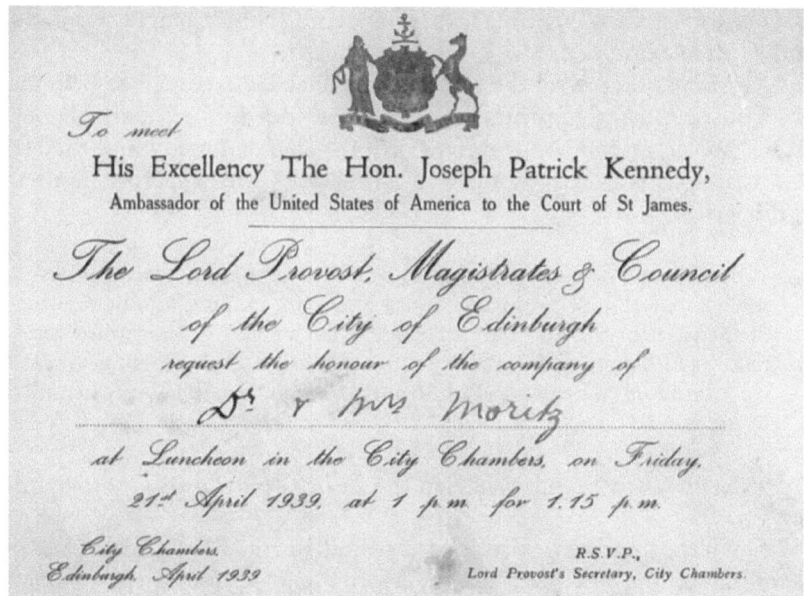

To meet

His Excellency The Hon. Joseph Patrick Kennedy,
Ambassador of the United States of America to the Court of St James.

The Lord Provost, Magistrates & Council

of the City of Edinburgh

request the honour of the company of

Dr & Mrs Moritz

at Luncheon in the City Chambers, on Friday,

21st April 1939, at 1 p.m. for 1.15 p.m.

City Chambers,   R.S.V.P.,
Edinburgh, April 1939   Lord Provost's Secretary, City Chambers.

FIGURE 6.2 Dr. and Mrs. Moritz were invited to meet the US Ambassador to the United Kingdom, Joseph Kennedy, when he visited Edinburgh in 1939. Almost 30 years later, Dr. Moritz would review the autopsy of Kennedy's son, President John F. Kennedy. (Moritz Family Collection)

In April 1939, Alan and Velma were invited to a luncheon at the City Chamber in Edinburgh with Joseph Patrick Kennedy, the US ambassador to the United Kingdom. Kennedy's son would later become president of the United States, and Moritz would be called on to review the investigation of his assassination.[32]

When not out of the country visiting institutes of legal medicine, Moritz conducted research in Edinburgh University's pathology department and helped with lectures to medical and law students. He also arranged and conducted lab demonstrations. Cities in Scotland had elected coroners, while the forensic pathologists and toxicologists were not employed by the government, had no primary authority and "only functioned when the police called [one] as a consultant," Moritz said.[33]

Medical students in Scotland also received intensive training in forensic medicine. "I think there was a course of 60 lectures, lecture demonstrations or clinics required for [the] third year of medical school," he said. "Well that was true in Scotland, it was less true in England. There was teaching in the English universities, but it wasn't associated with any institutes, there were no regular places where such bodies were examined."[34]

Moritz worked with the Edinburgh Police Department to help identify a suspect using imprints of a deformed foot in the inner sole of his shoe. "We described the criminal, his probable deformity and the characteristics of his gait from a pair of his shoes," Moritz wrote in a letter to Burwell.

> When he was caught we found to our delight that we were surprisingly accurate in all respects. Smith and I are making a joint report of the case for the Edinburgh Police Department. We determined the fellow's blood group from the sweat in the lining of his shoes but since we found him to belong to O [the most common type] we were afraid to use it.

The paper was to be published in the *Police Journal of Great Britain*, he said.[35]

Of all the forensic institutions he toured during his 2 years in Europe, Scandinavia and northern Africa, Moritz said he found the facility in Cairo and the city itself most interesting. "Cairo is a pretty wicked place, no doubt of that," he was quoted in a December 1941 article in the *Boston Globe*. "But it gets its reputation for producing the most murders of any city in the entire world because of the unwillingness of the police departments south of the Nile to bestir themselves in the solving of their own murders." He continued, saying that local police often throw murder victims into the north-flowing Nile and they "end up at Cairo and there the police can't pass the buck to other departments." Years later, he said Cairo institute, at the time he visited, had been set up by the British and those working there had been trained in England.[36]

THINGS TO AVOID

By August 1938, halfway through his 2-year fellowship, Moritz had gathered some important information about creating a new legal medicine department, including several things he thought should be avoided.

"I feel I have made a long journey and spent an inordinate amount of time to study organizations and methods that are fundamentally bad," he said in a letter to Dr. S.B. Wolbach, head of pathology at Harvard Medical School. "I have tried hard to keep an open mind because I felt that I must not let the narrow vision engendered by my specialized experience in medicine interfere with a just appraisal of this new field," he said. "I have forced myself to dig into many of the heterogeneous activities that constitute the practice of Legal Medicine."

He said the legal medicine programs he had visited thus far were too broad in their academic scope. "The result of this is that I am more firmly convinced than ever that the centralization of the practice of Legal Medicine robs the practitioner of his usefulness by making him a jack-of-all-trades." Autopsies, he continued, "are universally badly done and injudiciously interpreted because the men in Legal Medicine are not controlling their work by a knowledge of general pathology."

He found technicians working in areas outside their expertise, court testimony based on questionable and even inaccurate lab results, and official causes of death based on improper autopsy techniques. Moritz did say his experiences in Edinburgh were "valuable" because of Dr. Sydney Smith's "broad experience, common sense, and proper sense of the controlled observation." He also said the respect and success surrounding Smith and his department had generated an "attitude" that he hoped to emulate in the legal medicine program at Harvard.

In the same letter, he told Wolbach that he was eager to begin working on the new department, where he hoped being regarded as an expert would jumpstart cooperation with local law enforcement. "I do not want to start work in Boston handicapped by a lack of prestige that might be associated with a longer period of preparation if such prestige would affect my chances of getting control of active medico-legal work," he said. "I would like to come to Boston with the status of a medico-legal expert rather than to come there as a pathologist who would like to have some medico-legal work to do."

He closed his letter to Wolbach saying he was interested in writing a book. "Two things lead me to think that I should write a book as an alternative to coming home and going to work," he wrote.

> One is that I don't know any other profitable way to spend my time, and the other is that there is a need for such a book as I propose to write. There is no book to my knowledge that treats the post mortem pathology of forensic medicine against the background of general pathology. Such a treatment is especially desirable in considering cases of obscure sudden death, workmen's compensation cases, and accident insurance cases.[37]

While Moritz was in Europe, Frances Glessner Lee made sure his office was properly furnished and had a secretary, and she worked to add books and periodicals concerning criminology or forensic medicine to the McGrath Library of Legal Medicine, which she had created with an endowment in 1934.[38] Lee's desire to make sure Moritz was happy was not just limited to his work. Before Moritz and his family left for Europe in 1937, she made sure they were adequately equipped with furniture when they moved into their new home in the Jamaica Plain neighborhood of Boston. She also offered to store their car at her New Hampshire estate while they were away, but he turned down that offer.

Lee "cultivated us assiduously because she wanted the department to be a kind of Sherlock Holmes place and she was having trouble persuading me," Moritz said. "She invited Velma and me up ... for the weekend, and she was a very rich woman and had at one time, after she'd [divorced] her husband, entertained herself by establishing an antique store." Lee took the couple to a farmhouse on her estate, The Rocks, in the White Mountains of New Hampshire, which was "full of antiques that had been moved from that shop." She encouraged the couple to pick out pieces of furniture for their house when they moved to Boston. Some of the furniture turned out to be quite valuable and remains in the Moritz family.[39]

Pathology of Trauma, his textbook advancing forensic pathology as an academic specialty, was published in 1942. The textbook, dedicated to Lee, has been updated several times over the years and remains useful for anyone considering a career in forensic pathology.[40]

NOTES

1. Alan R. Moritz, transcript of interview by someone identified only as "Bonnie," Cleveland, Ohio, 1980 (Moritz Family Collection).
2. Mary Dowling Daley, "Law-Medicine Center Celebrates 30th Anniversary," *in brief*, Law Alumni Bulletin Case Western Reserve University, March 1984 (Case Western Reserve University Archives).
3. Alan R. Moritz, transcript of interview by someone identified only as "Bonnie," *Cleveland, Ohio,* 1980 (Moritz Family Collection).
4. Alan R. Moritz, interview by Mary Daley, November 18, 1983 (Case Western Reserve Archives).
5. Alan R. Moritz, "The Pathogenesis of Sudden Death," *The Transactions of the American Therapeutic Society* 34 (1934): 5, (Moritz Family Collection).
6. Alan R. Moritz, transcript of interview by someone identified only as "Bonnie," *Cleveland, Ohio,* 1980 (Moritz Family Collection); Jeffrey Jentzen, *Death Investigation in America: Coroner's, Medical Examiners, and the Pursuit of Medical Certainty* (Cambridge: Harvard University Press, 2009), 35–36.
7. Jeffrey Jentzen, *Death Investigation in America: Coroner's, Medical Examiners, and the Pursuit of Medical Certainty* (Cambridge: Harvard University Press, 2009), 35–36.

8. Jeffrey Jentzen, *Death Investigation in America: Coroner's, Medical Examiners, and the Pursuit of Medical Certainty* (Cambridge: Harvard University Press, 2009), 35.

9. Jeffrey Jentzen, *Death Investigation in America: Coroner's, Medical Examiners, and the Pursuit of Medical Certainty* (Cambridge: Harvard University Press, 2009), 37.

10. Jeffrey Jentzen, *Death Investigation in America: Coroner's, Medical Examiners, and the Pursuit of Medical Certainty* (Cambridge: Harvard University Press, 2009), 40; Alan R. Moritz, interview by Mary Daley, November 18, 1983 (Case Western Reserve Archives)

11. Bruce Goldfarb, *18 Tiny Deaths: The Untold Story of Frances Glessner Lee and the Invention of Modern* Forensics (Napierville, IL: Sourcebooks, 2020), 113.

12. Jeffrey Jentzen, *Death Investigation in America: Coroner's, Medical Examiners, and the Pursuit of Medical Certainty* (Cambridge: Harvard University Press, 2009), 40.

13. Jeffrey Jentzen, *Death Investigation in America: Coroner's, Medical Examiners, and the Pursuit of Medical Certainty* (Cambridge: Harvard University Press, 2009), 40; Alan R. Moritz, interview by Mary Daley, November 18, 1983 (Case Western Reserve Archives).

14. Minutes of the first meeting of the Committee to Consider the Future of Legal Medicine in Harvard University. April 13, 1936 (Center for the History of Medicine at Francis A. Countway Library, Harvard University).

15. C. Sidney Burwell, letter to J. Edgar Hoover, October 29, 1966 (Center for the History of Medicine at Francis A. Countway Library, Harvard University).

16. Alan R. Moritz, transcript of interview by someone identified only as "Bonnie," *Cleveland, Ohio*, 1980 (Moritz Family Collection).

17. C. Sidney Burwell, letter to Alan Gregg, April 10, 1937 (Center for the History of Medicine at Francis A. Countway Library, Harvard University).

18. Jeffrey Jentzen, *Death Investigation in America: Coroner's, Medical Examiners, and the Pursuit of Medical Certainty* (Cambridge: Harvard University Press, 2009), 41; Alan R. Moritz, transcript of interview by someone identified only as "Bonnie," *Cleveland, Ohio*, 1980 (Moritz Family Collection).

19. Alan R. Moritz, transcript of interview by someone identified only as "Bonnie," *Cleveland, Ohio*, 1980 (Moritz Family Collection).

20. Alan R. Moritz to Sidney Burwell, May 24, 1937 (Center for the History of Medicine at Francis A. Countway Library, Harvard University).

21. C. Sidney Burwell, letter to Alan Gregg, June 22, 1937 (Center for the History of Medicine at Francis A. Countway Library, Harvard University); Alan R. Moritz, transcript of interview by someone identified only as "Bonnie," *Cleveland, Ohio,* 1980 (Moritz Family Collection).

22. Alan Gregg, office diary, October 7, 1937 (New York: Rockefeller Foundation Archives, 1937); Alan R. Moritz to Sidney Burwell, December 7, 1937 (Center for the History of Medicine at Francis A. Countway Library, Harvard University).

23. C. Sidney Burwell, letter to Hugh Clegg, October 11, 1937 (Center for the History of Medicine at Francis A. Countway Library, Harvard University).

24. C. Sidney Burwell, letter to Frances G. Lee, October 11, 1937 (Center for the History of Medicine at Francis A. Countway Library, Harvard University).

25. Alan R. Moritz, transcript of interview by someone identified only as "Bonnie," *Cleveland, Ohio,* 1980 (Moritz Family Collection).

26. Alan R. Moritz, letter to C. Sidney Burwell, November 26, 1937 (Center for the History of Medicine at Francis A. Countway Library, Harvard University).

27. Alan R. Moritz, letter to Frances G. Lee, January 16, 1938 (Center for the History of Medicine at Francis A. Countway Library, Harvard University).

28. Alan R. Moritz, letter to C.S. Burwell, December 7, 1937 (Center for the History of Medicine at Francis A. Countway Library, Harvard University).

29. Alan. R. Moritz, letter to C.S. Burwell, March 2, 1938 (Center for the History of Medicine at Francis A. Countway Library, Harvard University).

30. John A. Moritz, interview by Rob Moritz, April 18, 2018, Benton, Ark.; Alan R. Moritz, transcript of interview by someone identified only as "Bonnie," *Cleveland, Ohio,* 1980 (Moritz Family Collection).

31. Alan R. Moritz, transcript of interview by someone identified only as "Bonnie," *Cleveland, Ohio,* 1980 (Moritz Family Collection).

32. Invitation to Alan R. Moritz and Velma to a luncheon with "His Excellency the Hon. Joseph Patrick Kennedy, Ambassador of the United States of America to the Court of St. James," on April 21, 1939, at the City Chamber in Edinburgh.

33. Alan R. Moritz, letter to Sidney Burwell, April 29, 1938 (Center for the History of Medicine at Francis A. Countway Library, Harvard University); Alan R. Moritz, transcript of interview by someone identified only as "Bonnie," *Cleveland, Ohio,* 1980 (Moritz Family Collection).

34. Alan R. Moritz, transcript of interview by someone identified only as "Bonnie," *Cleveland, Ohio*, 1980 (Moritz Family Collection).

35. Alan R. Moritz, letter to Sidney Burwell, April 29, 1938 (Center for the History of Medicine at Francis A. Countway Library, Harvard University).

36. Charles P. Haven, "Colleges Join Police Hunting Down Killers," *Boston Globe*, November 30, 1941 (Center for the History of Medicine at Frances A. Countway Library, Harvard University); Alan R. Moritz, transcript of interview by someone identified only as "Bonnie," *Cleveland, Ohio,* 1980 (Washington, DC: Moritz Family Collection, 1980).

37. Alan R. Moritz, letter to S.B. Wolbach, August 2, 1938 (Center for the History of Medicine at Frances A. Countway Library, Harvard University).

38. Alan R. Moritz, letter to Frances G. Lee, January 16, 1938 (Center for the History of Medicine at Francis A. Countway Library, Harvard University); Alan R. Moritz, letter to Frances G. Lee, January 25, 1939 (Center for the History of Medicine at Frances A. Countway Library, Harvard University).

39. Alan R. Moritz, transcript of interview by someone identified only as "Bonnie," *Cleveland, Ohio,* 1980 (Moritz Family Collection).

40. Alan R. Moritz, *Pathology of Trauma* (Philadelphia: Lea & Febiger, 1942).

CHAPTER 7

Nazi Germany

The Nazi Party was firmly in control of Germany, with Adolf Hitler as commander-in-chief, when Moritz visited medical institutions in a number of German cities. Germany would annex Austria in March 1938. Moritz spent time in the region before and after Austria was annexed.[1]

There was no mistaking the Nazi position on Jews. "We all knew that part of the Hitler program was the destruction of all Jews in Germany," Moritz said four decades later. "I think it was clear in 'Mein Kampf' that genocide was an important part of his program," he said, referring to Hitler's 1925 autobiography.

Seeing and understanding the advancements in forensic pathology in Germany, as well as in neighboring Austria and elsewhere in Europe, were of such vital importance in developing the Department of Legal Medicine at Harvard that Moritz had no choice but to visit. But while precautions were taken, he was always uneasy traveling.

He always carried a letter from the German Consulate in Cleveland, Ohio, saying, as he paraphrased, that "the distinguished professor Herr Doctor Moritz was making that visit and that the Consul would appreciate any courtesies that they might make." He also carried with him a letter stating that he was "non-Jewish." He admittedly "felt cheap carrying something like that with me, but I felt that since I was investing the time and money in making this survey, it would be foolish to have it jeopardized unnecessarily."

Along with the two letters on his person at all times, he also carried in his luggage papers from the US State Department that explained the purpose of his visit.

It was obvious that Jews were second-class citizens in Germany, where Moritz said "Jews not desired" signs were ubiquitous in restaurants and hotels. And while he never felt threatened, he was keenly aware that Nazi officials were watching him. "There wasn't a place in Germany or Austria that my luggage wasn't gone through," he said. He resorted to using the old-school detection technique of plucking a few strands of his hair and placing them "on the edge of an envelope or

     DOI: 10.4324/9781003539186-8

book, something of that sort" before he left his hotel room. When he returned, the hairs had almost always been moved.

Even though he knew he was being tracked, he still tried to be less conspicuous.

> I was told by the first professor I visited in Hamburg that it would save me trouble and make my visits to various places more comfortable for me if I would conform to the general requirement to always say "Heil Hitler" as a greeting ... If you were going to ask the bus driver which stop you should get off at, you'd say "Heil Hitler."

HARBINGERS OF HORROR

Many overt signs of deep-seated anti-Semitism in the day-to-day life of Germans would have been obvious to anyone who visited Hamburg in the late 1930s, but my grandfather's particular field of study exposed him to harbingers of the horrors to come. At the Institute of Forensic Medicine, which doubled as the government office for investigations of criminal, suspicious and unexplained deaths, he was given a tour guided "by one of the young staff members who was not very happy with the total situation."

The institute's morgue was overflowing, Moritz recalled.

"The morgue was ordinarily built to accommodate ... 40 bodies in compartments on either side. The room had been overbuilt to begin with because it was much wider than was required to maneuver carts to the bodies on the two sides and there were two long trestle tables running the full lengths."

Each trestle, he said, "had just as many bodies on them as they'd hold. My guess is perhaps somewhere from 40 and 60 bodies in excess of those that could be accommodated in the compartments."

He said,

"Each body had a cord around the neck with a tag on it and also around the wrist. The name and number was on [the wrist tag] and the presumptive cause or manner of death was on the tag around the neck. I picked up a tag around a neck, because, on this particular body, it was clear from the distortion of both arms that there were broken bones in both. And I picked up the tag on the neck to see what the presumptive cause of death was, and it was suicide."

He asked the guide if the body had been mishandled after death to account for the broken arms. "If not, how in the devil did this person commit suicide?"

The guide shrugged and told Moritz that the tags would indicate "that the majority of these people had either committed suicide or died suddenly of disease." The young staffer told Moritz that no autopsies would be performed "because the decision that led to the making of these tags—suicide—was made by an authority ... superior to any authority in the Institute." The deaths were not being investigated; the bodies were simply stored in the morgue "as a convenience to the authorities who would ultimately see to the disposal of the bodies."

The director of the institute told Moritz that his staff was also being asked to study genetics. In a little nook near the director's office was a small shelf closet filled with containers. On one side were containers of "ovaries removed from women, not dead women, and on the other side were testes [that had been] removed," according to my grandfather. The ovaries and testes "had been sent to [the director] to make a study of the genetic deficiencies that might well be disclosed in the spermatozoa or in the ova."

The director told Moritz that

> someone in the higher echelon of the medical department of the government was interested in genetic evidence of support to the assumption or fact that Jews had a genetic deficiency that might be disclosed by examination of the gonads, male and female.

Moritz asked the director if he planned to do the genetic research. "No, I'm not going to do it," the man responded.

"He obviously felt that he had to receive the material and act as though it was a matter of interest to him," Moritz said later. "He could well use as an excuse that he was very short-handed and this material would keep all right."

Decades later, Moritz was asked how people could work in such situations and conditions. My grandfather was matter-of-fact in his response: "I'm sure many of them stayed to have an occupation that enabled them to support themselves and their families."

Moritz's study tour took him to Vienna in 1939, the year after Austria was annexed to Germany and the Nazi persecution of Austrian Jews took hold. During the trip he said he was taken by Austrian officials to what he described as a "museum," where possessions confiscated from Jews were displayed and then sold by the government.

"There wasn't any particular explanation ever made other than they took everything away from the Jews sent to concentration camps, the camps where they systematically destroyed them. You can see where it would leave you slightly sick to your stomach."

TRAIN TO FRANCE

My grandmother and the three children left Edinburgh for Boston in 1939, but Moritz was still in Vienna when war broke out that summer. He claimed more than 30 years later to have been "on the last train to cross the French frontier," but that may have been an exaggeration. He was seated in a passenger compartment with a number of Jews who were fleeing Germany. "These were people who knew that this was their last chance to get out," he said.

"I suppose that for most of them, their next step would be to get over into Great Britain or some other way, down to Palestine," he said. "Some of them were going to Palestine."

The trip to Paris, which normally took 6–8 hours, was taking much longer as the train frequently stopped to let German troops board or to accommodate military trains. "As we came up closer to the French frontier, we would be put off on a siding to let troop trains or military supply trains move up."

As the trip dragged on, the tension heightened among the Jews with whom he shared the compartment. "They knew that the people in the green uniforms were getting on the train in increasing numbers as we approached the frontier, and everybody knew that they were going to be searched," Moritz said. This was especially ominous because the Jewish passengers had no luggage and "anything they were taking with them had to be secreted in their clothing or elsewhere."

Moritz, conversant in German, listened as the other passengers discussed their options for preserving their valuables. "The conversation wasn't getting anywhere. No one had any solutions." My grandfather had an idea.

Earlier in the trip he had met a courier with the US State Department, who conspicuously had a leather bag locked to his wrist. "We met in the passageway, and he'd invited me to come in and have a drink, which I did and fairly early."

After listening to the concerns expressed by the Jewish passengers, Moritz left the compartment and located the American courier. The train was about an hour from crossing the border into France.

> "I told him I was sure these people probably had jewelry, valuables that were not very bulky. If I got this stuff together in a handkerchief or something, something appropriate and came up, what would be the chance of him carrying it across the border?"

The courier "was a very nice fellow and said that he was quite sure that it could be done, if the collection of this stuff were done discreetly." The courier told him to not enter his compartment with the items if he thought he was being followed. "It was important that I not be seen entering or leaving," Moritz said.

Back in his compartment, Moritz explained the plan—including one possible drawback: If the passengers were delayed after the valuables were transferred to the courier, they would have to collect their property at the US Embassy in Paris. In preparation for that possibility, Moritz wrote down the names of each person in the compartment.

When they got to the border into France, the Jews were searched. The Germans did tell passengers to change trains and there was a concern that some "were likely to be pulled out because the Gestapo knew all about everybody that was in that compartment," he said.

"For some reason or other, they all disappeared for a while, while they were searched," he said. Eventually, he and everyone in the compartment were united after the train trip ended and he was able to return all their valuables to them. "Funny thing, these people were obviously, understandably, very grateful and they took my name and address because I was going right back to Boston as soon as I could get a ship, but I never heard from one of them."

That doesn't mean he was forgotten. In the fall of 1948 or spring of 1949, while a freshman at Haverford College in Philadelphia, Moritz's son John was asked by a professor if he was related to the Moritz who helped a group of German Jews smuggle valuables across the border from Germany into France in the late 1930s.[2]

NOTES

1. Unless noted, information for this chapter is from an interview of Alan R. Moritz, transcript of interview by someone identified only as "Bonnie," *Cleveland, Ohio*, 1980 (Moritz Family Collection).
2. John A. Moritz, interview by Rob Moritz, August 15, 2020, Benton, Ark.

CHAPTER 8

Harvard Years

After 2 years of study in Europe and North Africa, Moritz and his family were reunited in Boston in the fall of 1939, and he immediately began implementing his vision for a world-class Department of Legal Medicine at Harvard Medical School. The budget included $15,000 a year for salaries and supplies, which came from Frances Glessner Lee's $250,000 endowment, and $5,000 annually from the Rockefeller Foundation to pay two research fellows. The new department's offices, lab and library were on the third floor of the medical school's pathology building.

Two young forensic pathologists were soon recruited to the program as legal medicine fellows: Dr. Herbert Lund, a University of Pennsylvania Medical School graduate, and Dr. Edwin V. Hill, a graduate of Tufts Medical College. Moritz lectured to medical and law school students and promoted the importance of medical examiners at conferences, seminars and social gatherings organized by Lee. He also conducted and wrote scholarly articles for scientific journals. Soon two more legal medicine fellows were brought into the program.

Moritz saw the new academic program as having three primary responsibilities. The first was educational: to teach legal medicine to Harvard medical students and department fellows, as well as to medical students at Tufts and Boston University, and educate law enforcement officers in scientific crime detection of unusual or unknown deaths. The second was to consult with local medical examiners in their investigations of murders and unusual deaths. The third was to conduct research and publish the results.

In 1940, the first full calendar year of operation, the Department of Legal Medicine was consulted on 72 death investigations and conducted autopsies in 56 of those cases. Specimens and evidence were collected in the other 16 cases. A probable cause of death was determined in 53 of 56 autopsies. Cause of death was determined in half of the other 16 cases. Overall, the 72 death investigations included 22 homicides, 17 accidents, 11 natural causes and 9 suicides. The manner of death was not determined in 13 cases. The department was quickly proving its worth.

DOI: 10.4324/9781003539186-9

The department's first-year report said:

A comparison of the relative value of the evidence derived from these two types of consultation indicates that the chances of determining the cause of death are far greater when the Medico-Legal Consultant actually participates in the performance of the autopsy than when specimens are sent to the laboratory [1]

Many of Moritz's plans for the new department were reached quickly, but gaining the trust of medical examiners and law enforcement took some time. As he had discussed in letters to Lee and Dean Sidney Burwell while in Europe, consulting on death investigations was vital to educating the fellows. Still, medical examiners, coroners and law enforcement agencies in Boston and Suffolk County were territorial and distrustful of the new department. Suffolk County was especially important because that was where most of the homicides and unusual deaths occurred, but the county was divided into two medical examiner districts. Dr. Leary, the medical examiner, was well respected and a politically powerful figure, and his distrust of the motives of Harvard and Moritz was contagious.[2]

After attempts to address concerns raised by Leary and others failed, Moritz suggested creating a new third southern division of Suffolk County and getting the governor to appoint him the medical examiner of that new division. When that request was denied, Moritz decided to force the issue. That also backfired.

One night, he got word that a homicide had just occurred in Suffolk County. He drove to the scene, uninvited, only to have his worst fears realized. He saw deputies washing blood off the walls because they did not want to get the blood on their clothes. He also saw curious bystanders milling about inside the house and contaminating the crime scene. When he complained to the sheriff at the scene, he was told to shut up and leave.[3]

Eventually, Lee, Burwell and the Rockefeller Foundation's Alan Gregg persuaded Gov. Leverett Saltonstall to name Moritz a medical-legal expert with the Massachusetts Department of Public Safety. Under the new arrangement, Moritz and his department were able to assist Suffolk County and eventually most of New England in their investigations. Any findings by Moritz and his department could be accepted or rejected by the local investigating agencies, and the agencies could also claim the findings as their own if they wanted. Leary also was named a lecturer in the Department of Legal Medicine, a bit of political horse-trading that Moritz resented but accepted to get his department access to the necessary death investigations.[4]

As director of the Rockefeller Foundation's medical sciences division, Gregg kept a diary detailing his daily activities. On February 2, 1942, he

FIGURE 8.1 Alan Moritz at his gruesomely decorated desk at Harvard Medical School, shortly before his departure in 1949. (Courtesy Stanley A. Ferguson Archives of University Hospitals, Cleveland, Ohio)

noted his favorable impression of Moritz. He appreciated Moritz's early successes as director of the department, as well as his political acumen.

"Moritz is to be sworn in as Leary's assistant as medical examiner for Suffolk County—this is almost better than one hoped and the more so because Leary wrote one of the letters to the Governor advocating the appointment," Gregg wrote. "The fact that Moritz's course in legal medicine is given also to [Boston University] and Tufts students has aided Governor Saltonstall in making the appointment."

Gregg also noted that Moritz was "effective in an unspectacular way." The work he and his fellows had done investigating criminal cases had already "saved at least six innocent individuals from convictions for homicide and detecting the actual offender in nine other cases where the police would have made no further investigations."[5]

Local law enforcement agencies soon saw the value of his work when Moritz and his team began finding errors or uncovering clues that detectives had not discovered. "We had to win them over by helping them avoid blunders," Moritz told *Medical World News* in 1970.

Eventually, Moritz and his staff became so busy with calls to assist local agencies that they placed suitcases by the office door filled with various instruments and other equipment needed for death investigations. "We never can tell when we will be called to assist county medical examiners to investigate a death and so we are always ready," Moritz said.

In one case, a man was charged with murdering his wife after neighbors reported hearing the couple arguing loudly, according to the article in *Medical World News*. The victim had bruises on her face and was bleeding in the brain, and there was evidence of a struggle in their house where she was found dead. While the evidence suggested the woman was killed by her husband, the suspect's attorney argued that the medical examiner who performed the autopsy had not ruled out other possibilities for the bleeding in the victim's brain.

After the man's conviction, his attorney filed a petition asking that the dead woman's body be exhumed for another autopsy. Moritz performed that autopsy and discovered the woman had been suffering from a bacterial infection, which caused a blood clot to travel to her brain. "The evidence made it altogether reasonable to assume that the blood vessel had burst due to high blood pressure during the quarrel and that the bruises were self-inflicted when she lost consciousness and fell down," Moritz said in the article. "The husband was pardoned."[6]

In another case, Moritz and his team were asked to help local police after the skeletal remains of a woman with a rope around her neck were discovered in a wooded area. The remains were found lying on top of a shrub, which had been flattened by the weight of the body. Police thought the woman had probably been killed somewhere else and dragged to the area using the rope.

During his investigation, Moritz removed pieces from the crushed shrub under the skeleton and from nearby shrubs. He took the specimens to a botanist who determined the shrub under the skeleton had died sometime the previous June. Strands of the unusual rope found around the neck of the skeleton were also studied and it was determined that the rope was used to strangle the woman but not to drag her. The victim's approximate age was determined by X-raying her bones, and her dental records were ultimately used to identify her. With that information, the local investigators were able to make an arrest.[7]

This case matches the July 1940 murder of Irene Perry, the subject of a feature story in the *Boston Globe* in August 2024. In that case, which nagged at Lee for years because the suspect was ultimately acquitted, Moritz used a unique process to determine if the victim was strangled with the rope. According to the *Globe*, Moritz determined the first loop of rope around the victim's neck was 10.5 inches. He thought that was tight enough to strangle her, but he needed to be sure because the victim was so decomposed.

He then got 50 women between 18 and 25 to volunteer to have the circumference of their necks measured. None had a neck less than 12.5 inches. The women also agreed to let Moritz's team place a rope around their necks and slowly tighten it. He found that tightening the rope a half-inched caused "great discomfort," and 3/4 inch "could not be tolerated," according to the article. Based on that, Moritz concluded Perry had been strangled.

Perry had also been pregnant, which led Moritz to make the rather obvious suggestion that investigators attempt "to learn the identity of the man responsible for her pregnancy." Perry's married boyfriend, Frank Pedro, was charged with her murder after a length of the same 24-strand rope was found in his basement. Despite strong evidence, Pedro was acquitted by an all-male jury after his defense suggested that Perry might have been the victim of a botched abortion.[8]

Pedro's acquittal notwithstanding, the overall success of Moritz's team meant they would soon be responding to calls from across Massachusetts and neighboring states. The department was producing a new type of medical specialist, he said. "In the future, we are likely to produce more and more hybrid 'pathologists,'" Moritz said in the *Medical World News* article.

> We can call them pathologists to the extent that they are interested in the study of disease and its manifestations; but we will have to call them biochemical pathologists, neuropathologists, immunopathologists and the like in recognition of the fact that they will be using tools and perspectives drawn from these various disciplines, rather than from pathology as it existed 30 years ago.[9]

In May of 1942, Gregg wrote a letter to Lee thanking her for her support of the Department of Legal Medicine and praising her for her work in getting Moritz hired as director. Lee responded a month later saying she was glad Gregg approved of Moritz's work, so far, but she was reluctant to take too much credit for his being hired. "He was not a discovery of mine—the credit for that must go to Dr. Burwell, but I think he is rare and that we were most fortunate to find him."

Within a year, however, she told Gregg that Moritz "is not blessed by a large measure of political sagacity and easy manners."[10]

LEE AND MORITZ

As the reputation of the Department of Legal Medicine grew, the relationship between my grandfather and Frances Glessner Lee grew more complicated. The heiress's love of the police and obsession with death investigations not only changed Harvard but also greatly affected the trajectory of Moritz's career. Historians would later refer to Lee as "the mother of forensic science" and to Moritz as the "father of forensic pathology."[11]

Like Moritz, Lee was an advocate of replacing the elected coroner system with highly trained medical examiners. A statewide medical examiner system was established in Massachusetts in 1877, and a similar system was established in New York City in 1918 and Essex County, New Jersey, in 1927. Most of the rest of the United States, however, was under the coroner system.

Lee didn't have a background in public relations but certainly exhibited many of the necessary skills—persuasiveness, promotion, education and relationship-building. She thought the way to get lawmakers to consider replacing the coroner system with medical examiners was to educate the public. If the public understood the legal woes caused by coroners investigating unusual deaths and homicides and saw how much improved the investigations would be with trained medical examiners, they might pressure their lawmakers to change the necessary laws. So even before Moritz returned from Europe, Lee proposed an exhibit for the 1939–1940 New York City World's Fair.

In a letter to Moritz, she asked for suggestions on what such a display should include. Moritz suggested a series of hand-drawn panels illustrating some of the "more common situations in which expert medical knowledge is needed to obtain facts necessary for the administration of justice." He suggested a fatal wreck involving two vehicles, a homicide or suicide involving a gunshot, a death from carbon monoxide poisoning, a person found dead in the water, a death that looks suspicious but with no visible cause, and an accidental or work-related death.[12]

Lee's desire to get publicity for the new department, even before it was up and running, was also evident when she persuaded Moritz to travel from Europe, halfway through his 2 years there, to New York to lecture on legal medicine at a conference. Not only was the exhibit being prepared for the World's Fair, but she had Moritz scheduled to speak about the new department at a series of events, meetings and lectures. Moritz met with Massachusetts Gov. Saltonstall, State Police Commissioner

Paul Kirk and officials at the FBI laboratory in Washington. He also lectured at the Institute of Medicine of Chicago and to medical students in the Windy City.[13]

The two subsequently teamed up to create training seminars for law enforcement and medical examiners and advanced training for coroners. Moritz traveled to meet with—and Lee wrote letters to—politicians, medical professionals, law enforcement agencies, civic groups and other organizations in more than 25 states. Their work had some success with medical schools in California, Cincinnati, Virginia and Washington creating legal medicine departments. Several states—Connecticut, Louisiana, Maine, New York, North Carolina, Ohio, Oklahoma and Rhode Island—enacted coroner reform laws, but most states retained their archaic coroner systems with little or no educational requirements.[14]

Lee had begun to realize that Moritz was not a glad-hander and that self-promotion did not come naturally. She tried to make things easier for him after his return from Europe, but her well-intentioned suggestions sometimes felt more like micromanaging. In a letter to Moritz in advance of a dinner party with supporters of the new department at her New Hampshire estate, she described in specific detail the schedule of events and how he should speak to the group. The letter, which contained a little humor, also illustrates how excited she was about the department.

She wrote,

> I would like to have you make a little talk on legal medicine in general—what it is and why, what you have been doing in your two years abroad, what the needs in this country are, and what the prospects are at Harvard for fulfilling them.

> There will be many doctors, some lawyers and probably some of the New Hampshire Medical Referees, and we have asked the local undertaker, deputy sheriff and chief of police, together with the butcher, the baker and candle stick maker. It will be a chance for a little missionary work, but as you know it musn't be too technical, nor shall I say, too 'gory.' Ultimately New Hampshire may send us specimens or call us in consultation. If it isn't taxing you too much, I should think you could safely talk for thirty or forty minutes and that talk should include some definite account of cases. You will have a friendly and interested audience, one eager to hear what you have to say.

> I can't tell you what a comfortable and easy feeling I have about the prospect of my interest about the Medical School. I only hope you are half as happy about it as I am.[15]

A few weeks later, she suggested in a memo that Moritz start requesting payment for the various lectures and speeches he gave in support of the department, or on his advocacy of reforming the coroner system with trained medical examiners. "In my opinion it is poor policy to give anything free and the way you start is the way you will have to finish," she said. "Don't hold yourself or your information and experience too cheap!"[16]

THE "NUTSHELLS"

Lee, with her enthusiasm for law enforcement, was especially excited about Moritz and the department offering lectures and seminars to officers on scientific techniques for investigating murders and unusual deaths. She realized that most police detectives had little or no science or medical education, so technical and medical jargon used in the seminars might overwhelm them. She thought that mixing the highly technical seminars with a more hands-on and visual learning approach might help them understand the concepts better.

Lee thought back on a birthday gift she had created for her mother in 1913: a miniature replica of the Chicago Symphony Orchestra. Those carved wooden models included 75 miniature musicians and a 5-inch-tall conductor. She thought that type of miniature display would work as well in helping investigators study unusual death and homicide scenes because one of the purposes of the seminars was to improve observation and detection skills.[17]

With the replica of the orchestra in mind, Lee and a hired carpenter began making replicas—1-inch to 1-foot scale—of actual death scenes. As each grisly murder or death scene was being handcrafted, she sought advice from Moritz on how to make sure they were realistic and to keep the specific details in place so those studying could detect important details and come up with an answer on how the specific death occurred.

In one letter, Lee thanked Moritz for some suggested changes. "You have given me just the kind of help I hoped for and needed," she said. While working on the dioramas she found herself "constantly tempted to add more clues and details and I am afraid I may get them 'gadgety' in the process." While the scenes were incredibly realistic, Lee admitted she sometimes added some detail for her own entertainment. She urged Moritz to "watch over this and stop me when I go too far."

Lee told Moritz she was having difficulty placing a bloody footprint on a newspaper in one murder scene.

She said,

> While I would like very much to get the footprint in blood on the newspaper I cannot find any way of getting the newspaper in any position

to receive that footprint and since we seem to have about as many problems in this model as the students are likely to be able to solve I am going to reserve this newspaper-bloody-footprint for another model if you approve.

She added that an electrician was to arrive soon to electrify some of the exhibits.

In the same letter, she commented that she and Moritz were like fiction writers in creating not only the crime scenes but also the detail and clues.

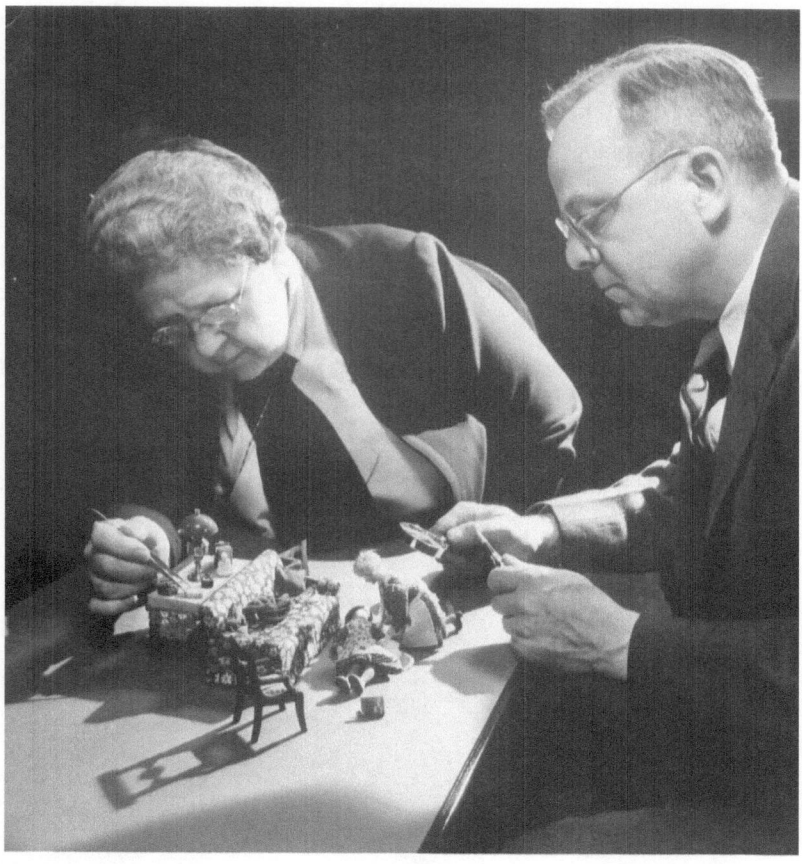

FIGURE 8.2 Dr. Moritz works with Frances Glessner Lee, benefactress of Harvard Medical School's Department of Legal Medicine, on her series of death scene dioramas known as the *Nutshell Studies of Unexplained Death*, 1948. (Center for the History of Medicine at Francis A. Countway Library, Harvard Medical School)

Since you and I have perpetrated these crimes ourselves we are in the unique position of being able to give complete descriptions of them even if there were no witnesses—very much in the manner of the novelist who is able to tell the inmost thoughts of his characters.[18]

Eventually, Lee and and the carpenter completed the *Nutshell Studies of Unexplained Death*—originally 19 or 20 of them, of which 18 survive. The scenes ranged from a man hanging from a barn rafter to a woman lying dead on the kitchen floor in front of an open icebox. Lee ultimately gave them to Maryland's Chief Medical Examiner's office.

Bruce Goldfarb, former custodian of the *Nutshells* for the Maryland ME's office, published the definitive biography of Lee in 2020 titled *18 Tiny Deaths*. He said Lee "spared no effect or expense to give her dioramas authenticity." Each scene, in a dollhouse-like box, was intricately detailed with things like handsewn curtains and dresses, knitted stockings and tiny buttons made of sequins. The paintings on the walls were also handmade; a tiny view of The Rocks, Lee's cottage in New Hampshire hangs over a fireplace in one scene. "For whisky bottles,

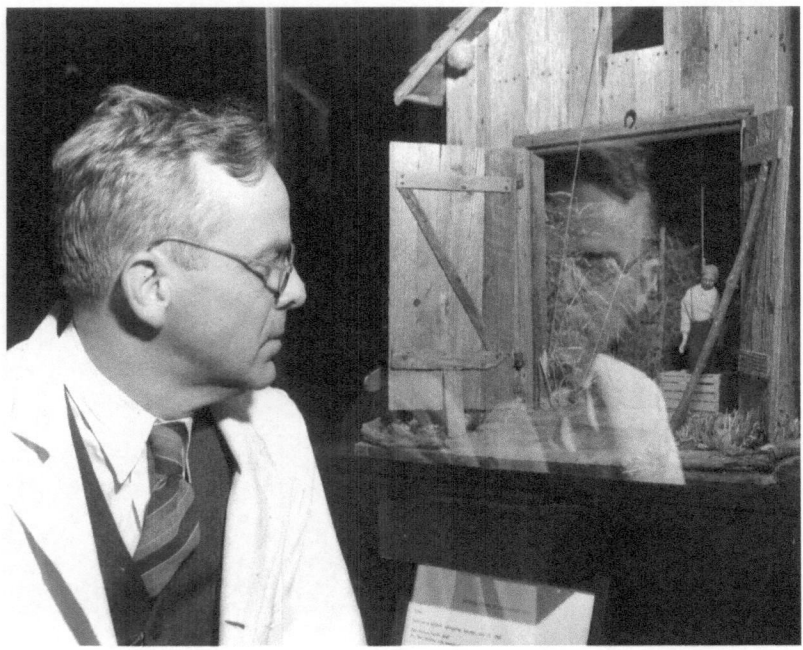

FIGURE 8.3 Dr. Moritz poses with one of the *Nutshell Studies*, 18 of which survived and are in the possession of Maryland's Office of the Chief Medical Examiner in Baltimore. (Center for the History of Medicine a Francis A. Countway Library, Harvard University)

to ornament the models, she acquired labels of Town Tavern and Crab Orchard brand liquor from the National Distillers Products Corporation from which she made miniatures," Goldfarb wrote.[19]

REPORT TO THE DEAN

By 1944, year five of the department, things had become more difficult and stressful. While the number of fellows had reached as high as five at a time, the US involvement in World War II had prompted two to resign and join the Army. Two other fellows had been hired away by other universities wanting to develop similar programs. Now down to just himself and two fellows to respond to the growing number of investigation requests, Moritz was still lecturing at Harvard, Boston University and Tufts and frequently testifying in court. He was also involved in what would become a groundbreaking study for the military on the pathology of burns.

Moritz's tenure at Harvard was at a crossroads in the spring of 1944. He understood that when the war ended, the number of qualified candidates for department fellowships would increase. He also realized that there were many other areas of concern within the Department of Legal Medicine that needed to be addressed.[20]

To compound his stress, in April he was offered a job as dean of the medical school at Western Reserve in Cleveland. He informed Burwell and Gregg of the offer, saying the position would allow him to continue research and teaching and put him on track to possibly become director of the Institute of Pathology when Karsner retired in about 5 years.

In a candid May 4 letter to Karsner, Moritz said the decision on whether to accept the offer from Western Reserve had caused anxiety and insomnia. "My consumption of Nembutal in the past few weeks has been large," he said.[21]

On May 15, Moritz presented Burwell with a review of the department's first 5 years. While the report was necessary for the department's future growth, Moritz also used it and the job offer from Western Reserve to determine Harvard's commitment to the department and to his career.

"It is possible that the University did not fully realize the extent to which it was committing itself in undertaking the development of a department of Legal Medicine," Moritz wrote. "It would be better to abandon the project entirely than to persist in an attempt so handicapped as to be doomed to failure."

More money would be needed to hire additional staff, he recommended in the report, because the department's success had created new and unforeseen responsibilities for himself and the department fellows.

He also expressed concern that his department wasn't getting the same academic and scientific respect as other departments in the medical school, and that support was still lacking from the law school, which had been promised when he was hired.

"It has become apparent that there is urgent need for certain additions to the professional personnel of the department, and for certain changes in the relations of this department to other departments of the Medical School," the report said. "If these additions and changes cannot be made I doubt the department can serve a sufficiently useful function to justify its continued existence."

Moritz also said the scope of his job had broadened significantly in the 5 years since the department launched. He was teaching fellows and medical students, supervising research, and supervising or conducting several hundred autopsies a year as a pathologist to the department of public safety and associate medical examiner of Suffolk County. He also was responsible for "public enlightenment" and "found it necessary to devote a large amount of time in traveling and speaking to attract graduate students to the Department of Legal Medicine and to bring to the attention of physicians, lawyers, police and other public officials the need for improvement in the practice of Legal Medicine."

Moritz admitted he put too much responsibility on himself when he created the department. Another "serious fault" in the department was that there was no one "qualified in the chemical and toxicological aspects of investigating cases of chemical injury and poisoning," the report said.

> Although poisoning is not a common form of murder it is an exceedingly frequent and important form of accidental and occupational injury, and as such becomes the responsibility of the department of Legal Medicine in the investigation of medico-legal deaths. It is intolerable to the head of the department and to the University that the School of Medicine should undertake a responsibility for medico-legal practice that it is unable to discharge with competence.[22]

The report surprised and alarmed Burwell and everyone at Harvard, up to President James Conant. They feared one of their stars might leave. Moritz said the report was "not an ultimatum" but admitted their response would help him decide whether to take the job at Western Reserve. The report was "an appraisal of the status of the Department of Legal Medicine and the making of the appraisal was stimulated by the invitation recently received by me to come to Cleveland," he wrote to Burwell.

"If the things that need to be done cannot be done, it would be both to my interests and to the interests of the University if we face the facts as soon as possible," he said.

> It would then be to my interests to prepare myself for a return to the field of general pathology and it would be to the interests of the University to make plans for the eventual incorporation of Legal Medicine and its funds into the Department of Pathology.[23]

In response to Moritz's 5-year review, the Rockefeller Foundation provided an additional $75,000 to the department over 10 years, and Lee raised her annual funding from $1,000 to $3,000 for 5 years. Moritz decided to stay.[24]

INVESTIGATION SEMINARS

In early 1945, the Department of Legal Medicine, in association with Boston University and Tufts College, began offering the death scene educational seminars to medical examiners, coroners and pathologists. In the fall of 1945, Lee's *Nutshells* were added to the seminars and courses started for law enforcement officers. Eventually, a seminar was held for journalists.

Each attendee was assigned two of Lee's crime scene models. After reading the information provided and carefully studying the scenes they would report their conclusions to Moritz and he would let them know if they were correct.[25] By 1949, the seminars were being offered regularly for a week, 3 days or intensive 1-day courses. They were popular and attended by law enforcement officials, lawyers, medical examiners and coroners from across the country and Canada.

A 1948 seminar in Boston that was attended by journalists from across New England included a lecture by Moritz on when and why "competent official medical investigation of certain deaths" is of public interest. Moritz also lectured on the objectives and procedures of a homicide investigation and errors made in interpreting evidence.[26]

Police officers who completed the seminar later created an independent organization called Harvard Associates in Police Science, and Lee was named the group's first president. HAPS, now incorporated and located in Baltimore, continues to hold annual seminars and the *Nutshells* are still studied by law enforcement officers and others.

The seminars helped spark the public fascination with crime scene investigation, but improving the archaic coroner system was the common goal of the unique—and not always smooth—working relationship between Moritz, the rural Nebraska boy who became one of the best-educated medical professionals of his time, and Lee, the home-schooled heiress.[27]

From October 2017 to January 2018, the miniature death scenes were the subject of an exhibit at the Renwick Gallery of the Smithsonian American Art Museum in Washington, DC. The exhibit, *Murder Is Her Hobby: Frances Glessner Lee and The Nutshell Studies of Unexplained Death*, was billed as "the surprising intersection between craft and forensic science."[28]

CONANT'S VISIT TO IPSWICH

In 1943, Alan and Velma Moritz built a two-bedroom cottage on about 10 acres, half an old apple orchard and half pine trees, near Ipswich, Massachusetts, about 40 miles north of Boston. The couple and their children had spent three summers in rented lodgings in the small coastal village known for clams, early American architecture and white sand beaches. Alan and Velma decided they wanted a more permanent retreat as the children became more self-sufficient.

The cottage was on Argilla Road, not far from a beach and the renowned Crane Estate. Dean Burwell and his wife, Edith, also had a summer home on Argilla Road, and the couples were friendly. In August 1945, the Burwells hosted Harvard President James Conant and his wife, Patty, for a weekend in Ipswich. The purpose, according to Moritz, was to provide the Conants a little rest and relaxation. They needed it.

Conant had been appointed to the National Defense Research Committee, which oversaw military research, including the Manhattan Project, which developed the first atomic bombs. He later became chairman of the committee and was part of the team that recommended that President Harry Truman use the new weapons in hopes of ending the war that continued in the Pacific Theater after Germany's unconditional surrender in May 1945.

On August 6, under the president's order, a 5-ton atomic bomb was dropped on Hiroshima, Japan. Three days later, a similar bomb was dropped on Nagasaki.

"The reason Conant needed a break ... I think all those fellows who had something to do with the development of the atomic bomb must have had some misgivings," Moritz said years later. The previous month, on July 16, Conant had been present at the Alamogordo Bombing and Gunnery Range in New Mexico for the first detonation of an atomic bomb.

During the weekend in Ipswich, Burwell brought Conant to the Moritzes' cottage as well. What Moritz remembered most distinctly

FIGURE 8.4 Alan and Velma Moritz at their cottage in Ipswich, Massachusetts, in the mid-1940s. (Moritz Family Collection)

about the weekend was not any particular comment Conant made about the recent bombings or the Manhattan Project. Instead, he recalled vividly a conversation the two had about birds nesting under the eaves of the porch, where screens were to be installed a few days hence.

"We watched the mother bird flying back and forth, feeding these young ones, and I said I didn't know what we were going to do about this," Moritz recounted. (My grandfather identified the birds as starlings, and a nest of baby starlings in August would be late but not unheard of in Massachusetts.) Moritz suggested he might move the nest, but Conant, who had an interest in ornithology, was adamantly opposed. "Oh, no, you can't move that," Moritz said Conant told him. "The parents will abandon the [baby] birds."

Moritz explained to Conant that the porch was where the family spent most of their time during the heat of the late summer, and without screens "the mosquitoes and greenheads are going to make this porch absolutely no good to us."

"That's too bad," Conant said. "I guess next year you'll have to put up the screens earlier, so the birds don't get in."

Years later, as he recalled the conversation, Moritz was still struck by the fact that "the idea of destroying those little birds was just unthinkable" to one of the architects of nuclear war.

My grandfather had done his own share of military research. The files at Harvard Medical School contain gruesome photos of the dogs that were sacrificed to his study of flamethrowers. So, decades later, he was sympathetic to the Manhattan Project scientists who "all must have had nightmares."

And Moritz believed that they could all take solace that their fearsome weapon did bring about the end of the war. If the bombs had not been dropped, Moritz said, "there'd probably been another million casualties of American soldiers because the Japanese were set to defend the homeland to the last ditch and we were going to take the homeland, the home islands."[29]

Conant, who was president of Harvard University from 1933 to 1953, was presented the civilian Medal of Merit with a bronze oak leaf cluster by President Truman in 1948. He was later named United States High Commissioner of Germany by President Eisenhower.[30]

NOTES

1. "First Annual Report of the Department of Legal Medicine Harvard Medical School, January 1, 1940–December 31, 1940" (Center for the History of Medicine at Francis A. Countway Library, Harvard University).

2. Frances Glessner Lee, letter to Alan R. Moritz, November 15, 1938 (Center for the History of Medicine at Francis A. Countway Library, Harvard University); Sidney Burwell, "Memorandum of Conversation with Mrs. Lee on June 2, 1938," (Center for the History of Medicine at Francis A. Countway Library, Harvard University); Alan R. Moritz, transcript of interview by someone

identified only as "Bonnie," *Cleveland, Ohio,* 1980 (Moritz Family Collection); "Of Crime and Change and the Doctor's Doctor," *Medical World News,* March 13, 1970, 34; Alan Gregg, work diary, October 16, 1939 (Rockefeller Foundation Archives); Jeffrey M. Jentzen, *Death Investigation in America* (Cambridge, MA: Harvard University Press, 2009), 43.

3. Bruce Goldfarb, *18 Tiny Deaths: The Untold Story of Frances Glessner Lee and the Invention of Modern Forensics* (Napierville, IL: Sourcebooks, 2020), 168.

4. Sidney Burwell, "Memorandum of a Conversation with Mrs. Lee Concerning the Situation of Legal Medicine, June 15, 1937" (Center for the History of Medicine at Francis A. Countway Library, Harvard University).

5. Alan Gregg, office diary, February 2, 1942 (Rockefeller Foundation Archives)

6. "Of Crime and Change and the Doctor's Doctor," *Medical World News,* March 13, 1970, 34–35.

7. "Scientists to Teach Crime Detection," *New York Times,* April 15, 1945 (Center for the History of Medicine at Francis A. Countway Library, Harvard University)

8. Patricia Wen, "The Heiress at Harvard Who Helped Revolutionize Murder Investigations – and the Case She Couldn't Forget," *Boston Globe,* August 14, 2024.

9. "Of Crime and Change and the Doctor's Doctor," *Medical World News,* March 13, 1970, 39.

10. Alan Gregg, letter to Frances Glessner Lee, May 21, 1942 (Center for the History of Medicine at Francis A. Countway Library, Harvard University); Frances Glessner Lee, letter to Alan Gregg, June 4, 1942 (Rockefeller Foundation Archives); Alan Gregg, "Memo of Interview of AG with Mrs. Frances Lee," March 19, 1943 (Rockefeller Foundation Archives).

11. "Of Crime and Change and the Doctor's Doctor," *Medical World News,* March 13, 1970, 31; "Murder is Her Hobby: Frances Glessner Lee and The Nutshell Studies of Unexplained Death," *Smithsonian American Art Museum,* accessed March 6, 2022, https://americanart.si.edu/exhibitionsnutshells

12. Alan R. Moritz, letter to Frances Glessner Lee, December 6, 1938 (Center for the History of Medicine at Francis A. Countway Library, Harvard University).

13. Frances Glessner Lee, letter to Sidney Burwell, May 27, 1938 (Center for the History of Medicine at Francis A. Countway Library, Harvard University); Sidney Burwell, "Memorandum

of Conversation with Mrs. Lee October 3, 1938" (Center for the History of Medicine at Francis A. Countway Library, Harvard University).

14. "First Annual Report of the Department of Legal Medicine Harvard Medical School, January 1, 1940–December 31, 1940" (Center for the History of Medicine at Francis A. Countway Library, Harvard University).

15. Frances Glessner Lee, letter to Alan R. Moritz, September 18, 1939 (Center for the History of Medicine at Francis A. Countway Library, Harvard University).

16. Frances Glessner Lee, letter to Alan R. Moritz, September 27, 1939 (Center for the History of Medicine at Francis A. Countway Library, Harvard University).

17. Katherine Ramsland, "The Truth in a Nutshell: The Legacy of Frances Glessner Lee," *The Forensic Examiner* (Summer 2008): 16–19; "The Story of a House," *Official Blog of Glessner House*, January 7, 2013, accessed August 14, 2024, https://glessnerhouse .blogspot.com/2013/01/frances-glessners-miniature-orchestra .html; Elizabeth Evitts Dickinson, "The Woman Who Invented Forensics Training With Doll Houses," *The New Yorker*, November 5, 2017, accessed November 9, 2017, https://www.newyorker.com /culture/culture-desk/the-woman-who-invented-forensics-training -with-doll-houses; Earl Banner, "She Invested a Fortune in Police, Entertained Them Royally at Ritz," *Boston Globe*, February 4, 1962.

18. Frances Glessner Lee, letter to Alan R. Moritz, August 21, 1945 (Center for the History of Medicine at Francis A. Countway Library, Harvard University).

19. Bruce Goldfarb, *18 Tiny Deaths: The Untold Story of Frances Glessner Lee and the Invention of Modern Forensics* (Napierville, IL: Sourcebooks, 2020), 210–216.

20. Alan R. Moritz, "The Status of the Department of Legal Medicine of Harvard Medical School After the First Five Years of Its Existence: Report to the Dean by the Professor of Legal Medicine," May 15, 1944 (Center for the History of Medicine at Francis A. Countway Library, Harvard University).

21. Alan R. Moritz, letter to Sidney Burwell, April 17, 1944 (Center for the History of Medicine at Francis A. Countway Library, Harvard University); Alan R. Moritz, letter to Alan Gregg, April 14, 1944 (Rockefeller Foundation Archives); Alan R. Moritz, letter to Howard T. Karsner, May 4, 1944 (Center for the History of Medicine at Francis A. Countway, Harvard University).

22. Alan R. Moritz, "The Status of the Department of Legal Medicine of Harvard Medical School After the First Five Years of Its Existence: Report to the Dean by the Professor of Legal Medicine," May 15, 1944 (Center for the History of Medicine at Francis A. Countway Library, Harvard University).

23. Alan R. Moritz, letter to Sidney Burwell, May 15, 1944 (Center for the History of Medicine at Francis A. Countway Library, Harvard University)

24. Sidney Burwell, letter to Alan Gregg, December 7, 1948 (Rockefeller Foundation Archives)

25. Frances Glessner Lee, "Legal Medicine at Harvard University," *Journal of Criminal Justice and Police Science* (Winter 1952): Vol. 42, 674–678.

26. Program for "Seminar on Scientific Criminal Investigation for New England Journalists," Department of Legal Medicine, Harvard Medical School, June 17, 1948 (Center for the History of Medicine at Countway Library, Harvard University); Sidney Burwell, letter to Alan Gregg, December 7, 1948 (Rockefeller Foundation Archives).

27. Erin N. Bush, "Death in Diorama: The Nutshell Studies of Unexplained Death," accessed September 24, 2021, http://www.deathindiorama.com/legacy.html; Pete Martin, "How Murders Beat the Law," *The Saturday Evening Post*, December 10, 1950, 32–50; Elizabeth Evitts Dickinson, "The Woman Who Invented Forensics Training With Doll Houses," *The New Yorker*, November 5, 2017, accessed November 9, 2017, https://www.newyorker.com/culture/culture-desk/the-woman-who-invented-forensics-training-with-doll-houses

28. "Murder is Her Hobby: Frances Glessner Lee and The Nutshell Studies of Unexplained Death," *Smithsonian American Art Museum*, accessed March 6, 2022, https://americanart.si.edu/exhibitionsnutshells

29. Alan R. Moritz, transcript of interview by someone identified only as "Bonnie," *Cleveland, Ohio,* 1980 (Moritz Family Collection).

30. "James B. Conant: American Educator and Scientists," *Britannica*, accessed August 15, https://www.britannica.com/biography/James-B-Conant.

CHAPTER 9

Burn Studies

Alan Moritz believed the wartime research work he and his colleagues did on "thermal trauma"—burns—would be his most important scientific legacy. "We did more work than add another brick to the wall; we created a wall that had not existed before," he said.[1] This chapter addresses research carried out specifically for the war effort. Other burn-related cases that happened during World War II merit their own chapters.

When the United States entered World War II after the bombing of Pearl Harbor on December 7, 1941, many Harvard faculty members mobilized in support of the war effort, like they had dutifully done at the outset of World War I. Many of the faculty went to Europe to provide medical treatment to troops as part of the American Defense-Harvard Group. Moritz's friend Dr. Elliott Cutler, a professor of surgery at Harvard and a brigadier general in the US Army Medical Corps, served as chief consultant in surgery in the European Theater of operations. Other Harvard scientists conducted research for the military in a variety of areas, including explosives and radio electronics.[2]

Moritz, at 42, was offered an opportunity to go to Europe as a lieutenant colonel in the US Army Medical Corps but decided to stay in Boston because he felt he could be of more use conducting research, according to his older son, John. While continuing to lead the Department of Legal Medicine, Moritz worked as an investigator for two committees reporting to the National Defense Research Council.[3]

Working alone or with a team of scientists, Moritz spent the war years researching the effects of burns caused by electricity, chemicals and radiation. Burns caused by heat and cold, including the effect of flamethrowers, were studied to determine the "degree and duration of heat and cold that are required to cause irreversible tissue damage, a medical problem that had not been adequately probed and that was occurring with increasing frequency in troops exposed to flamethrowers and to stratospheric cold."[4]

DOI: 10.4324/9781003539186-10

Moritz said,

> The exciting thing to me was that we produced new, precise information by precise methods, and this is what anybody who is strongly drawn to pathology tried to do. Every physician is a kind of detective, trying to solve problems by following clues. But the methods of the clinician are relatively imprecise, and so are his solutions, understandably. The pathologist hopes that what he discovers will help patients, but his main interest is in the accuracy, not the application of his findings. A passion for precision—that's the earmark of the pathologist.[5]

Dr. Leopoldo Cancio, a retired US Army colonel and director of the US Army Institute of Surgical Research Burn Center in San Antonio, said Moritz's research was still relevant in the 2020s, and he has cited his findings many times in his own research on burns.

"They are foundational studies," Cancio said in an interview for this biography. "They form the basis for key understandings that we have about burn injury and inhalation injury." Moritz and those who assisted him—most notably F.C. Henriques Jr., a physical chemist at Harvard—"were the main people who developed concepts of depth of injury as related to time of exposure and temperature of material or the process affecting the skin," Cancio said. "And then [his] other major contribution was understanding how heat affects the airways or does not affect the airways during the process of ventilation injury."[6]

FLAMETHROWERS

By July 1940, World War II was already raging in Europe and flamethrowers were being used. News of the weapon's use caught the interest of US Secretary of War Henry Lewis Stimson, who ordered the Chemical Warfare Service, a branch of the US Army that developed chemical weapons, to develop a flamethrower for US troops. The weapon had limited use near the end of World War I.

Flamethrowers were first used by US soldiers in the Pacific Theater because they could be carried on the back of a soldier and were effective in capturing "strongly fortified and entrenched positions," David Van Wyck wrote in a 2020 article in the journal *Military Medical Research*. While using a flamethrower to kill a combatant was viewed by many as barbaric and cruel, the US Chemical Warfare Service noted that some deaths appeared to be painless and went so far as to describe such a death as a "mercy killing," according to Van Wyck.

That "mischaracterization arose from a series of first-hand accounts describing what were believed to be quick, painless and unmarred deaths, as well as from a poor and incomplete misunderstanding of flamethrower lethality," Van Wyck wrote, noting that the US military had not by then done an in-depth study on the lethal effects of flame-throwers. "As a result, indirect mechanisms, such as hypoxia and carbon monoxide poisoning were generally absent from accounts of the flame-thrower's fatal effects."[7]

An undated memo from the Army Institute of Pathology found in Moritz's archived files at Harvard Medical School said "there have been reports to the effect that in some instances the victims of flame-thrower attack have failed to disclose any external evidence of injury." The memo details the procedures medical officers qualified as pathologists were required to follow when collecting samples from those who were killed by flamethrowers. "It is from such cases that tissues for pathologi-cal examination are most earnestly desired," the memo states.[8]

In a May 1942 proposal to Dr. Sidney Burwell, dean of Harvard Medical School, Moritz detailed plans for an experiment on "the local and systemic effects of burning." Heat from a flame and from heated water would be applied to the legs of anesthetized pigs suspended in canvas hammocks. The temperature on the legs of the pigs would be recorded during the process. The proposal said that after the legs are burned, the tissues—"skin, fat, muscle, bone marrow, blood vessels and nerves"—would be analyzed. The reaction of the pig's skin to differ-ent temperatures and the rate of tissue repair, if evident, would also be studied.[9]

In 1945, the National Defense Research Committee hosted the "Symposium on the Toxicological Aspects of the Flame Thrower," in Washington, DC, and a study by Moritz and Henriques was "one of the major reports on flamethrower casualties," according to Van Wyck. The study, "an experimental investigation of the physiological mechanisms concerned in the production of casualties by flamethrower attack," exposed anesthetized dogs and pigs to flamethrowers. Results indicated that the animals exposed directly to the flame died within 60 seconds. Indirect exposure to the flame and the resulting rise in temperature had a variety of lethal effects, including cardiac arrest and shock, depending on the animal's core temperature. Van Wyck's article said the study was questioned by some because pigskin, while similar, is not identical to human skin. Other studies presented at the symposium looked at suffo-cation as a contributing cause of death among victims of flamethrowers.[10]

Gruesome black-and-white photos of the research are preserved in Harvard Medical School's files. Moritz also subjected himself to burn research. "In fact, he would come home at night with quarter-size, half-dollar-size burns on his forearm from testing various materials," his son John said in a 2018 interview. One dog that was destined for burn research instead came home with Dr. Moritz. Named Reddy, he became a beloved pet for John, Anne and Richard.[11]

While Moritz's burn research using dogs and pigs was praised by the military, which requested the studies, animal advocates would become highly critical as the urgency of wartime receded. In the early 1960s, Moritz, who had returned to Western Reserve in Cleveland, learned that animal rights organizations, including the Humane Society of the United States, had launched an animal cruelty campaign against the researchers and were singling out at least one of the studies he had done while at Harvard. In a letter to Bernard F. Trum, director of the Animal Research Center at Harvard Medical School, Moritz explained that the research on the "casualty producing potential of the flame thrower in circumstances that would duplicate field conditions as closely as possible" was requested by the National Defense Research Council, and he defended the studies' valuable results.[12]

Moritz acknowledged that because of the urgency of the NDRC's request, he and Henriques "went directly to animal experiments without performing a number of preliminary tests that probably would have been made in ordinary circumstances." He added that that after reviewing the process, "many, if not most of the animal experiments, would have been eventually necessary to answer the questions raised even [if] there had been time to have preceded the animal experiments by more elaborate non-biological analytical observations."

In the letter to Trum, Moritz criticized those who were raising questions about the research. He said he and NDRC believed the studies were needed to protect soldiers and that "these same critics would be even more acrimonious had it turned out that the information had been needed" but the military not been worried about the effects of flamethrowers on the soldiers. "I suggest that those who are least qualified to play the game are usually the most vocal Monday morning quarterbacks," he wrote.

In 1964, Dr. Maurice Visscher, chairman of the physiology department at the University of Minnesota Medical School, wrote a letter asking Moritz for advice on how to counter claims by animal rights groups concerning the Harvard burn studies and comments he made at a National Research Council symposium on burns in 1951. "They quote you as exposing animals to 500° C temperature under 'light anesthesia' and allowing them to die in 24 to 48 hours, without analgesics."

Visscher, co-founder and president of the National Society of Medical Research, told Moritz that the NSMR was gathering information for a response to the Humane Society's accusations and looking for specific examples "in which the [Humane Society] is not telling the truth."[13]

Moritz responded to Visscher in a letter that all animals were given "an anesthetic dose of sodium pentothal" before the tests and all animals that survived with burns were "kept under sodium pentothal so long as they survived."[14]

In 1966 Congress passed and President Lyndon Johnson signed the Laboratory Animal Welfare Act, the first federal law protecting the welfare of animals used for scientific research. The law has been amended a number of times since.[15]

In total, Moritz's research resulted in ten groundbreaking papers on thermal burns and the absorption into the skin of toxins from those burns. Eight of the studies are in a series titled "Studies of Thermal Injury," and those studies would be cited in numerous articles on burn research for decades to come.[16] "They are pretty detailed and there is a lot of material in each one of those papers," Dr. Cancio, director of the US Army Institute of Surgical Research Burn Center, said.[17]

Moritz's burn studies were the first of their kind and most have not and cannot be duplicated for a number of reasons, including the difficulty in reproducing the amount of heat used and a prohibition on conducting such research on "companion animals," Cancio said. "So you've got to go back to those original papers," he told me. "You can't take somebody else's word for it. You have got to read your grandfather's papers."

Cancio said he was particularly interested in the studies involving human volunteers and was surprised to learn that Moritz and his colleagues were among the volunteers who burned themselves. "Oh my gosh, you can't volunteer yourself as an experimental subject on your own study nowadays," he said.[18]

Not all of Moritz's work for the military involved burns. He also worked with Capt. Norman Zamcheck of the US Army Medical Corps to study the death reports of nearly 1,000 soldiers who died of unknown causes.

The soldiers had been considered in good health yet died suddenly or within 24 hours of becoming sick. The study was similar to one Moritz had done more than a decade earlier when he reviewed some of the more than 2,500 consecutive autopsies performed or studied in the Institute of Pathology at Western Reserve University and University of Hospitals in Cleveland. That study, titled "Pathogenesis of Sudden Death," was published in 1934 in the *Transactions of the American Therapeutic Society*.[19]

The study requested by the military and published in November 1946 in the *Archives of Pathology* found most of the soldiers who died were considered "overweight" or "very heavy" compared to other servicemen. About 350 of the deaths were caused by heart disease. Also, most of those who died were 25 or older, and about a third of the overall deaths were caused by meningitis, as well by infections, bleeding in the brain and pneumonia.[20]

Moritz flatly refused at least one military research project. It is mentioned in a 2016 article by Adam Kline and Robyn Dexter titled "Secret Weapons, Forgotten Sacrifices," which was published in 2016 in the US National Archives & Records Administration's *Prologue* magazine. The article details the various ideas and proposals made during World War II to the US Office of Scientific Research & Development, which was tasked with finding new weaponry for the war effort.

Kline and Dexter wrote:

> When two colonels inquired in 1944 about "using methane bombs to freeze a neighborhood," Alan R. Moritz of Harvard's medical school dismissed the proposition, saying that such a weapon would only harm those within "the immediate vicinity." He also mentioned that methane gas would cause severe injury. He stated that using incendiary rounds to ignite a kilogram of methane gas would release "approximately 13,000 kilocalories," as opposed to the mere 250 kilocalories taken in by warming liquid methane.[21]

While Moritz's studies on burns were conducted for the military, his expertise was sometimes displayed in the courtroom. In 1946, he testified in the trial of an Army lieutenant charged with branding the letters "T" and "F" on a woman's breasts. He "told a Suffolk superior court jury the [cigarette] butt brands were permanent and that cuts the girl claims were inflected with a razor likewise will not completely fade," the *Republican*, a newspaper in Springfield, Massachusetts, reported. Moritz also testified that the "center sections of the many burns were 'third degree variety.'"

The newspaper article said the judge accepted Moritz as a "medical expert on burns after he recounted his work on more than 5,000 autopsies and disclosed he had experimented for the war department on burns during the war." The article continued, saying that Moritz "said he had burned both himself and friends to get scientific data on the subject."

While the article about the trial was straightforward, the headline was a bit sensational: "Helen's Brands Will Be Visible All of Her Life: Dr. Alan Moritz's Testimony Shows Love Orgy Won't Be Forgotten."[22]

ANIMAL DOPING

At least once, Dr. Moritz conducted animal research that didn't involve burns, nor was it conducted for the military. In 1947, the Massachusetts Racing Commission was battling the illegal practice of "doping" racehorses and racing dogs with stimulants, and three commissioners approached Moritz about the possibility of research into the detection of stimulants and depressants in racing animals. The Department of Legal Medicine agreed to conduct drug testing research, believing the research on animals might also benefit drug testing in humans.[23]

Within a year, new testing techniques were announced that allowed for faster detection of smaller amounts of drugs. The findings were hailed by the racing commissioners and quickly put into practice. The techniques also were soon being used in Boston hospitals.

A press release announcing the Department of Legal Medicine's research findings was issued by Harvard Medical School on August 6, 1948, and an article on the new drug testing techniques and their use on humans ran about a week later in the "Science in Review" column of the *New York Times.*

The *Times* reported that emergency physicians were regularly faced with drug overdose patients, often from sleeping pills containing barbiturates such as luminal, sodium amytal, Seconal and phenobarbital. The department's research "has found a way of correlating the blood concentration of a barbiturate with the amount taken and of correlating the time of taking with the clinical effect." Additional research "should reveal the speed and means by which the body disposes of various drugs. Thus the task of determining the cause of death in fatal cases of poisoning would be simplified."[24]

The "new techniques are already in use in Boston hospitals in the treatment of unconscious emergency patients," the article went on. "Quick diagnosis is important in cases of poisoning. By a new method of analyzing blood, Harvard's Laboratory of Legal Medicine now determines in half an hour whether the unconscious patient brought to the hospital took an overdose of something."[25]

The new drug testing procedures on animals were approved by the state Racing Commission. The organizations that worked with the Department of Legal Medicine on the study were the Eastern Racing Association, the Revere Racing Association, the Taunton Greyhound Association and the Massasoit Greyhound Association.[26]

NOTES

1. "Of Crime and Change and the Doctor's Doctor," *Medical World News*, March 13, 1970, 36.
2. Corydon Ireland, "Harvard Goes to War," *The Harvard Gazette*, November 10, 2011, https://news.harvard.edu/gazette/story/2011 /11/harvard-goes-to-war/; John A. Moritz, interview by Rob Moritz, April 21, 2018, Benton, Ark.

3. John A. Moritz, interview by Rob Moritz, April 21, 2018, Benton, Ark.

4. "Of Crime and Change and the Doctor's Doctor," *Medical World News*, March 13, 1970, 36–37

5. "Of Crime and Change and the Doctor's Doctor," *Medical World News*, March 13, 1970, 37.

6. Leopoldo C. Cancio, telephone interview by Rob Moritz, August 28, 2020.

7. David W. Van Wyck, "Beyond the Burn: Studies on the Physiological Effects of Flamethrowers during World War II," *Military Medical Research* 7, no. 1 (February 27, 2020): 8, accessed July 18, 2024, https://mmrjournal.biomedcentral.com/articles/10.1186/s40779 -020-00237-9.

8. Army Institute of Pathology, Memo in Alan R. Moritz's Archived Materials, n.d. (Center for the History of Medicine at Francis A. Countway Library, Harvard University).

9. Alan R. Moritz, letter to C. Sidney Burwell, May 6, 1942. (Center for the History of Medicine at Francis A. Countway Library, Harvard University).

10. David W. Van Wyck, "Beyond the Burn: Studies on the Physiological Effects of Flamethrowers during World War II," *Military Medical Research* 7, no. 1 (February 27, 2020): 8, accessed July 18, 2024, https://mmrjournal.biomedcentral.com/articles/10.1186/s40779 -020-00237-9.

11. John A. Moritz, interview by Rob Moritz, April 21, 2018, Benton, Ark.

12. Alan R. Moritz, letter to Bernard F. Trum, July 2, 1963 (PATH015 Alan R. Moritz, MD, Papers, Stanley A. Ferguson Archives, University Hospitals of Cleveland).

13. Maurice B. Visscher, letter to Alan R. Moritz, August 26, 1964 (PATH015 Alan R. Moritz, MD, Papers, Stanley A. Ferguson Archives, University Hospitals of Cleveland).

14. Alan R. Moritz, letter to Maurice B. Visscher, August 31, 1964 (PATH015 Alan R. Moritz, MD, Papers, Stanley A. Ferguson Archives, University Hospitals of Cleveland).

15. "Government Passes Tougher Laws on Use of Animals in Laboratories," *The Crimson*, August 15, 1967, accessed July 8, 2024, https://www.thecrimson.com/article/1967/8/15/government -passes-tougher-laws-on-use/.

16. Richard Ford, proposal for research letter to The Office of Naval Research, Medical Sciences Section, April 16, 1951. (Center for the History of Medicine at Francis A. Countway Library, Harvard University); Cancio interview.

17. Leopoldo C. Cancio, telephone interview by Rob Moritz, August 28, 2020.
18. Leopoldo C. Cancio, telephone interview by Rob Moritz, August 28, 2020.
19. Alan R. Moritz, "The Pathogenesis of Sudden Death," reprinted from the *Transactions of the American Therapeutic Society* XXXIV (1934), 97-101. (Moritz Family Collection).
20. Alan R. Moritz and N. Zamcheck, "Sudden and Unexpected Deaths of Young Soldiers; Diseases Responsible for Such Deaths During World War II," *Archives of Pathology* (November 1, 1946): Vol. 16, Issue 11, 459–494.
21. Adam Kline and Robyn Dexter, "Secret Weapons, Forgotten Sacrifices: Scientific R & D in World War II," *Prologue Magazine* 48, no. 1 (Spring 2016): 28–29, National Archives, accessed July 18, 2024, https://www.archives.gov/publications/prologue/2016/spring/office-scientific-research-development-world-war-ii.
22. "Helen's Brands Will Be Visible All of Her Life: Dr. Alan Moritz's Testimony Shows Love Orgy Won't Be Forgotten," *The Republican*, Springfield, MA, July 8, 1946.
23. Harvard University Press Release, Afternoon Papers of Friday, August 6, 1948. (Center for the History of Medicine at Francis A. Countway Library, Harvard University).
24. Waldemar Kaempffert, "Narcotics Study: Experts Reveal New Ways of Treating Drug Poisoning," *New York Times*, August 14, 1948, E-9.
25. Waldemar Kaempffert, "Narcotics Study: Experts Reveal New Ways of Treating Drug Poisoning," *New York Times*, August 14, 1948, E-9.
26. Alan Moritz, letter to Dr. Richard Fitz, July 21, 1948 (Center for the History of Medicine at Francis A. Countway Library, Harvard University).

CHAPTER 10

Cocoanut Grove

The Moritz family spent Thanksgiving of 1942 in a rented cottage in Ipswich, Massachusetts, the seaside village where they would soon build their own cottage. On Sunday morning, November 29, Alan, Velma and the three children began the 40-mile drive to their home in Jamaica Plain.

Not long into their trip, their car was pulled over by a state trooper who asked to speak with Dr. Moritz outside the car. After a brief discussion, Velma was told she would need to drive the children the rest of the way home. The trooper had been sent to fetch Dr. Moritz because his help was needed in a mass casualty situation in Boston's Bay Village neighborhood.[1]

While my grandmother drove my father and the twins home, my grandfather was taken to the scene of what remains the deadliest nightclub fire in US history. Late the previous night, a fire had erupted in the popular Cocoanut Grove nightclub, killing nearly 500 people and injuring several hundred more. Moritz, graduate fellows from the Department of Legal Medicine and other pathologists who were enlisted to help had the gruesome task identifying the bodies—and determining causes of death, which was more complicated than it might seem.

The fire had started in the club's basement, known as the Melody Lounge. Witnesses told investigators that they first noticed the fire in a decorative palm tree on the wall and it quickly traveled to the ceiling. In less than 10 minutes, the fire, fueled by highly flammable decorations on the walls and ceiling, spread throughout the nightclub as patrons scattered in all directions.[2]

As news of the tragedy and the mind-boggling death count was being reported in the United States and the world, Boston public safety officials were baffled by the fire itself. It had moved with incredible speed and ferocity and produced some unusual gasses, yet it did not burn as much of the nightclub as they would have thought, Paul Benzaquin wrote in a 1960 *Boston Globe* article.

Many of the victims had been blinded by thick smoke and had been trampled or crushed trying to find their way out of the building. Others died from burns. What surprised investigators most was that about half

DOI: 10.4324/9781003539186-11

79

of the victims had little or no burns, but their bodies were reddish in color. That suggested highly toxic fumes may have caused their deaths. The question, then, was what caused those deadly fumes?[3]

Tests conducted at Harvard Medical School by Moritz and Dr. Frank Dutra, a fellow in the Department of Legal Medicine, determined that those deaths were most likely caused by acrolein, a toxin emitted by the burning of the artificial leather which lined the walls and covered chairs and stools in the nightclub. The two presented their findings to a panel that had been created to investigate the fire.

In high concentrations, acrolein works as an anesthetic and can cause people to fall unconscious and die. The families of many of the victims "took comfort from the medical opinion that few Grove victims suffered the terrible torture of burning alive," Benzaquin wrote. "Post mortems suggested that most of such victims were already dead or mercifully unconscious when overtaken by the fire. Those who suffered the worst were the ones who survived the fire but succumbed to their burns later in hospitals."[4]

Before research into the cause of the deaths could begin, however, Moritz and dozens of other forensic pathologists and medical examiners had the grim task of identifying the bodies. The *Boston Globe* reported on December 3, 1942, that all the victims were identified within 89 hours and 40 minutes.

> By dental structure, jewelry, scraps of clothing, military "dog tags," fingerprints and the cooperation of parents and friends, officials found names of every one in the piles of death which were carried Saturday night and Sunday morning in ambulances, trucks and emergency tumbrils to the Northern and Southern Mortuaries.

"Methods of identification were efficient and quick, many of them remarkable in their ingenuity," the article continued. Moritz worked at the Southern Mortuary with Suffolk County Medical Examiner Timothy Leary and "set up a program which made identification simple and less harrowing." After separating men from women, the bodies "were then reclassified by height, color of hair, weight, color of clothing, type of jewelry," the article said. "Dr. Alan Moritz, state pathologist, who returned from a week-end vacation Sunday afternoon to assist Dr. Leary, said this system of cross reference eliminated untold confusion."[5]

LESSONS LEARNED

The horrific event at the Cocoanut Grove led to the widespread adoption of stricter building codes in the United States, and the fact that no subsequent fire in a public venue has come close to its death count is a testament to the lessons learned. Moritz and his Legal Medicine team also learned from the response and developed protocols on how to conduct future mass-casualty investigations. More protocols were added following the July 1944 circus fire in Hartford, Connecticut. In that incident, a fire broke out while some 6,000 people were under a large canvas "big top" to enjoy a performance of the Ringling Brothers and Barnum & Bailey Circus. Nearly 170 died when the burning tent fell onto the crowd.[6]

For years, the department's benefactress Frances Glessner Lee had been interested in the possibility of using dental records to identify decomposed and burned bodies. In 1903, when she was 25 years old, the Iroquois Theater in Chicago caught fire and more than 600 people were killed. In 1943, she told Gregg she was working on a proposal that would "standardize the record systems of dentists," so they could be used, if necessary, for identification purposes. She also proposed a "dental project," with research being done to determine if teeth from a dead person's body could be used to estimate the time or manner of death and whether they could be used for identification. The study would also look at the "natural decomposition" of teeth, as well as what happens to teeth when immersed in liquids, incinerated, subjected to acids or alkalis and trauma.[7]

There is no indication that the Department of Legal Medicine acted on Lee's proposals. However, Moritz clearly embraced the promise of forensic dentistry. In the second edition of "Pathology of Trauma," published in 1954, he wrote that medical examiners should look at the teeth when trying to identify a decomposed body or one burned beyond recognition. "After fingerprints, teeth probably constitute the richest single source of identifying characteristics of an otherwise unrecognizable corpse." He said most adults have had a dental examination, and dentists typically keep accurate records of dental disease and repair.

> Generally speaking, the dental charts prepared by pathologists from the examination of a corpse are rarely worth the paper upon which they are written. If a useful dental record of a corpse is desirable it should be prepared by a dentist.[8]

In the same chapter, Moritz stressed the importance of observation during an autopsy and recalled how a victim of the Cocoanut Grove fire was identified. The body, he said, was burned beyond recognition but her age, sex and size were similar to a girl reported to have been in the nightclub at the time of the fire. An autopsy clinched the identification because "the contents of her stomach corresponded to those of an unusual meal that the missing girl was known to have shared with her family approximately three hours before the outbreak of the fire."[9]

In April 1947, a death investigation seminar by Moritz and his department included a course on the procedures used to identify hundreds of victims of the Cocoanut Grove and the Hartford circus fires. Scientific procedures used to determine the chemicals in the fumes after the Cocoanut Grove fire were also discussed. J.H. Arnette, a chemist with the Texas State Police laboratory, attended that seminar and, about a week later, a cargo ship carrying 2,000 tons of fertilizer exploded in the port of Texas City. Nearly 600 people were killed and another 100 were believed to have died but their remains were never found. Using techniques he learned from the seminar at Harvard, Arnette established a command center at the scene and used tags to help in the identification of victims before they were removed from the scene.[10]

In 1950, Dr. Richard Ford, who followed Moritz as director of the Department of Legal Medicine, told Maryland police officers that state leaders in Massachusetts were considering a proposal that would require civilians to wear fireproof identification tags. The ID tags would be beneficial in helping identify bodies after a nuclear attack—a constant concern during the Cold War—or other mass casualty events. He said every large city should have a public-disaster plan in place, and the plan should include the designation of a temporary mortuary and personnel on standby to transport the dead to the facility.[11]

The kind of disaster response plan that Boston had to create on the fly in 1942 is now standard for cities across the United States, and they are reviewed and modified on a regular basis.

NOTES

1. John A. Moritz, interview by Rob Moritz, April 21, 2018, Benton, Ark.
2. Daniel J. Flemming, "The Cocoanut Grove Revisited: US Navy Records Document How 492 Died in a Deadly Nightclub Fire 75 Years Ago," *National Archives* 49, no. 3 (Fall 2017), accessed November 17, 2021, https://www.archives.gov/publications/prologue/2017/fall/cocoanut-grove.
3. Paul Benzaquin, "Holocaust!: The Shocking Story of the Boston Cocoanut Grove," *Boston Globe*, January 21, 1960.
4. Paul Benzaquin, "Holocaust!: The Shocking Story of the Boston Cocoanut Grove," *Boston Globe*, January 21, 1960.
5. "All Grove Dead Identified 89 Hours After Fire Struck: Efficient Medical Detective Work Attributed to Wartime Organization," *Boston Globe*, December 3, 1942, 21.

6. "The Texas City Disaster: April 16, 1947," *Texas City Local Firefighters Local 1259*, accessed August 8, 2024, https://www.local1259iaff.org/disaster.html; Vicki Daniel, "The Social History of Disaster Victim Identification in the United States, 1865 to 1950," *Academic Forensic Pathology: The Publication of the National Association of Medical Examiners Foundation,* May 10, 2020.

7. Alan Gregg, "Memo of interview of AG with Mrs. Frances Lee," March 19, 1943 (Rockefeller Foundation Archives); From Frances Glessner Lee to the Department of Legal Medicine, Harvard Medical School, "Plans for a Dental Project," n.d. (Center for the History of Medicine at Francis A. Countway Library, Harvard University).

8. Alan R. Moritz, *Pathology of Trauma*, 2nd ed. (Philadelphia: Lea & Febiger, 1954), 392.

9. Alan R. Moritz, *Pathology of Trauma*, 2nd ed. (Philadelphia: Lea & Febiger, 1954), 393.

10. Vicki Daniel, "The Social History of Disaster Victim Identification in the United States, 1865 to 1950," *Academic Forensic Pathology: The Publication of the National Association of Medical Examiners Foundation,* May 10, 2020; "The Texas City Disaster: April 16, 1947," *Texas City Local Firefighters Local 1259*, accessed August 8, 2024, https://www.local1259iaff.org/disaster.html; "Hartford Circus Fire," *connecticuthistory.org*, July 6, 2019, accessed August 15, 2024, ttps://connecticuthistory.org/the-hartford-circus-fire/; "State Toxicologist: Ex-Abilenian One of Chief Witnesses in Clary Trial," *Abilene Reporter-News*, June 1, 1948; "The Texas City Disaster: April 16, 1947," *Texas City Local Firefighters Local 1259*, accessed August 8, 2024, https://www.local1259iaff.org/disaster.html

11. "Identity Tags Urged for All: Massachusetts Weighs Items in Bomb-defense Plan," *Baltimore Sun*, October 24, 1950 (Center for the History of Medicine at Francis A. Countway Library, Harvard University).

CHAPTER **11**

"Death on a Silver Platter"

Of the thousands of deaths Dr. Moritz worked on during his long career, none seemed to trouble him more than the Noxon case, which, strangely, became a *cause célèbre* both for advocates for the rights of the disabled and for advocates of euthanasia. My grandfather was conflicted, too— not about his medical conclusion or morality but on the question of reasonable doubt in the face of conflicting expert testimony.[1]

John F. Noxon Jr., a 46-year-old corporate attorney and veteran of World War I, was accused in September 1943 of deliberately electrocuting his 6-month-old son, who had Down syndrome. The case became a front-page staple in the Boston newspapers, although the death of baby Lawrence Noxon had occurred 140 miles to the west, in Pittsfield, Massachusetts, near the New York border. The arrest and prosecution of an affluent and politically connected lawyer—one himself disabled by polio after he returned from the war—on a charge of first-degree murder was also followed closely by the *New York Times* and many other newspapers in the Northeast.[2]

Noxon, who enjoyed tinkering with radios, told police he had been changing the tubes in a radio, described in some reports as a large console, in the library of his home. He said his wife brought the baby into the room and placed him on a metal tray on the floor to prevent any damage to furniture or floor if he wet his diaper. Noxon's wife left the room and eventually he, too, left the room to get something—either a screwdriver or new tubes for the radio, depending on media reports. He told police he was gone between 5 and 10 minutes. As he returned, he "noticed the odor of something burning" and found his son dead on the floor with his forearm, just above the wrist, entangled in the electric cord of a lamp Noxon had been using to see inside the radio. It was soon determined that the cord was old and frayed.[3]

An early report in the *Times* said "a wire had been tied around the baby's arm and the fatal charge was effected when the child, in damp underclothing, was placed on a metal tray." [4]After discovering the baby dead, the Noxons summoned their family doctor, Albert C. England, who was considered a medical examiner but not a pathologist under

DOI: 10.4324/9781003539186-12

Massachusetts' coroner system. Dr. England issued a certificate of death by electrocution, and the child's body was taken to a funeral home and embalmed.[5]

England, however, was troubled by the circumstances of the boy's death and discussed it with the local police chief, who opened an investigation. After meeting with the Noxons, the police chief called in Moritz to perform an autopsy on the baby. My grandfather was then director of the Department of Legal Medicine at Harvard Medical School and a pathologist for the Massachusetts Department of Safety, and he was regarded as an expert on burns due to his research for the War Department and his experience identifying victims of the Cocoanut Grove nightclub fire the previous year.

Five days after Lawrence Noxon's death, his father was charged with murder.

Moritz testified for more than a week as a prosecution witness in the trial that commenced in late February of 1944, 5 months after the boy's death. The following is a section of the front-page article in the *Boston Globe* on March 7, 1944, detailing Moritz's testimony about the autopsy findings:

> "On the left forearm was a lesion 2 1/2 inches long," he said.
> "In the center the skin had been broken up and destroyed. The color was predominantly green and yellow.
> "Next to the center the skin had a cooked appearance, gray in color."
> Moritz was grasping a point on his own left arm just below the elbow on the outside of the arm.
> "Next to where the skin looked cooked there was a brilliant red line that could be traced all around," said Moritz.
> "The skin was discolored outside the red line, purple, shading to blue and pink.
> "There were narrow lines radiating out into the skin, some an inch and a half, others a half-inch long. All were in pairs rather than single lines.
> "Part of these marks was dark red and the skin was depressed.
> "The skin was gray, yellowish and had a cooked appearance around these pairs of lines."
> The courtroom crowd sat holding their breath as Moritz, graphically waving his left arm and pointing out spots, gave this description.
> "The major burn on the left arm covered about four square inches.
> "On the back of the left arm was a dumbbell-shaped set of red discolorations with several slender bright red lines between them.
> "The skin around the mark had a cooked appearance.
> "In the under-portion of the right arm was an area of discoloration, a mixture of brown and pink. In the center of that area, about three-quarters of an inch long, were small marks in the surface of the skin.
> "Nearer the elbow were two small holes in the skin shaped like an inverted T. The edges were sharp.

"Below these two were another pair of small holes in the skin, shaped like exclamation marks between a 32d and 16th of an inch each."
Moritz stepped to the blackboard and drew "exclamations points" with chalk for the jury.
"At the very center of the discolored area [there] was another small hole also shaped like an exclamation point.
"This was the only one of the five I have described that penetrated through the skin.
"At the bottom of the area of discoloration was a line of discoloration which we found out was an area of cooking and shrinking of the skin." [6]

Moritz remained convinced, even decades later, that Noxon meticulously planned the boy's death "so that it would seem to be an accident. He electrocuted him."[7]

A mistrial was declared after a juror collapsed and could no longer continue hearing the case. (The Massachusetts Legislature passed an alternate juror law in 1945 to avoid the necessity of such mistrials.) Moritz also testified in the second trial, which began in June 1944. In July, John Noxon was found guilty of first-degree murder and sentenced to death.[8]

Despite his unwavering conviction that Noxon was indeed guilty of premeditated murder, my grandfather joined an ultimately successful campaign for leniency that seems to have been inspired mainly by a kind of professional humility. The defense, led by former Massachusetts Gov. Joseph Ely, had presented testimony from well-qualified experts—including Dr. Milton Helpern, who for 20 years was chief medical examiner of New York City—who concluded that the boy's death could have been the accident his father claimed it was. Dr. Moritz couldn't shake his feeling that the jury didn't give the defense's witnesses their due.

"Not that the evidence was faulty; I still had the opinion I had. But if I'd been on the jury, I … could not have thought this man was guilty beyond a reasonable doubt," he said in 1980.[9]

After Noxon was sentenced to death, Moritz attended hearings requesting that Noxon be pardoned or issued clemency. For a star prosecution witness of Moritz's reputation to ask for leniency for a man sentenced to death for killing his own son merited Page One treatment.[10]

"I didn't enjoy that part of it either," Moritz said.

It was very difficult for me to go down there to this hearing. … It was front-page news with the implication that I had changed my mind about it. I hadn't changed my mind about anything, except feeling that if I were on the jury, I couldn't have voted as the jury did."[11]

Moritz also wrote to three successive governors to urge mercy. In a letter preserved in the archives at Harvard Medical School, he asked Gov.

Leverett A. Saltonstall to grant clemency and release Noxon. Saltonstall left office in January 1945 without taking action, so my grandfather continued his petitions. Several newspapers refer to letters Moritz wrote to Saltonstall's successor, Maurice J. Tobin, and Tobin's successor, Robert F. Bradford. Tobin, who served a single 2-year term as governor, commuted Noxon's sentence to life as he left office in January 1947.[12]

Moritz still wasn't satisfied. Front-page stories appeared in Pittsfield's newspaper, the *Berkshire Eagle,* and in other New England newspapers in 1947 and 1948 reporting on the letters Dr. Moritz wrote. On July 22, 1947, a front-page article in the evening edition of the *Boston Globe,* headlined "Ask Pardon for Noxon," had a quote from Moritz above the headline: "I do not believe a truly open-minded jury could have found Noxon guilty beyond reasonable doubt." The paper noted that Moritz had been a "Chief Witness for the Prosecution at the Trial."[13]

The next day, the *Berkshire Eagle* published a front-page story with a headline that underscored my grandfather's role in the petition: "Moritz Letters Stir Controversy."[14]

In September 1947, former Gov. Ely filed a 40-page pardon petition for Noxon. In December 1948, Gov. Bradford recommended leniency, and on January 4, 1949, Noxon was paroled from his life sentence and released from jail. [15]

Noxon was "a man of considerable means, well connected both financially and politically," Moritz recalled, and Dr. Helpern was just one of several "highly competent pathologists" who, after examining the same evidence, had come to a different conclusion. "I think I would have felt that if people of this quality differed from the state's expert, I would think there was a possibility of his innocence," Moritz said.[16]

Helpern wrote extensively about the Noxon case in his 1977 memoir, "Autopsy." He described the Berkshire County Courthouse as "a primitive place" and the trial atmosphere as "positively medieval." Helpern wrote that "the community was after Noxon. They didn't like him and were out to get him, a phenomenon I'd witnessed in New England before."[17]

Helpern, like my grandfather, believed there was strong evidence for both prosecution and defense. "I testified to the effect that it was equally possible for the child to have sustained this electrical burn in an accidental way as in a homicidal way," Helpern wrote. "There was nothing inherent in the autopsy or the appearance of the burn on the forearm that helped to decide this either way—you just couldn't tell the difference."

He was complimentary of my grandfather's work and professionalism, pointing out that they came to the same conclusion about the verdict—as did Judge Abraham E. Pinanki.

"Alan Moritz was aghast at the guilty verdict," Helpern wrote.

He had gone there armed to the teeth with evidence to substantiate the homicide allegation .... He was a most impressive witness, with prestigious qualifications. Yet afterward, he asked, "How could they convict him? I don't think the jury should have believed only my testimony, even though I believed it implicitly, and ignored that for the defense."[18]

THE MORAL QUESTIONS

The conviction of John Noxon Jr. and the subsequent commutation of his death sentence are seen by some observers as evidence of how American society and the legal system have marginalized people with disabilities. Supporters of euthanasia have also referenced the case when arguing that so-called "mercy killings" have a long history and even some measure of public support.

Baby Lawrence Noxon's genetic condition has weighed heavily on everyone who has examined the case, from the 1940s forward. I won't polish the language my grandfather used more than 30 years later: "It was a very unpleasant case because you couldn't help but have some sympathy with this man's ... Mongolian child," he said. "It's merciful if it dies of something because it's a child that is nothing more than an idiot. They usually die by the time they get in their 20s," he said, citing a life expectancy that was still true for people with Down syndrome in the 1970s. [19]

In an essay titled "Death on a Silver Platter: Masculinity, Disabilities, and The Noxon Murder Trials of 1944," Ivy George and James W. Trent Jr. concluded that Noxon ultimately received leniency because he was affluent and politically connected. The essay, published in the 2017 book *Phallacies: Historical Intersections of Disability and Masculinity*, suggests that Noxon's own disability played a role in popular support for granting him mercy.

George and Trent wrote:

"Embedded in the charges, trial, commutation, and parole are issues of class (Noxon was well to do), gender (Noxon was a successful man), religion (Noxon was a High-Church Protestant), and politics (Noxon was a Democrat). And all of these variables play into the events between 1943 and 1949. But Noxon was also a disabled polio survivor whose image of walking or standing with two canes was printed in newspapers across the nation. The image and words about him are embodied in the label, 'crippled.' In none of the several dozen articles about these events is there a failure to mention 'crippled Noxon.'"[20]

Noxon, wrote George and Trent, was perceived as "a real man, a triumph and an inspiration even if he kills his differently disabled child."

They concluded that Noxon, despite maintaining his innocence, most likely saw his son as "helpless and defenseless, with no social or economic potential." In the 2005 book *A Concise History of Euthanasia: Life, Death, God and Medicine*, the Euthanasia Society of America and the Voluntary Euthanasia Legislation Society cited the Noxon case among others as indicators that "society was ready to approve euthanasia laws."

> The jury had found him guilty because Noxon kept insisting that the son's death was an accident, despite evidence that a radio wire was found on the child's arm, and the child was on a metal tray and wearing a wet diaper. On the other hand, Noxon suffered from polio, and sympathizers pointed out that he had a justifiable worry about trying to raise such a disabled child.[21]

"MERCY KILLING"

About a year after Noxon was paroled, a doctor's "mercy killing" of a New Hampshire woman with terminal cancer made headlines. Dr. Hermann Sander was charged with first-degree murder after he admitted to injecting 40 cubic centimeters of air into the veins of a 59-year-old patient whose cancer was so advanced that she could not eat or drink. The arrest and subsequent trial sparked a national debate over the morality of euthanasia.

The *Boston Daily Record* interviewed Moritz for an article published shortly before Sander's trial began in January 1950. Asked about lethal injections of air, Moritz said there was "no data available in this country, as far as I know, which would determine exactly what constitutes a 'lethal injection' of air into a person's veins." Sander had admitted injecting his patient with air four times, and he insisted that she died peacefully. He documented what he did in the patient's treatment notes, and officials at the hospital later alerted police about what Sander had done.

After a 14-day trial, a jury deliberated about an hour before declaring Sander not guilty of murder.[22]

NOTES

1. Alan R. Moritz, transcript of interview by someone identified only as "Bonnie," *Cleveland, Ohio,* 1980 (Moritz Family Collection).
2. Donald B. Willard, "Noxon Held Without Bail Denies Mercy Killing," *New York Times*, September 28, 1941, 1.

3. "Noxon Death Shock Went Through Arms," *Berkshire Eagle*, October 22, 1943, 1–2.

4. "Lawyer Arrested in Death of His Son," *New York Times*, September 28, 1942, 27.

5. George Ivy and James W. Trent Jr., "Death on a Silver Platter: Masculinity, Disabilities, and the Noxon Murder Trials of 1944," in *Phallacies: Historical Intersection of Disability and Masculinity*, ed. Kathleen M. Brian and James W. Trent Jr. (Oxford: University Press, 2017), 220.

6. Dorothy G. Wayman, "Noxon Defense Forces Moritz to Suspend His Testimony," *Boston Globe*, March 7, 1944, 1.

7. Alan R. Moritz, transcript of interview by someone identified only as "Bonnie," *Cleveland, Ohio,* 1980 (Moritz Family Collection).

8. Alan R. Moritz, transcript of interview by someone identified only as "Bonnie," *Cleveland, Ohio,* 1980 (Moritz Family Collection); Stephen Chermak and Frankie Y. Bailey, eds., *Crimes of the Centuries: Notorious Crimes, Criminals, and Criminals Trials in American History,* Vol. 2, (Santa Barbara, CA: ABC-CLIO, 2016), 585.

9. Alan R. Moritz, transcript of interview by someone identified only as "Bonnie," *Cleveland, Ohio,* 1980 (Moritz Family Collection).

10. "Noxon's Pardon Papers are Prepared for Counsel," *Berkshire Eagle*, July 22, 1947, 1.

11. Alan R. Moritz, transcript of interview by someone identified only as "Bonnie," *Cleveland, Ohio,* 1980 (Moritz Family Collection).

12. Alan R. Moritz to Gov. Leverett A. Saltonstall, July 11, 1944. (Center for the History of Medicine at Francis A. Countway Library, Harvard University).

13. "Noxon's Pardon Papers are Prepared for Counsel," *Berkshire Eagle*, July 22, 1947, 1; "Ask Pardon for Noxon," *Boston Globe*, July 22, 1947, 1.

14. "Moritz' Letters Stir Controversy," *Berkshire Eagle*, July 23, 1947, 1.

15. Stephen Chermak and Frankie Y. Bailey, eds., *Crimes of the Centuries: Notorious Crimes, Criminals, and Criminals Trials in American History,* Vol. 2 (Santa Barbara, CA: ABC-CLIO, 2016), 585.

16. Alan R. Moritz, transcript of interview by someone identified only as "Bonnie," *Cleveland, Ohio,* 1980 (Moritz Family Collection).

17. M. D. Milton Helpern and M. D. Bernard Knight, *Autopsy: The Memoirs of Milton Helpern, the World's Greatest Medical Detective* (New York: St. Martin's Press, 1977), 103–104

18. M. D. Milton Helpern and M. D. Bernard Knight, *Autopsy: The Memoirs of Milton Helpern, the World's Greatest Medical Detective* (New York: St. Martin's Press, 1977), 104.

19. Alan R. Moritz, transcript of interview by someone identified only as "Bonnie," *Cleveland, Ohio,* 1980 (Moritz Family Collection).

20. George Ivy and James W. Trent Jr., "Death on a Silver Platter: Masculinity, Disabilities, and the Noxon Murder Trials of 1944," in *Phallacies: Historical Intersection of Disability and Masculinity*, ed. Kathleen M. Brian and James W. Trent Jr. (Oxford: University Press, 2017), 229; Ian Dowbiggin, *A Concise History of Euthanasia: Life, Death, God and Medicine* (Lanham, MD: Rowman & Littlefield Publishers, Inc., 2005), 87.

21. Ian Dowbiggin, *A Concise History of Euthanasia: Life, Death, God and Medicine* (Lanham, MD: Rowman & Littlefield Publishers, Inc., 2005), 87.

22. "Mercy Killing Arouses Nation," *Boston Daily Record*, January 7, 1950 (PATH015 Alan R. Moritz, MD, Papers, Stanley A. Ferguson Archives, University Hospitals of Cleveland).

CHAPTER **12**

Leaving Harvard

Despite the Department of Legal Medicine's successes and its growing national reputation, Moritz continued to be frustrated by the lack of cooperation from other Harvard programs. Forensic pathology training, Moritz thought, was too specialized, and he told Dean Burwell in early 1946 that Legal Medicine and Pathology needed a closer relationship. The only way to be competent in forensic pathology was to also be competent in general pathology, he said, and he kept himself relevant through his simultaneous position as pathologist-in-chief at nearby Peter Bent Brigham Hospital.

He told Burwell that specializing in forensics "to the exclusion of other aspects of pathology is basically unsound." The "University should have a mechanism for bringing its graduate trainees in pathology in contact with the problems that are peculiar to forensic medicine and I do not believe this can be done successfully by departmentalization of forensic pathology."

He told Burwell he did not see how the relationship between his department and the rest of the medical school could be improved, short of his resigning. He reasoned that if he did leave, the problem could be addressed in one of two ways.

> One would be able to merge the Department of Legal Medicine with that of general pathology and to appoint to the staff of that department either on a part-time or full-time basis a pathologist who would maintain control of a sufficient amount of case work in a medico-legal pathology to ensure teaching material.

In this scenario, he said, undergraduate and graduate classes in forensic pathology would then be merged with that of general pathology to the benefit of both.

The second option would be to "link the medical examiner's office at the city hospital to the Department of General Pathology and require a general pathologist at the hospital to perform the work of a forensic pathologist," he said.

                    DOI: 10.4324/9781003539186-13

> If such an arrangement were made the house officers in pathology at the City Hospital would be automatically ensured of some training in the field of legal medicine and an arrangement would exist whereby graduate students could be accepted for special training.[1]

Burwell immediately notified Harvard President Conant of Moritz's concerns. He also told Conant that Moritz was considering a professorship of pathology offered by Northwestern University in Chicago. "I need not say that I am distressed by this," Burwell said. He went on to suggest that it might be time to consider merging forensic pathology into the medical school's Pathology Department and suggested creating an ad hoc committee to study the idea. Moritz, of course, should be on that committee, he added. It is not known whether the ad hoc committee was formed and what, if any, recommendations were made.[2]

Moritz's frustration was apparent to Frances Glessner Lee, who was happy that Moritz continued to work part-time as pathologist-in-chief at Peter Bent Hospital. She told Alan Gregg of the Rockefeller Foundation that, during a lunch meeting in April 1947, she had asked Moritz "point blank" if he thought he was going to succeed S.B. Wolbach, chairman of the pathology department at Harvard. His reply was, "They have not asked me." Lee then told Gregg that Moritz's "heart is still in pathology and always will be."[3]

In May 1947, Moritz presented Gregg and the Rockefeller Foundation with a report on the status of the department, the first in several years. "This spring brings us to the end of the first relatively normal year of post-war operations and seems to be an appropriate time to take stock of the past and plan for the future," he wrote.

Much of the report centered on looming issues that Moritz feared might cause problems down the line. He said the demand for forensic pathologists and medical examiners was not as great as originally projected when the department began a decade earlier because, despite all efforts, most states were still relying on the archaic coroner system. "It was recognized early in 1940 that a demand for persons qualified in the field of legal medicine must exist if there is to be any continuing justification for accepting candidates for such training."

Since arriving at Harvard, he had traveled "hundreds of thousands of miles to talk to state, county, and city medical societies, to medical and law facilities, to lawyers, to police, and to politicians," explaining that coroners were not trained as medical examiners and local and state laws needed to be changed. He said he had visited 26 states "in an effort to stimulate legislative enactment necessary to create a demand for persons trained in legal medicine." He and his department had helped draft legislative reforms for at least ten states, but the laws had been changed in just three of those states.

He wrote in the report,

> Until laws relating to the office of coroner or medical examiner in a significant number of states have been changed, there will be relatively little demand for the kind of professional product that can be turned out by the Department of Legal Medicine.

Moritz also continued to be frustrated by the lack of support his department was receiving from Harvard's law school. Before the outbreak of World War II, attempts were made to improve the working relationship, but they fell apart. Moritz had lectured at the law school and conducted some mock trials involving "cases of medico-legal interests." He also lectured on "scientific evidence and medico-legal problems," but few law students attended the lectures, which were voluntary and not for credit.

In one short-lived effort, a researcher was hired by the law school to study medico-legal issues. The researcher, Dr. Hubert W. Smith, was a graduate of both Harvard's law school and its medical school.

Moritz wrote,

> Although Smith worked hard and manifested considerable originality, he did not arouse any significant amount of interest in legal medicine within the faculty of the Law School and there was little inclination on the part of the faculty to provide for a continuation of Smith's work after the war.

Moritz did say in the May 1947 status report that he had recently been asked by the law school to give another series of lectures. While attendance would again be voluntary, he "hoped that this adventure will stimulate further interest in legal medicine at the Law School."[4]

Evidence that a successful relationship between legal medicine and law was possible added to Moritz's frustration. His friend Dr. Wiley D. Forbus was director of a new legal medicine program at Duke University in North Carolina, and he was enjoying the support of both the medical school and the law school. "But we didn't have the cooperation from the law school that was necessary to make it the kind of thing that went on at Duke," Moritz said decades later.[5]

TRYING TO KEEP HIM

By the late fall and early winter of 1948, it was becoming obvious that something needed to be done to keep Moritz from leaving. Burwell, wanting to be proactive and to nail down a long-term commitment, suggested that the Rockefeller Foundation consider a grant of $295,000 to the department "to be used in support of the work of Dr. Alan Moritz as Frances Glessner Lee Professor of Legal Medicine until his retirement in 1966."[6]

Burwell also enlisted Ernie Griswold, dean of the Harvard Law School, to send a letter to Gregg discussing the importance of the department and how it had benefited law students and would in the future.[7]

But while Burwell was pressing for additional funding to keep Moritz until retirement, Gregg had already determined that keeping Moritz would be tricky. A week before the Thanksgiving holiday, Moritz met with Gregg to provide another update on the department. Moritz again said he was "concerned over the uncertainty of the future" and wanted to know what would happen when the department's current funding appropriation ended in five years. The department, at that time, received $7,000 annually from Harvard and $7,000 from the Rockefeller Foundation.

Moritz told Gregg that fewer than 4% of the 300,000 unexplained or criminal deaths each year in the United States were being investigated by properly trained medical examiners or detectives. The rest were either not investigated or investigated by coroners lacking essential training. In order to provide that training, he said, the department would need more funding.[8]

After their meeting, Gregg wrote in his diary that Moritz's future at Harvard was unclear unless his concerns were addressed. "I would judge that Moritz will have an opportunity to go to Cleveland which he will find hard to decline unless the future at Harvard is somewhat clearer."[9] Gregg also informed Burwell that the Rockefeller Foundation would probably not agree to his $295,000 in funding request to keep Moritz at Harvard for almost two more decades. The foundation, however, was willing to fund the department for 5 more years and at $20,000 annually. A meeting with Moritz was then scheduled for January 13, 1949, to discuss his future and the budget proposal.[10]

During the January meeting, Gregg and Burwell sought assurances from Moritz about his commitment to Harvard and left the meeting believing he would stay. Burwell "thought one of the things the foundation would like to be assured of was Dr. Moritz's own attitude toward his own future in Legal Medicine; was he, in fact, primarily and fundamentally interested in this field," according to minutes of the meeting sent to the Rockefeller Foundation. Moritz had responded to Burwell's question "emphasizing the point that he considered the opportunities for a unique contribution in Legal Medicine to be excellent; that he proposed to try and make that contribution...."[11]

Gregg, during the meeting, "expressed great interest" in Moritz and told him of his plan to ask the Rockefeller Foundation to raise the department's annual funding to $20,000. News of the additional funding and their desire to improve the cooperation between his department and the Department of Pathology and law school were all well received by Moritz.[12]

LETTER OF RESIGNATION

The optimism felt by Gregg and Burwell after the meeting evaporated at the end of the month when they got the news they had worked to avoid. On January 31, Moritz's mentor Howard Karsner announced his resignation as director of Western Reserve's Institute of Pathology to take a job in DC as medical research adviser to the Navy. Dr. Harry Goldblatt, who was once in line to succeed Karsner at the institute, had left Western Reserve in 1946 to become director of medical research at Cedars of Lebanon Hospital in Los Angeles. Moritz was offered the director position and quickly accepted.[13]

Moritz's decision to return to Western Reserve surprised Gregg, Burwell and Conant. "I greatly regretted Moritz's decision, and I was surprised by it because I thought that after our talk he decided to stay," Gregg told Burwell. As a precaution, Gregg said, he deliberately delayed writing Conant to tell him about their January 13 meeting "to be doubly sure" that Moritz was not going to resign. On the day Gregg finally wrote Conant what he described as a "routine letter," Moritz announced his departure. "And it turned out I was wrong," he said.[14]

During an event they attended in Washington later in February, Conant told Gregg that he was disappointed that some at Harvard Medical School had "not appreciated the importance of Legal Medicine" and Moritz's long-term vision for the department.[15]

Burwell, in a letter to Gregg, said Moritz would be difficult to replace. Moritz was "a great addition to the Harvard Medical School and he has put his energy into a pioneering development of which I think the School will be increasingly proud." But Burwell understood Moritz's decision, recalling a recent conversation with Gregg.

> As we said in your office it is a crucial decision for him since whichever way he jumps, he is in effect, determining the [road] he will follow for the rest of his professional career. When he really put it to the test, he decided that he would rather do Pathology.

At first, Burwell told Gregg, he thought Moritz's resignation would "endanger all that had been accomplished" by the department in the past decade. But, "as I thought about it in a more philosophical state I was sure that much of what Dr. Moritz had done will survive to be a foundation of a new growth of Legal Medicine." He went on to say he hoped "very earnestly" that the Medical School would "go forward further with the development of Legal Medicine."[16]

In his resignation letter to Gregg, Moritz described "two principal reasons, one negative and one positive," for his decision to leave Harvard.

> The former is that although I take great satisfaction in the successful results of my endeavors in behalf of legal medicine, I know that I have been and would probably become increasingly discontented to spend such a large portion of my time doing things that I do not enjoy, however necessary and important they may be.

He went on to say his replacement as director of the Department of Legal Medicine

> must continue to be a propagandist and must create a national demand for improvement in medicolegal practice. Otherwise, he cannot in good faith accept people for post-graduate training. Confronted as I am with an alternative, I find myself reluctant to spend the major part of the next fifteen years of my life at this kind of activity.

The positive reason for leaving was the environment at Western Reserve had changed significantly in the 12 years since he had left to take the director's position at Harvard. He now saw opportunities to accomplish things in legal medicine in Cleveland that were not available at Harvard. "I find a community of young, capable and energetic professors whose plans for the future are most attractive." He told Gregg that he expected Western Reserve to become "one of the outstanding medical centers of the continent within the next two decades," and that from "a physical and organization standpoint the Institute of Pathology in Cleveland is the finest workshop that I know of for teaching and research in the field of pathology."

Moritz continued, telling Gregg that he was proud of his accomplishments at Harvard.

> I would regret it exceedingly if I thought that my leaving would wipe out the progress that this department has made, but I do not believe that this will be the case. I feel sure that a large part of what has been done is permanent and that under new leadership, the department will continue to influence national improvement in the practice and teaching of legal medicine.[17]

In a letter to Lee, he said his decision to leave was not easy. At the end of his career, he expected to "regard what I have done on behalf of the field of legal medicine as the most important contribution that I have made to society." Moritz acknowledged that Lee, as well as officials at Harvard and the Rockefeller Foundation, would most likely be "disturbed to a great or lesser degree by my leaving." He said he had "devoted twelve years, which is approximately one-third of the productive period of my life, to legal medicine and I am now faced with the crucial decision of what I want to do during my last fifteen years."

His new job at Western Reserve "will probably be less important from the standpoint of social welfare but will undoubtedly give me more pleasure in the doing." He concluded, saying that Cleveland had become an important medical center "and has potentiality for becoming much more important."[18]

The *Boston Herald* in an editorial on September 5, 1949, praised Moritz for his work at Harvard. "He established at Harvard Medical School a department of legal medicine unique in this country and far in advance of anything abroad," the editorial said. "The department has demonstrated the need of scientific investigation of homicides and unexpected and sudden deaths."

> It has given free service to the state of legal pathology, with medical experts available night and day to identify the guilty and exonerate the innocent. It has served in detecting public health hazards, as in the case of a bank teller who was found to have died from malignant diphtheria. And it has trained experts in legal medicine who have taken to other states the advances made here.

The editorial concluded, saying Moritz "leaves here a work magnificently begun, and the men he trained to carry it on."[19]

Moritz recommended as his successor Dr. Richard Ford, a graduate of Harvard Medical School and a World War II veteran who worked as a research fellow in the department. Ford's nomination was supported by Lee, and he was appointed Suffolk County medical examiner for the Southern District in 1950.[20]

In early June 1950, less than a year after he left Harvard, Moritz was asked to return to Boston as Shattuck Professor of Pathological Anatomy and head of the Department of Pathology at Harvard Medical School and pathologist-in-chief at the Peter Bent Brigham Hospital. His salary would have been $15,000 a year. Included in the offer was a pledge to reorganize and modernize the Department of Pathology facilities and up to $100,000 was pledged for the project.[21]

Moritz declined the offer. "There is an extraordinarily fine sense of institutional responsibility on the part of the Western Reserve faculty that is not prevalent at Harvard. Perhaps it is because Western Reserve is on the make and Harvard has arrived." He also said, "I think it will be more fun to play on the Cleveland team."[22] Years later he said his career would have been much different if the offer had been made sooner. "I probably would have never left Boston if that decision had been made a year earlier, but now it was too late." But he harbored no regrets or resentments, saying he was "delighted with the situation in Cleveland," where he spent the rest of his career.[23]

THE DEPARTMENT'S DEMISE

In August 1959, Harvard University President Nathan M. Pusey and Dr. George Packer Berry, dean of the medical school, created an ad hoc committee to look at the future of the Department of Legal Medicine "and address the question of the department's balance between academic work and service to the community."

Frances Glessner Lee was then past 80 and bedridden. Her continued financial support of the department was in doubt.

In April 1961, the committee reported that the Department of Legal Medicine was spending most of its energy and manpower assisting local law enforcement on death investigations. Some training seminars were still being provided, but very little research was being conducted. Lee died on January 27, 1962. She was 83.

By 1963, Harvard estimated the Department of Legal Medicine's "contributions to the state's Department of Public Safety at some $50,000 per year, consulting on nearly 400 post-mortem cases" and concluded that to be an "unacceptable burden on the school." In November of that year, the ad hoc committee recommended to the Administrative Board of Medical School that the department be converted to a division of forensic pathology in the Department of Pathology. Harvard's Center for the History of Medicine describes it this way: "Following internal personnel upheavals and personal difficulties, Richard Ford was relieved of all administrative responsibilities, and his appointment ended in 1965."[24] Ford died by suicide in 1970 at age 55.[25]

NOTES

1. Alan Moritz, letter to Sidney Burwell, February 1, 1946 (Center for the History of Medicine at Francis A. Countway Library, Harvard University).
2. Sidney Burwell, letter to James B. Conant, February 5, 1946 (Center for the History of Medicine at Francis A. Countway Library, Harvard University).
3. Alan Gregg, office diary, April 16, 1947 (Rockefeller Foundation Archives).

4. Alan R. Moritz, report on the Department of Legal Medicine to Alan Gregg, May 23, 1947 (Center for the History of Medicine at Francis A. Countway Library, Harvard University).

5. Alan R. Moritz, interview by Mary Daley, November 18, 1983 (Case Western Reserve Archives).

6. Sidney Burwell, letter to Alan Gregg, December 8, 1948 (Center for the History of Medicine at Francis A. Countway Library, Harvard University); Alan Gregg, letter to Sidney Burwell December 21, 1948 (Rockefeller Foundation Archives).

7. Erwin N. Griswold, letter to Alan Gregg, December 8, 1948 (Center for the History of Medicine at Francis A. Countway Library, Harvard University).

8. Alan Gregg, office diary, November 17, 1948 (Rockefeller Foundation Archives).

9. Alan Gregg, office diary, November 17, 1948 (Rockefeller Foundation Archives).

10. Sidney Burwell, letter to Alan Gregg, December 8, 1948 (Center for the History of Medicine at Francis A. Countway Library, Harvard University).

11. Gregg, office diary, January 13, 1949 (Rockefeller Foundation Archives); "Memorandum of Meeting with Dr. Alan Gregg, Dr. Alan Moritz and Dr. Burwell in Dr. Gregg's Office in New York on January 13, 1949 at 3:00" (Rockefeller Foundation Archives).

12. "Memorandum of Meeting with Dr. Alan Gregg, Dr. Alan Moritz and Dr. Burwell in Dr. Gregg's Office in New York on January 13, 1949 at 3:00" (Rockefeller Foundation Archives).

13. Alan R. Moritz, transcript of interview by someone identified only as "Bonnie," *Cleveland Ohio*, 1980 (Moritz Family collection); "Goldblatt, Harry," *Encyclopedia of Cleveland History*, accessed August 10, 2024, https://case.edu/ech/articles/g/goldblatt -harry; Alan. R. Moritz, "Howard T. Karsner, MD, 1879–1970," *The American Journal of Pathology* 61, no. 1 (January 1971): 3–5 (Case Western Reserve Archives).

14. Alan Gregg, letter to Sidney Burwell, February 4, 1949 (Rockefeller Foundation Archives).

15. Alan Gregg, office diary, February 9, 1949 (Rockefeller Foundation Archives).

16. Sidney Burwell, letter to Alan Gregg, February 1, 1949 (Rockefeller Foundation Archives).

17. Alan R. Moritz, letter to Alan Gregg, February 1, 1949 (Center for the History of Medicine at Francis A. Countway Library, Harvard University).

18. Alan R. Moritz, letter to Frances Glessner Lee, January 31, 1949 (Center for the History of Medicine at Francis A. Countway Library, Harvard University).
19. "Dr. Moritz Goes," *Boston Herald*, September 5, 1949 (Case Western Reserve University Archives).
20. "Richard Ford (1915–1970)," *Center for the History of Medicine at Francis A. Countway Library*, Harvard University, accessed August 10, 2024, https://collections.countway.harvard.edu/onview/exhibits/show/corpus-delicti/richard-ford
21. George P. Berry, letter to Alan R. Moritz, June 8, 1950 (Path015 Alan R. Moritz, MD, Papers, Stanley A. Ferguson Archives, University Hospitals of Cleveland).
22. Alan R. Moritz, letter to George P. Berry, June 25, 1950 (Path015 Alan R. Moritz, MD, Papers, Stanley A. Ferguson Archives, University Hospitals of Cleveland).
23. Alan R. Moritz, "Alan R. Moritz: Autobiographical Notes in Extension of Information Contained in Curriculum Vitae. Prepared at Request of Miss K., Archivist of the University Hospitals," mid-1970s (Path015 Alan R. Moritz, MD, Papers, Stanley A. Ferguson Archives, University Hospitals of Cleveland).
24. "The Ad Hoc Committee Report," *Center for the History of Medicine at Francis A. Countway Library*, Harvard University, accessed April 9, 2021, https://collections.countway.harvard.edu/onview/exhibits/show/corpus-delicti/ad-hoc-committee-report.
25. "Dr. Richard Ford, 55, A Suicide; Witness in Many Murder Trials," *New York Times*, August 4, 1970, accessed August 10, 2024, https://www.nytimes.com/1970/08/04/archives/dr-richard-ford-55-a-suicide-witness-in-many-murder-trials.html.

CHAPTER **13**

Going Hollywood

Crime and mystery stories have been a staple of popular culture since Edgar Allen Poe's "The Murders in the Rue Morgue" was published in 1841. For nearly two centuries, there has been an eager audience for police detectives, private eyes, lawyers and secret agents solving who-dunnits with keen intellect and an eye for detail. The plots for novels, short stories, feature films and television series are often "ripped from the headlines"—fictionalized tales based on unusual or infamous true crimes.

In 1976, a new category of crime-detecting hero emerged on TV: "Quincy M.E." Played by character actor Jack Klugman, best known as the slovenly sportswriter Oscar Madison in the TV series *The Odd Couple*, Dr. R. Quincy—his first name was never revealed—was a Los Angeles County medical examiner who wasn't content to perform autopsies.

In 1983, the final year of the show's run, my grandfather was asked by an interviewer whether he was the inspiration for Quincy. Dr. Moritz was quick to distance himself from a character he found frankly absurd. "Well, anyone who functions as Quincy does wouldn't have time to do his work," Moritz said. "No, I suppose every medical examiner gets offended when asked if he's like Dr. Quincy simply because it doesn't work that way."[1]

Strictly speaking, Quincy was not the first forensic pathologist with a starring role in popular fiction. That honor appears to belong to Dr. McAdoo, another character with no first name, who was played by Bruce Bennett in the 1950 Metro-Goldwyn-Mayer feature film *Mystery Street*. And there is no dispute about this: Dr. McAdoo *was* inspired by Dr. Moritz. The character in the film was head of forensic pathology at Harvard Medical School, the very job my grandfather had originated and left a few months before the film was released.[2]

Mystery Street was directed by John Sturges, who would go on to direct classics *Bad Day at Black Rock*, *The Magnificent Seven* and *The Great Escape*.[3] Reviews were generally positive.

Los Angeles Examiner:

                    DOI: 10.4324/9781003539186-14

"It's jam-packed with some swell performances, and a wonderfully relaxed direction of a suspenseful, tightly-written story."

Time Magazine:

Mystery Street is a low-budget melodrama without box-office stars or advance ballyhoo. It does not pretend to do much more than tell a straightaway logical story of scientific crime detecting. Within such modest limits, Director John Sturges and Scripters Sydney Boehm and Richard Brooks have treated the picture with such taste and craftsmanship that it is just about perfect.

Philadelphia Evening Bulletin:

No one can accuse MGM of following a pattern in producing Mystery Street. This murder melodrama has a fresh new angle and within the confines of its modest limits is satisfactory entertainment. ... it strikes a new, gruesome note that will delight connoisseurs of such things.[4]

Mystery Street had originally been proposed as a documentary on the founding and work of Harvard's Department of Legal Medicine to be titled "Murder at Harvard." But, according to Bruce Goldfarb's *18 Tiny Deaths*, Frances Glessner Lee "did not desire personal publicity but wanted popular attention focused on the field of legal medicine." It was Lee, Goldfarb wrote, who suggested telling the story of Irene Perry's murder, the case that had involved botany, rope, neck circumference and dental records.[5] The project evolved into a fictionalized drama, with Moritz serving as a technical adviser at the insistence of Harvard's top administrators.[6]

MGM must not have been ready for a story about scientists with lab coats, as Bennett's Dr. McAdoo was the second lead of the film. Top billing went to young Mexican heartthrob Ricardo Montalban as police Lt. Peter Morales, who teamed up with Dr. McAdoo to solve the murder of a woman on Cape Cod. But Bennett, a shot-putter in the 1928 Olympics whose subsequent screen career lasted nearly 50 years, seemed to think forensic pathology had potential, especially for the new medium of television. Newspaper articles in Boston, Los Angeles and New York said Moritz and Bennett had developed a friendship and that Moritz provided the actor with real-life case files for what Bennett envisioned as a series for film or TV.[7]

Edwin Schallert wrote in the *Los Angeles Times* on September 20, 1951, that Bennett had retained William B. Sackheim to write the first film featuring a character based on Moritz, in which Bennett would star.[8] Sackheim, a film and television producer, later became known for his work on light TV comedies *Gidget* and *The Flying Nun*, as well as the crime drama *Delvecchio*.[9]

On the same day as Schallert's article, Thomas M. Pryor wrote in the *New York Times* that Bennett "has acquired from Dr. Moritz the screen and television rights to 325 case histories compiled by the doctor." The article said Bennett "has signed William B. Sackheim to write a screen treatment from several of the histories concerning the role medical science played in solving the crime, and intends to offer them as a package-deal basis," with Bennett starring in both the films and TV shows. "Dr. Moritz, now a professor and chief of pathological research at Western Reserve University, will supervise the scripts to check them for technical accuracy."[10]

Hedda Hopper, a nationally syndicated celebrity gossip columnist, wrote in October 1951 that Moritz was "Bennett's house guest and the two got to be buddies." She too described some kind of transaction. When Moritz "left Harvard to return to Western Reserve's department of pathology, he sold Bennett his source material. This is to be a package with Bennett playing the role of Dr. Moritz in the series."[11]

In an interview more than 30 years after the release of Mystery Street, Moritz acknowledged that some case files were provided to Bennett, but whether they were sold and what happened to the grand plan are details lost to history.[12]

PERRY MASON

Moritz had befriended a much bigger celebrity while still at Harvard in the 1940s. Mystery writer Erle Stanley Gardner, who had introduced his best-selling "Perry Mason" character in 1933, began to attend Moritz's lectures and seminars. Ten years older than Moritz, Gardner described himself as a pupil in a glowing thank-you handwritten in a first edition of the Perry Mason novel *The Case of the Cautious Coquette*.

To Dr. Alan R. Moritz
My friend and instructor from the pupil who raised hell with discipline but will nevertheless try to be worthy.
Yours,
Erle Stanley Gardner
May 1949[13]

Moritz's friendship with Gardner continued after he left Harvard and returned to Western Reserve, and the novelist attended and spoke at several seminars Moritz conducted in Cleveland. In a letter dated May

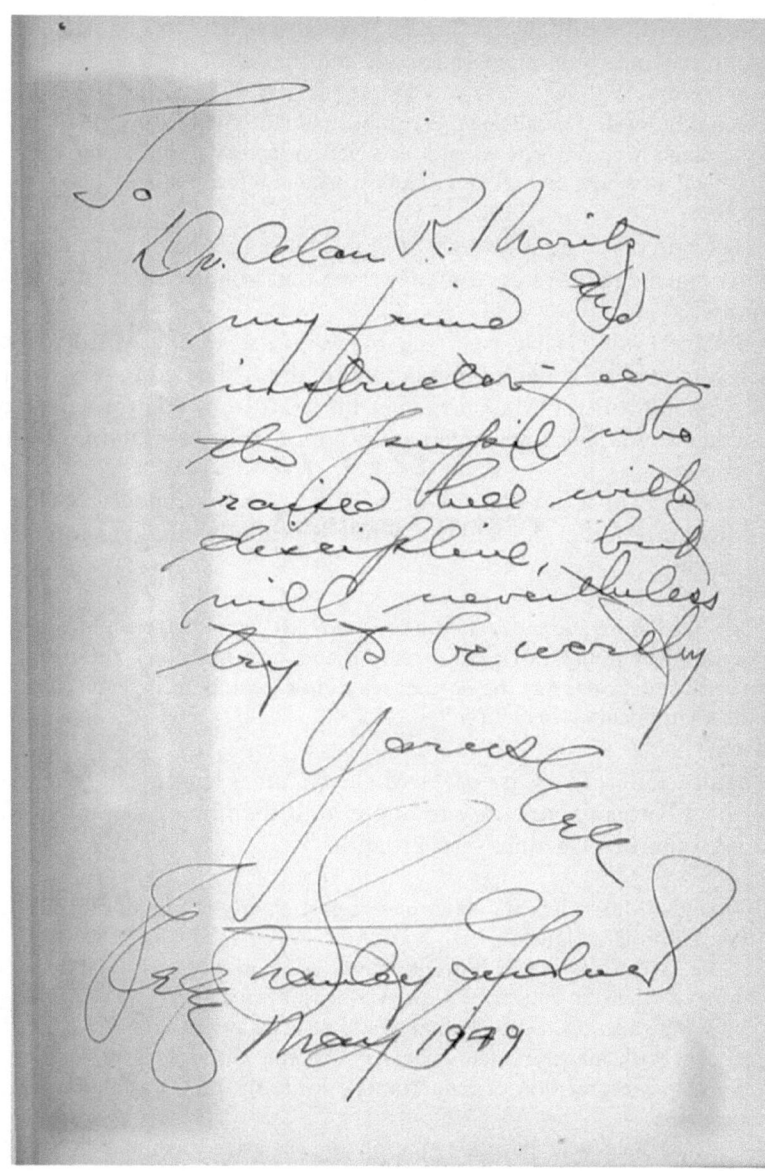

FIGURE 13.1 Erle Stanley Gardner inscribed a first edition of his 1949 Perry Mason novel *The Case of the Curious Coquette*: "To Dr. Alan R. Moritz My friend and instructor from the pupil who raised hell with discipline but will nevertheless try to be worthy." (Moritz Family Collection)

5, 1950, Gardner said he had heard Moritz would be in Los Angeles for a legal medicine conference and suggested that it

> would be swell if arrangements can be made for you to come down to the ranch for a day or two and see a fiction factory in operation, also to bend an elbow and see if we can't work out a few publicity plans.

Gardner said his current project "will be coming along one of these days and arrangements have been made to see that you get the first copy off the press."[14]

Gardner was clearly referring to *The Case of the Musical Cow,* which was published the following month and dedicated to Moritz. The book was not a Perry Mason thriller but features a dog trainer named Rob Trenton who becomes mixed up in a murder mystery while on a trip to Europe.[15]

Musical Cow is not one of Gardner's best-reviewed novels. In his letter to my grandfather, he said that while reading the final version before publication,

> I realized more and more that in order to have a character who had to be saved by police work rather than by his own ingenuity, there was a certain deficiency of the normal masculine glandular appendages in the anatomical construction.[16]

The dedication in *The Case of the Musical Cow* is lengthy, but there will never be a better opportunity to quote it all than in a biography of the man who sparked Gardner's imagination:

> When the Massachusetts Police have a particularly tough murder case they call in Dr. Alan Moritz.
>
> Dr. Moritz considers himself primarily a pathologist. I look upon him as a scientific detective. Whatever he is, he has a razor-keen mind.
>
> Where a less perceptive mind would hack away at an objective, Dr. Moritz, with his keen mental perception, cuts through to his objective with the precision of a micrometer knife slicing off a laboratory specimen.
>
> Some men who have a string of degrees after their names have difficulty in applying what they know. They can teach but they can't perform.
>
> Dr. Moritz, however, is different. His mind is a highly trained scientific instrument of exact precision. His education consists of no mere array of facts gleaned from the pages of books, but is truly a background of encyclopedic knowledge. His mind is constantly, insistently probing in its search of truth.
>
> As a pathologist, he might well be content merely to examine the vital organs and determine the cause of death, to study the bones of a

skeleton and ascertain the age, height and sex. But he does far more than this. When he probes beneath a skeleton in search of clues in the grass, he functions as a scientific detector of crime; his investigations are remorselessly thorough.

He will quite likely come up with some dry, broken blade, which to the uninitiated seems nothing but a piece of withered grass. It is the detective insight of Dr. Moritz which enables him to decide that this blade of grass was broken during a struggle which preceded the murder; that the botanical laboratory will be able to tell him this particular vegetation matures during the last week in July, and that it was broken about a week before maturity.

Then quite casually, Dr. Moritz will suggest to the police that they start searching for a man about 55, who is susceptible to arthritis of the spine and of the right knee, and as a result walks stiffly and with a slight limp; a man who left his home about the 25th of July, and has not been seen since.

But what interests me more than anything else is the manner in which Dr. Moritz can hold a class spellbound while he lectures in a conversational tone of voice.

People learn and remember the things in which they are interested. They are prone to forget the things which fail to interest them.

During my career as a trial lawyer, I learned the necessity of holding the interest of a jury during an argument, and I am free to confess that I resorted to gesture, pose, change of pace, voice inflection, even the baiting of opposing counsel, in order to accomplish my purpose. Therefore, when I was privileged to enroll in one of Dr. Moritz's classes on Homicide Investigation at the Harvard Medical School Seminars, I could not help but marvel at the manner in which this man had the undivided attention of the class without using a single bit of oratorical trickery. There were virtually no gestures, no raising of the voice, no motion of the body. Dr. Moritz sat calmly at the head of the table and talked. While from time to time he has an interesting trick of changing the pace of his voice, the thing which really holds the interest of his audience is the manner in which the man catalogues, classifies, and expresses his ideas. His thoughts are interesting because the man himself is interesting. He sees beneath the surface, and I think he is impatient of any theory which cannot be put to practical use.

I am aware that it is popular to belittle the police in a detective novel. The reader closes the book with a sigh, saying to himself, "Well, I wasn't quite as smart as the detective, but at least I was a lot smarter than that dumb cop."

And because this approach has come almost stereotyped in the field of mystery fiction, the cumulative effect of hundreds of such stories has been manifestly unfair to the police. In this book I have therefore—and perhaps by way of atonement—tried to portray the State Police as they actually are: an extremely efficient body of men who are a credit to their profession.

In getting an authentic background, I observed the State Police in half a dozen of the eastern states. I slept in their barracks, I attended their training classes, I went out on road patrol, and I tagged along while they were investigating crimes.

I hope that the reader will find the picture of the police in this book to his liking, and that, to some extent, it may atone for the almost universal portrayal of police as stupid, bungling incompetents.

Herewith, I convey my respects to a marvelous body of men, and to Dr. Alan Moritz for the work he has done in helping train many of these men so that they are more familiar with the extent to which expert medical minds can assist them in their investigations.

And above all, I wish to acknowledge my indebtedness to Dr. Alan Moritz for an intellectual stimulation which has meant fully as much to me as the instruction I received while attending the seminars at which he has lectured.

And so I dedicate this book to DR. ALAN R. MORITZ[17]

It would not be the last time Gardner waxed rhapsodic about Alan Moritz. In 1952, Gardner wrote an article that appeared in the *San Francisco Examiner* under the headline "Beware the Eye-Witness: More Than One Innocent Person Has Been Convicted of a Crime Because Somebody 'Saw' Something that Didn't Happen."

In it, Gardner described Moritz as an "expert pathologist and practical detective whose exploits make the detective of fiction seem clumsy indeed." Gardner recounted a 1948 case involving the discovery of bones by a New Hampshire hunter. He detailed the innovative techniques Moritz used when called to the scene to investigate:

> Dr. Moritz built a glass cage around the remains, lifted the whole thing and packed it off to a laboratory. The bones he found were the skeletal remains of a female human being. They had been lying there for years. Pine needles had fallen, then turned to humus. Seeds had fallen in the humus and taken root. Every single bit of that evidence was carefully preserved and scientifically noted. Studies showed the seed had sprouted five years earlier. Scientific tests showed it would have taken pine needles three years to have formed a humus which would have enabled a seed of this type to sprout.
>
> So, bit by bit the police determined when the body must have started its long process of decay. Then armed with dates, they started checking disappearances. A single tooth proved to hold an interesting clue. The texture of the rotted garments added another clue. Soon the entire answer was available to the police, the identity of the corpse, the date of death and the manner of death.[18]

Velma Moritz was vocal in her opinion that her husband's value to Gardner deserved more than the occasional thank-you, but my father said Dr. Moritz never sought any payment.[19]

SAM SHEPPARD

In Cleveland, the last half of 1954 was consumed by one of the most sensational trials of the 20th century, the murder trial of Dr. Sam Sheppard. Moritz, a professional acquaintance of Sheppard's, was brought in to help law enforcement and prosecutors investigate the case, which would become so infamous that it inspired 120 episodes of a television series called *The Fugitive* (1963–1967) and a 1993 feature film of the same name.

Sheppard, 30 and a respected specialist in orthopedic surgery and neurosurgery, was accused of beating to death his 31-year-old wife, Marilyn, in her bed in the early morning of July 4, 1954.

Sheppard told police that Marilyn had gone to bed upstairs after a party at their home in Bay Village, an upscale suburb on the shore of Lake Erie, while he had fallen asleep on a downstairs couch. Sometime in the night, her screams woke him, and he ran upstairs and saw someone with a light-colored shirt in the bedroom. He was then knocked out from behind. When he came to, Sheppard claimed, he saw the intruder downstairs and chased him out the back door and down to the lakefront beach. The two fought and Sheppard was again knocked unconscious.[20]

Sheppard was taken into custody on the night of July 30, 1954, and charged with first-degree murder.[21] The arrest occurred the same day the *Cleveland Press* published a front-page editorial asking why it was taking so long to decide whether to file charges.[22]

Bay Village Police Chief Frank Story told reporters that Sheppard's arrest was "long overdue." He said it "should have happened right after the murder was discovered."[23]

The subsequent trial provoked a media frenzy that foreshadowed O.J. Simpson's acquittal of murder charges four decades later.

At the time of Marilyn Sheppard's murder, Moritz was the director of the Institute of Pathology at Western Reserve University. In his 2001 book *The Wrong Man*, James Neff suggests that Moritz's involvement in the case was the result of a publicity stunt by an afternoon newspaper. Public demand for information about the high-profile murder was feverish, according to Neff, and coverage in newspapers and on TV was aggressive, vast and thorough. News of the murder also garnered headlines across the United States.

"The Sheppard case had invigorated the competition among the city's three dailies," Neff wrote, and readers "could not get enough details." The *Cleveland News had cleverly conjured a news story out of nothing. It was a stunt, an 'open letter' to Cuyahoga County officials, asking them to seek assistance from Alan Moritz, M.D., chief pathologist at Western Reserve's medical school and a renowned forensic scientist.*

When Cuyahoga County Prosecutor Frank Cullitan "invited Moritz to join the investigation, and he agreed, the *News* wrote about it, taking prominent credit for the news it manufactured."[24]

Bob Considine, a correspondent with International News Service, wrote in a November 1954 column that, in the days after the murder, Dr. Sheppard had expressed interest in submitting to a "truth serum." It was a controversial technique even then, and he sought some conditions. First, the injection would be done at a hospital friendly to Sheppard. Second, there would be no publicity about the procedure. Moritz agreed but had his own condition: that he be allowed to pick the person who administered the injection. Sheppard, according to Considine's report, signed off on the deal but said he would have to get everything approved by his attorney, Bill Corrigan.[25]

Moritz and Corrigan met "at Cleveland's ultra ultra Union League Club for luncheon," Considine reported. Afterward, Corrigan called Sheppard on the phone.

"For a long time [Corrigan] listened to Dr. Sam extol the wonders of truth serum," the article said. "He waited for Sam to reach a semi-colon, and when he did Bill said laconically: 'Interesting. But if you insist on this test, I'm walking out.'"[26]

Sheppard decided against the truth serum, and the procedure suggested by Moritz was never performed.[27]

An appeals court said the "court's failure to insulate itself from the Cleveland press coverage, which created ... a Roman circus, was certainly a blatant and serious failing of the trial."[28] The US Supreme Court in 1966 reversed the conviction. Sheppard was acquitted in a second trial in late 1966. Sheppard was represented in the appeal and second trial by legendary lawyer F. Lee Bailey, then in his early 30s.[29] Bailey would become part of the legal "dream team" that won O.J. Simpson's acquittal in 1995.

THE DEATH OF SUPERMAN

By the late 1950s, Moritz was a nationally recognized expert in death investigations called on by law enforcement agencies and by private individuals. In the latter category was Helen Bessolo, who asked that Moritz and Dr. Frank Cleveland, a pathologist with Kettering Laboratories in Cincinnati, conduct an autopsy on her son, George Reeves, who was TV's original Superman.[30]

Reeves, 45, was found dead from a gunshot wound to the head in his Los Angeles home on June 16, 1959. The actor, who 20 years earlier had a minor role as one of Scarlett O'Hara's suitors in *Gone with the Wind*, gained fame as the Man of Steel in the hit TV series *Adventures of Superman*. The show ran from 1952 to 1958.[31]

Los Angeles Police Department detectives, relying on Reeves' fiancée, said Reeves had financial problems and was depressed because he was having trouble finding good roles after his popular TV series ended. Two autopsies concluded he had committed suicide, but rumors persisted that the actor had been murdered—possibly by the Mafia. There were also media reports that the bullet that killed Reeves was found in the ceiling while the casing was underneath his body and that no gunpowder residue was found on his hand.

Reeves' remains were originally interred in the Westwood Memorial Cemetery mausoleum in Los Angeles in late June. Five months later, his mother sought an autopsy by an expert from outside of California. Bessolo specifically requested Dr. Moritz, then at Western Reserve University in Cleveland, and Dr. Cleveland. The autopsy was conducted at Cincinnati General Hospital. Moritz and Cleveland also concluded that Reeves killed himself.

Although the third autopsy agreed with the first two, the rumors were hardly put to rest. In 1996—37 years after Reeves' death and a decade after my grandfather died—authors Sam Kashner and Nancy Schoenberger published a book called *Hollywood Kryptonite: Accident, Suicide, or Cold-Blooded Murder—The Truth about the Death of TV's Superman*.

Kashner and Schoenberger wrote that Moritz sent a number of photographs from the autopsy to Bessolo, and the photos were later obtained by the media and can now be found online. The authors also describe in curiously intimate detail a dinner meeting between Moritz and a Los Angeles detective a couple of days before the autopsy was performed. The detective asked Moritz to call LAPD Chief William Parker immediately after the autopsy if any findings conflicted with the suicide ruling by Theodore Curphey, the Los Angeles coroner. According to Kashner and Schoenberger, the detective wrote Parker's personal phone number on the back of the fortune from a fortune cookie and gave it to Moritz.

After the autopsy, according to the book, Moritz was seen looking at the slip of paper before making a phone call to tell Parker that Reeves had indeed killed himself.

Dr. Moritz told the *Los Angeles Herald Examiner* that he and his colleagues "had found nothing to contradict the original findings of Dr. Curphey and the Los Angeles coroner's office," according to "Hollywood Kryptonite."

Once again, there was no mention of powder burns or stippling on Reeves's hands or temple. The autopsy was conclusive. No one wanted to extrapolate on the absence of power burns, especially since the corpse was no longer in pristine condition. Chief Parker had sent one of his police detectives to make sure that Moritz wasn't about to drop a bombshell. He was satisfied with the outcome.[32]

NOTES

1. Alan R. Moritz, transcript of interview by Mary Daley, November 18, 1983 (Case Western Reserve Archives).
2. "On View: Mystery Street," *Center for the History of Medicine* at Francis A. Countway Library, Harvard University, accessed August 5, 2024, https://collections.countway.harvard.edu/onview/exhibits/show/corpus-delicti/richard-ford/mystery-street.
3. "John Sturgis: American Director," *Britannica*, accessed August 5, 2024, https://www.britannica.com/biography/John-Sturges#ref1198799.
4. Press Reviews of "Mystery Street," 1951 (Path015 Alan R. Moritz, MD, Papers, Stanley A. Ferguson Archives, University Hospitals of Cleveland).
5. Bruce Goldfarb, *18 Tiny Deaths: The Untold Story of Frances Glessner Lee and the Invention of Modern Forensics* (Napierville, IL: Sourcebooks, 2020), 242.
6. Press Release of "Mystery Street," 1951 (PATH015 Alan R. Moritz, MD, Papers, Stanley A. Ferguson Archives, University Hospitals of Cleveland).
7. "Mystery Street," *IMDb*, accessed August 6, 2024, https://www.imdb.com/title/tt0042771/; "Bruce Bennett: Biography," *IMDB*, accessed August 6, 2024, https://www.themoviedb.org/person/30303-bruce-bennett?language=en-US; Letters between Alan R. Moritz and Bruce Bennett (Moritz Family Collection and Center for the History of Medicine at Francis A. Countway Library, Harvard University).
8. Edwin Schallert, "Bruce Bennett Obtains Scientific Subject; Lon McCallister Gets Break," *Los Angeles Times*, September 20, 1951 (Case Western Reserve Archives).
9. "Emmy-Winning Writer-Producer William Sackheim Dies at 84," *Television Academy Emmys*, December 14, 2004, accessed August 6, 2024, https://www.emmys.com/news/emmy-winning-writer-producer-william-sackheim-dies-84.
10. Thomas M. Pryor, "Litvak to Direct Second Fox Film," *New York Times*, September 20, 1951.

11. Hedda Hopper, "Looking at Hollywood: Scott Heston in Key West," *New Orleans Times-Picayune*, October 24, 1951 (Case Western Reserve Archives).

12. Alan R. Moritz, transcript of interview by Mary Daley, November 18, 1983 (Case Western Reserve Archives).

13. Erle Stanley Gardner, inscription in *The Case of the Cautious Coquette,* dir. Ron Satlof (New York: William Morrow & Company, 1949) (Moritz Family Collection).

14. Erle Stanley Gardner, letter to Alan R. Moritz, May 5, 1950 (Case Western Reserve Archives).

15. Erle Stanley Gardner, *The Case of The Musical Cow* (New York: William Morrow & Company, 1950).

16. Erle Stanley Gardner, letter to Alan R. Moritz, May 5, 1950 (Case Western Reserve Archives).

17. Erle Stanley Gardner, *The Case of The Musical Cow* (New York: William Morrow & Company, 1950), v–vii.

18. Erle Stanley Gardner, "Beware of the Eye-Witness: More than One Innocent Person Has Been Convicted of a Crime because Somebody "Saw' Something That Didn't Happen," *San Francisco Examiner*, August 17, 1952.

19. John A. Moritz, interview by Rob Moritz, August 15, 2020, Benton, Ark.

20. Ray De Crane, "Doctor's Wife Murdered in Bay Village," *Cleveland Press*, July 5, 1954, https://engagedscholarship.csuohio.edu/newspaper_coverage/7.

21. "Dr. Sheppard Shocked as Warrant Is Served," *Cleveland Press*, July 31, 1954, https://engagedscholarship.csuohio.edu/newspaper_coverage/342.

22. "Why Isn't Sam Sheppard in Jail?" *Cleveland Press*, July 30, 1954.

23. "Bay Move Hailed by Celebrezze," *Cleveland Plain Dealer*, July 31, 1954, https://engagedscholarship.csuohio.edu/newspaper_coverage/340.

24. James Neff, *The Wrong Man* (New York: Random House, 2001), 76.

25. Bob Considine, "On the Line," *Waterbury Republican*, November 4, 1954 (Case Western Reserve Archives).

26. Bob Considine, "On the Line," *Waterbury Republican*, November 4, 1954 (Case Western Reserve Archives).

27. "Dr. Sheppard Bars Truth Test, City Takes Over Probe, Story Sure He Knows Slayer," *Cleveland Press*, July 21, 1954.

28. Bill James, *Popular Crime: Reflections on the Celebration of Violence* (New York: Scribner, 2011), 208.

29. Bill James, *Popular Crime: Reflections on the Celebration of Violence* (New York: Scribner, 2011), 205–222.

30. Sam Kashner and Nancy Schoenberger, *Hollywood Kryptonite: Accident, Suicide, or Cold-Blooded Murder – The Truth About the Death of TV's Superman* (New York: St. Martin's Press, Paperback, 1997), 238.

31. Peter Hoskin, "The Dark Side of Tinseltown," *The Spectator*, London, June 6, 2009, accessed August 6, 2019, https://search.pro-quest.com/docview/201192862?accountid=10017.

32. Sam Kashner and Nancy Schoenberger, *Hollywood Kryptonite: Accident, Suicide, or Cold-Blooded Murder – The Truth About the Death of TV's Superman* (New York: St. Martin's Press, Paperback, 1997), 238–241.

CHAPTER 14

Back in Cleveland

On his first day back at Western Reserve as director of the Institute of Pathology and director of the medical school's Department of Pathology, Dr. Moritz discovered that Karsner had left a welcoming gift in the restroom next to his office: a shoe-shine kit and a bottle of Pepto-Bismol. Sixteen years later, when Moritz moved out of the office to become provost of Western Reserve, he left the same gift for his successor, Dr. John R. Carter.

"I said that I trusted that he'd keep up the practice of his antecedents by keeping his shoes shined and his stomach in order—that he'd need both of them," Moritz said years later.[1]

To say Moritz was eager to return to Cleveland would have been an understatement. For some time he had been paying attention to reports that Dr. Sam Gerber, the nigh-eternal Cuyahoga County coroner, wanted to upgrade the morgue. The facilities were antiquated and needed to be modernized and expanded to keep up with the new technology and a rising caseload. Moritz liked that idea and saw it as something that could be of benefit when he took charge of the Institute of Pathology. So even before September 1, 1949, his last official day at Harvard, Moritz made several trips to Cleveland to develop key alliances that he hoped would ultimately help Western Reserve, and himself, create a top-notch legal medicine facility that trained pathologists in several subspecialties. He also wanted to establish a program in Cleveland to educate coroners, law enforcement and others on the techniques needed to properly conduct criminal and unexplained death investigations.[2]

In 1948, months before he announced he was leaving Harvard to become director of the Institute of Pathology at Western Reserve, he traveled to Cleveland to attend a meeting on the location of a planned new County Morgue building. During the meeting, he "favored a site near (Western Reserve) because of its natural integration of the school's present facilities with the functions of the morgue," the *Cleveland News* reported. Gaining the support of Gerber, a physician and lawyer, was critical.[3]

DOI: 10.4324/9781003539186-15

"Professionally, Gerber [was] an excellent administrator and he was determined to have high-quality people working in the coroner's office," Moritz said years later. Gerber was also an advocate of continuing education for coroners and crime scene investigators.

Gerber "wanted a good office in contrast to what [he] had before," Moritz said, but it would take some time for him to "make up his mind whether he wanted to move out in University Circle or whether he wanted to stay down there in the political arena of the courthouse and city hall." Eventually, the Academy of Medicine, the Cleveland Bar Association and the university aligned in support of building a new morgue near Western Reserve, and Gerber came around to the idea.[4]

The relationship between Moritz and Gerber proved invaluable on a number of fronts. In the fall of 1949, shortly after Moritz arrived back at Western Reserve, the two announced a new plan that made it easier for the 88 coroners in Ohio to receive pathological services from the state's three medical schools. Coroners in southern Ohio would receive pathology assistance from the University of Cincinnati; coroners in northern Ohio would receive pathological services from Western Reserve; and coroners in the central part of the state from The Ohio State in Columbus. Massachusetts was the only other state which had such a service, and it had started 10 years earlier, Moritz noted in announcing the new arrangement.[5]

While cementing an alliance with the coroner, Moritz also befriended Ollie Schroeder, a law professor at Western Reserve who had learned first-hand of Moritz's interest in creating a true legal medicine program. As a second-year student at Harvard Law School, "I sat in the lectures that Dr. Moritz gave in [the] medical school," Schroeder recalled years later. "They were free lectures; you got no credit for them because the law school wouldn't recognize that" as a proper law course. "But I was there, and he was very good and I enjoyed it."

Moritz's conversations with Schroeder quickly turned to the possible creation of a legal medicine program in Western Reserve's law school. Because placing the department in Harvard's medical school and trying to get law students interested had not worked, Moritz opted for a different approach. "Dr. Moritz said the leadership in bringing together the medicine and the law must come from the law school," Schroeder said.[6]

Coroner Gerber was named to Western Reserve's medical school faculty in 1952. The new coroner's office and morgue, a three-story building that cost $700,000, opened next to the Institute of Pathology in May 1953. The morgue included 13 laboratories and about $70,000 worth of new equipment. It also had a small amphitheater-shaped lecture room.

While Moritz was developing the curriculum, Schroeder worked to get the legal-medicine program incorporated into the law school. The

Law-Medicine Center, with Schroeder as director, offered its first course in the summer of 1953. The course, to assist lawyers in the preparation of civil actions involving medical questions, was taught by Dr. Lester Adelson, a friend of Moritz's and a professor of pathology at Western Reserve's medical school. Adelson also had recently been named deputy coroner. The second course, "Scientific Proof in Criminal Cases," was designed for prosecutors and law enforcement officers. Some of the classes were held in the new coroner's offices and in the morgue.[7]

The Law-Medicine Center provided forensic sciences classes to law and medical students, as well as to police officers, coroners, prosecutors, judges and practicing attorneys. Eventually, it shifted its focus from forensics to professional education and the intersection of law and medicine.[8]

In early 1954, Moritz said, a series of seminars involving new methods in crime investigation, as well as how to work as a team, were taught over a 6-day period. The seminars were attended by pathologists, prosecutors, doctors, toxicologists and police investigators from across the country. They were taught by 35 members of the Western Reserve law school and medical school, as well as the Cuyahoga County coroner's office.

"There seems to be a common misapprehension that successful criminal investigation is usually the work of a single genius ... a Sherlock Holmes, a Nero Wolfe or an Ellery Queen ... Nothing could be further from the fact," Moritz said.

A syndicated radio show called *The Ohio Story* aired an episode called "Crime Doctors" on Ohio stations in July 1954. In it, Moritz discussed the importance of the seminars and of the Law-Medicine Center. He also detailed a case where a woman was found shot to death outside her home.

After a brief investigation muddled by circumstantial evidence and faulty assumptions by the local police and the coroner, the victim's husband was arrested and charged with murder. Neighbors said she had complained that her husband had threatened her several times and had beaten her a year before. Police found a 30-30 shell casing on the ground near the body, but they could not locate the bullet. The husband owned a 30-30 rifle that had recently been fired.

Not long after the husband's arrest, the state attorney's office reached out to Moritz for assistance. During an autopsy, Moritz discovered tiny bullet fragments lodged into bone when the bullet passed through the woman's body. "Bullets have a way of leaving their fingerprints, too," he said. Analysis of the fragments determined that several kinds of metal, including antimony, were present in the 30-30 bullets. Bullets sold in the area did not contain antimony.

A few weeks later, a man walked into the police station and confessed to shooting the woman. He said it occurred while he was deer-hunting in the area. He had used a homemade bullet "packed with soldering metal, containing antimony," Moritz told the radio audience.[9]

The Law-Medicine Center's seminars grew in popularity, and it was soon attracting impressive presenters like Commander George H. Hatherill, head of the criminal investigation department at Scotland Yard. Western Reserve became the first university in the United States to treat legal medicine as a full academic discipline. The collaboration that had eluded Moritz at Harvard came together at Western Reserve.

Moritz continued presenting seminars for the next decade, traveling to attorney and police association meetings, medical and law schools, colleges and universities. At least twice he used this title for his lectures: "Tales That Dead Men Tell."

Moritz said,

> The main thing that I wanted was there to be a much greater recognition through the country—through the law, the Bar Association and the medical schools—of the importance to the welfare of the country of competent information about unexplained deaths, deaths due to violence of one kind or another, the search for information, search for evidence, that required some special experience to produce.[10]

In 2025, the Law-Medicine Center remains open at what is now Case Western Reserve University and is the oldest program for the study of legal medicine and health law in the United States.[11]

INSTITUTE OF PATHOLOGY

Moritz also restructured the Institute of Pathology by hiring several well-known pathologists from across the country and expanding the number of pathology specialties being offered, according to a chapter he wrote on the history of pathology and legal medicine in *Medicine in Cleveland and Cuyahoga County: 1810–1976*. The number of post-MDs enrolled at the institute grew quickly. Students saw an "opportunity that had not heretofore existed in Cleveland to acquire special expertise in various subspecialties of pathology, for example, pediatric pathology, neuropathology, exfoliative cytology, immunopathology, electron microscopy and forensic pathology," Moritz wrote. Many were attracted by a newly created PhD program in a pathology discipline and the ability to "attain certification by the American Board of Pathology in anatomic and clinical pathology with minimum time loss."

By the time he stepped down as director of the Institute of Pathology in 1965, 56 post-MD trainees in pathology had obtained anatomic or clinical pathology certification. Of those, 30 went on to work at medical schools in the United States or overseas and eight were hired by Western Reserve. The other 18 were practicing pathology in community hospitals, in the military or the public health service. "It can be said that the 1949–1964 period was one in which Cleveland became recognized as a nationally important source of teachers and investigators in the field of pathology," Moritz wrote.[12]

During his 16 years as director of both the Institute of Pathology and Western Reserve's medical school Pathology Department, Moritz worked as a program director of the Center on Aging Research, and he was chairman of the General Research Support Grants Committee. He also served on several committees administering institutional grants for heart and cancer clinical studies.[13]

Moritz was also active in the American Board of Pathology, the organization that issues exams and certifications for the specialty of pathology. From 1956 to 1969, he was a trustee for the ABP, and he served as president in 1958. In 1959, first certification examination was offered by the ABP. Twenty-five took the exam and were certified, while 19 grandfather certificates were awarded, including one to Moritz.[14]

SEMI-RETIREMENT

In 1964, Moritz was approaching typical retirement age. He put out the word that he planned to step down as director of both the Institute of Pathology and the medical school's pathology department in June 1965. The administration at Western Reserve, in an apparent effort to placate Moritz without losing him to full retirement, named him vice president. Moritz did, however, keep his director positions until a replacement could be found. He also was allowed to continue as a professor of pathology at the medical school.[15]

In June 1965, John Carter, a pathology professor at the university, was named director of the Institute of Pathology and Department of Pathology and Moritz was named provost of the university. While he had not "retired," as some newspapers reported, he had left full-time academics and had taken an administrative position. As provost, Moritz was the chief administrative officer of all university education research and student services. He continued as provost after Western Reserve and Case Institute of Technology merged in 1967 to form Case Western Reserve University.[16]

In late 1968, Moritz stepped down as provost and was named director of professional affairs at University Hospitals of Cleveland. He continued to hold his position as a professor of pathology at Case Western's School of Medicine. In July 1970, he was appointed to the newly created position of chief of staff at University Hospitals of Cleveland. Again, he kept his post as a professor of pathology at the medical school.[17]

NOTES

1. Alan R. Moritz, transcript of interview by Mary Daley, November 18, 1983 (Case Western Reserve Archives).

2. Alan R. Moritz, transcript of interview by someone identified only as "Bonnie," *Cleveland, Ohio,* 1980 (Moritz Family Collection); Mary Dowling Daley, "Law-Medicine Center Celebrates 30th Anniversary," *in brief,* Law Alumni Bulletin, Case Western Reserve, March 1984 (Case Western Reserve Archives); Alan R. Moritz, transcript of interview by Mary Daley, November 18, 1983 (Case Western Reserve Archives).

3. "Dr. Moritz Will Raise Institute's Stature," *Cleveland Press,* February 7, 1949 (Case Western Reserve Archives); Mary Dowling Daley, "Law-Medicine Center Celebrates 30th Anniversary," *in brief,* Law Alumni Bulletin, Case Western Reserve, March 1984 (Case Western Reserve Archives).

4. Alan R. Moritz, transcript of interview by Mary Daley, November 18, 1983 (Case Western Reserve Archives).

5. "Ohio Medical Schools Will Aid Coroners," *The Newark Advocate,* November 14, 1949.

6. Oliver Schroeder, transcript of interview by Mary Daley, October 31, 1983 (Case Western Reserve Archives).

7. "Gerber, Samuel R., M.D," *Encyclopedia of Cleveland History,* accessed August 14, 2024, https://case.edu/ech/articles/g/gerber -samuel-r-md; Odell M. Smith, "Cleveland," *Baltimore Sun,* May 7, 1954; John G. Blair, "Baltimore," *Baltimore Sun,* May 7, 1954.

8. Oliver Schroeder, transcript of interview by Mary Daley, October 31, 1983 (Case Western Reserve Archives).

9. Robert Waldrop, "The Crime Doctors," *The Ohio Story,* Episode 1171, aired July 15 (PM) and July 20 (AM), 1954, on the Ohio network (Case Western Reserve Archives).

10. Mary Dowling Daley, "Law-Medicine Center Celebrates 30th Anniversary," *in brief,* Law Alumni Bulletin, Case Western Reserve, March 1984 (Case Western Reserve Archives).

11. "About Our Center," *Law Medicine Center,* accessed August 14, 2024, https://case.edu/law/centers-institutes/law-medicine-center/ about-our-center.

12. Alan R. Moritz, "Pathology and Legal Medicine," in *Medicine in Cleveland and Cuyahoga County, 1810–1976*, ed. Kent Brown (Cleveland, OH: The Academy of Medicine of Cleveland, 1977), (Path015 Alan R. Moritz, MD, Papers, Stanley A. Ferguson Archives, University Hospitals of Cleveland), 188-231.
13. News Release, Western Reserve University, August 21, 1964 (Case Western Reserve Archives).
14. William G. Eckert, "The Forensic Pathology Specialty Certifications," *The American Journal of Forensic Medicine and Pathology* 9, no. 1 (1988): 85–89; University Medical Center News Release, "Dr. Alan R. Moritz Named Chief of Staff at University Hospitals," July 14, 1970 (Case Western Reserve Archives).
15. News Release, Western Reserve, University, "Dr. Beck and Dr. Moritz Are Retiring from WRU Teaching," May 21, 1965 (Case Western Reserve Archives).
16. News Release, Western Reserve University, June 4, 1965 (Case Western Reserve Archives); "WRU Elects Dr. Moritz Its First Provost," *The Plain Dealer*, June 6, 1965 (Case Western Reserve Archives).
17. "CWRU Provost to Resign Office," *The Plain Dealer*, December 3, 1968 (Case Western Reserve Archives); "Dr. Alan R. Moritz Named Chief of Staff at University Hospitals," *University Medical Center News Release*, July 14, 1970 (Case Western Reserve Archives).

CHAPTER 15

Family Mystery

Something happened in early 1955 that would baffle and haunt Alan Moritz for the rest of his life. The tragedy and its irony would be front-page news.

Alan and Velma were living in a large house on 5 acres east of Cleveland at Gates Mills. The property had an apple orchard, and he indulged his hobbies with a large garden and woodworking shop. The couple's three children were young adults, and the eldest, John, and his wife, Earlene, had produced the first grandchild the previous September.

Both sons were serving overseas. The Army had drafted John and had stationed him in northern Japan, so his wife and baby son were living with her parents west of Cleveland. Richard had enlisted in the Navy and was stationed in southern Japan. Richard's twin, Anne, had graduated from Bradford Junior College in Massachusetts and was living at home and attending Dyke Business School in Cleveland. She was engaged to be married in just a few weeks to a young man from nearby Kirkland, Ohio, who was a student at Colgate University in New York.[1]

In mid-February, Alan and Velma traveled to Los Angeles, where he spoke to the American Academy of Forensic Sciences. The couple then flew to Lincoln, Nebraska, where they visited his parents. Their next stop was to be the University of Kansas in Lawrence, where Moritz was to be a visiting professor of pathology from March 7-March 12.[2]

On Wednesday, March 2, a neighbor, Catherine Burwell, drove by the Moritzes' house on Battles Road in Gates Mills and noticed milk bottles were still outside the door. Because she knew Anne was staying at the house while her parents were out of town, she stopped and knocked on the door. A dog barked but no one answered.

Burwell—no relation to the Harvard Medical School dean—looked through a front window into a downstairs bedroom, where she saw Anne lying motionless on the bed. Burwell drove back to her house and called Velma's brother, Perry Boardman, who lived in Cleveland. She then returned to the house and waited for Boardman and his daughter, Barbara, to arrive. The three broke into the house through a basement window and confirmed that Anne was dead. She was 21.

DOI: 10.4324/9781003539186-16

FIGURE 15.1   Anne Boardman Moritz, shortly before her death in 1955 at age 21. (Moritz Family Collection)

It was "the hardest blow my mom and dad ever had," son John said decades later.

Anne Moritz's death was front-page news the next day in both the *Cleveland Plain Dealer* and the *Cleveland Press*, which both misspelled her first name. The articles quoted Cuyahoga County Deputy Coroner Lester Adelson on the probable cause of death: an "overwhelming virus infection." Friends, he told the reporters, said Anne had a cold in the days before her death but appeared to be feeling better.[3]

"The natural defenses of the body broke down and the virus reached the heart," Adelson was quoted in the *Cleveland Press*. Death by such a virus, Adelson said, "is as rare as being struck by lightning." A less likely cause, he said, might have been "a rare type of heart disease."

The newspaper article also pointed out that Anne's father was known for investigating unusual and unexplained deaths. "Ironically, Dr. Moritz's Institute of Pathology is one of three pathology centers in the country making an intensive study of this virus for the U.S. Public Health Service."[4]

Dr. and Mrs. Moritz returned home immediately. They instructed their sons not to come home from Japan for the funeral.

Despite Adelson's conclusion, Dr. Moritz was never convinced that his daughter's sudden death was caused by a viral infection. Desperate for answers, he reached out to his network of pathologists, sending them copies of her case file along with tissue samples, but no one could determine an exact cause. "You know the pathologist that my father was. When his only daughter died, every damn thing possible was done to figure out why," John Moritz said.

Anne's tragic death and Alan's unwillingness to accept a medical examiner's determination of the cause weighed on him and Velma for another three decades, and they died without a satisfactory explanation.

"FAMILY CURSE"

It would be 50 years after Anne's death, and 19 years after Dr. Moritz's death, before a likely cause was discovered: a mutation crawling through the far-flung family tree. My father, John Moritz, would refer to it as the "family curse."

In the fall of 2005, one of John's grandsons, a college freshman and an athlete, had a physical examination that included an electrocardiogram. An irregularity in his EKG led to the detection of a disorder known as Long QT Syndrome, a genetic heart arrhythmia that can lead to cardiac arrest. It had first been described in 1957, 2 years after Anne's death.[5]

Long QT was subsequently detected in John and in two of his four sons, a second grandson and a granddaughter. Richard, Anne's twin, died of cancer in 1995, and Long QT was not detected in any of his four children.

Family speculation that Long QT could explain Anne's death began immediately. While the genetic disorder was the talk of the immediate family and was being treated with beta blockers, whether it had come from the Moritz or Boardman side of Dr. Moritz's family was still in question.

A few years later, a television station in Nebraska produced short biographies of accomplished Nebraskans, and John Moritz was interviewed for a feature on his father. After the program aired, John received a phone call from Janet Osborne, a distant cousin still living in Nebraska. Janet's grandmother and Dr. Moritz's mother were sisters, daughters of John and Amelia Richards.

Janet wanted to alert John to the possibility that Long QT was in his family. In an email to John, Janet revealed that her 19-year-old daughter, Nicole, had died from cardiac arrest in 1992 after several fainting spells.

Doctors did not determine the cause of Nicole's death until 3 months later, when Long QT was detected in her grandmother, Janet Osborne's mother, during an EKG. Janet and four other Richards descendants were subsequently diagnosed with Long QT as well.[6]

While no one can be positive that Long QT Syndrome killed Anne Moritz, John is satisfied that the half-century mystery of his sister's death has been solved.

NOTES

1. Unless otherwise noted, information for this chapter came from an interview with John A. Moritz by Rob Moritz, August 15, 2020, Benton, Ark.
2. "Blame Virus in Death of Ann Moritz," *Cleveland Plain Dealer*, March 3, 1955.
3. "Blame Virus in Death of Ann Moritz," *Cleveland Plain Dealer*, March 3, 1955.
4. "Death of Ann Moritz Called Medical Rarity," *Cleveland Press*, March 3, 1955.
5. Jean-Louis Vincent et al., *Textbook of Critical Care*, 6th ed. (Philadelphia: Elsevier Health Sciences, 2011), 578.
6. Janet Osborne, email to John Moritz, June 20, 2013.

CHAPTER 16

"Classical Mistakes"

"Pathologist Scolds Doctors for Criminology Mistakes" read a headline in the *Chicago Sun-Times* on Friday, October 12, 1956. The newspaper had sent its science beat reporter, Robert S. Kleckner, to cover Dr. Moritz's speech the previous night during the annual meeting of the American Society of Clinical Pathologists at the Drake Hotel in Chicago.[1]

Moritz had received the society's Ward Burdick Award for his distinguished work in the field of pathology, and it was tradition for the honoree to present a medical lecture when receiving the award. His lecture, titled "Classical Mistakes in Forensic Pathology," was the product of decades of observation and frustration.

Moritz "minced no words" as he "blamed both police and some pathologists for slipshod work that complicate solution of deaths," the news story said. While the lecture was long and detailed, Kleckner, facing a deadline and with limited space, focused on 2 of the 14 mistakes Moritz enumerated:

- Failing to examine the body and its clothing at the scene of a suspicious death.
- Embalming the body before a pathologist can conduct an examination.

Kleckner, whose article ended up on page 18, could not have known that he was witnessing a milestone in forensic pathology. The complete lecture would be published in the December 1956 issue of the *American Journal of Clinical Pathology*, and it promptly became a legendary treatise for forensic pathologists and those studying to join their ranks well into the 21st century. You can Google it.[2]

"Classical Mistakes," Jeffrey Jentzen wrote in *Death Investigation in America* in 2009, "defined the specialty of forensic pathology and outlined the role of the forensic pathologist." The essay "instantly became the standard for teaching forensic medicine to students and practicing pathologists," wrote Jentzen, emeritus professor of forensic pathology in

DOI: 10.4324/9781003539186-17

the Department of Pathology at University of Michigan. "It served the dual purpose of documenting Moritz's contributions to the specialty and legitimizing the practice of forensic pathology for generations to come."[3]

The influence that one lecture has had on the science of forensic pathology almost defies description. In 1981, 25 years after it was originally published, "Classical Mistakes" was reprinted in the *American Journal of Forensic Medicine and Pathology*.[4] Fourteen more years later, in *Academic Forensic Pathology*, Dr. Joseph H. Davis drew from "Classical Mistakes" to discuss Moritz's specific warning against trying to play Sherlock Holmes when investigating unknown or unusual deaths. "Should we wish not to be the subjects of what Moritz discussed, we must broaden our investigative techniques and enlarge our 'simple case' files with relevant redundant supporting data," Davis wrote in 1995.[5]

Davis, a professor of pathology emeritus at the University of Miami, retired director of Miami-Dade County Medical Examiner and past president of the National Association of Medical Examiners, returned to Moritz's list for his 2011 article "Mistakes and Failures in Forensic Pathology" in *Academic Forensic Pathology: The Official Publication of the National Association of Medical Examiners*. Moritz's article "is as true today as it was thirty-seven years ago" and "should be required reading at least once per year by all pathologists, regardless of experience," he wrote.[6]

In 2015, *Academic Forensic Pathology* published an article by Dr. William R. Oliver titled "Moritz Revisited: Modern Mistakes About How We Think About Forensic Pathology." Oliver did not replicate "Classical Mistakes"; instead, he looked at how Moritz's observations still applied despite 60 years of technological and scientific advances.

Reading "Classical Mistakes" is imperative, Oliver said, because

> many of the younger practitioners are both unaware and uninterested in the intellectual heritage of their profession, in spite of excellent histories available. Such myopia is unfortunate because issues faced by Moritz are as alive today as they were four generations ago.

Moritz's treatise "it is still one of the most valuable articles a young forensic pathologist could read," Oliver concluded.[7]

Forensic pathologist Dr. Thomas Young's 2019 book, *The Sherlock Effect: How Forensic Doctors and Investigators Disastrously Reason Like the Great Detective*, is an homage to one of Moritz's "Classical Mistakes." "Although [Moritz] was not well known to the general public, many of his ideas shaped the development of the death investigation in the United States," Young wrote.[8]

Young, a fellow of the American Academy of Sciences and the National Association of Medical Examiners, argues that many forensic pathologists today incorrectly investigate deaths like Sherlock Holmes, who solved mysteries by reasoning backward. Holmes used logic and intuition to trace the many past steps that led to the known result. But Holmes was fiction, with every clue controlled by creator Sir Arthur Conan Doyle. In his book, Young details a number of real-life death investigations that were botched by deductions rather than medical evidence—exactly as Moritz feared.

"When Dr. Moritz delivered his speech in 1956, he could not have anticipated how bad this problem would eventually become," Young wrote.[9]

In "Classical Mistakes," Moritz warned of the "mistake of substituting intuition for scientifically defensible interpretation." He described this error as "one of the most dangerous mistakes in forensic pathology, and one that is particularly prevalent among experienced forensic pathologists who, for one reason or another, acquire a propensity for what might be called 'categorical intuitive deduction.'"

"This Sherlock Holmes type of expert may see certain bruises in the skin of the neck and conclude without doubt that they were produced by the thumb and forefinger of the right hand of the stranger," my grandfather said.

> He ignores the essential component for proof of the correctness of any such scientific deduction, namely, the nonoccurrence of such lesions or changes in control cases. Such a pathologist usually has the happy faculty of failing to remember the many similar bruises of necks that were known to have been produced by mechanisms other than pressure by the thumb and fingers.

The Holmesian pathologist is "a delight to newspaper reporters owing to the fact that he 'makes good copy,'" Moritz said.

> He may be highly esteemed by the police and by the prosecuting attorney because he is an emphatic and impressive witness. His prestige, together with his exclusive access to the original evidence, places him in an exceedingly powerful position in the courtroom. Rarely can the defense attorneys find anyone with comparable experience to evaluate the postmortem findings.

Any defense expert who disagrees with the modern-day Sherlock may be dismissed by jurors as merely being "hired to say something that would help the accused."

Chillingly, Moritz concluded,

> It is difficult to estimate how much harm is done by these people. I know of a man who was hanged largely on the weight of such

uncritical evidence. ... The stakes are too high to play hunches in forensic pathology.[10]

The "Classical Mistakes" lecture and the subsequent article began with Moritz discussing what he describes as "unique features of the mistakes" commonly made.

One is the frequency with which mistakes are made by good patholo-gists. Another is the frequency with which a seemingly trivial error turns out to have disastrous consequences. Perhaps fewer mistakes would be made if there were widespread appreciation for what consti-tutes a mistake in the performance of a medicolegal autopsy, and why it is a mistake.

Moritz admitted that he had made some of the classical mistakes him-self. He recognized other mistakes in the work of other pathologists, autopsy procedure reports "or from performing second autopsies on exhumed bodies."[11]

The 14 Classical Mistakes identified by Alan Moritz are:

1. Not being aware of the objective of the medical and legal aspects of the autopsy.
2. Performing an incomplete autopsy.
3. Permitting the body to be embalmed before performing an autopsy.
4. Deciding not to conduct an autopsy when the body is mutilated or decomposed.
5. Not recognizing or misinterpreting changes to the body after death.
6. Not adequately examining the clothing and other things worn by the person at the time of death.
7. Considering one's opinion and interpretation, rather than being objective and relying on the facts, when conducting the autopsy and reporting the findings. [1]
8. Not examining the body at the scene of the crime.
9. Replacing intuition for scientifically defensible interpretation.
10. Not taking enough photographs of the evidence.
11. Not using good judgment when taking or handling specimens for toxicology testing.
12. Allowing minor errors to jeopardize the overall autopsy process and results.
13. Minor mistakes (forgetting to do certain things).
14. Talking too soon, too much or to the wrong people.[12]

NOTES

1. Robert S. Kleckner, "Pathologist Scolds Doctors for Criminology Mistakes," *Chicago Sun-Times*, October 12, 1956, 18.
2. Alan R. Moritz, "Classical Mistakes in Forensic Pathology," *The American Journal of Clinical Pathology* 12 (December 25, 1956): 1383–1397.
3. Jeffrey Jentzen, *Death Investigation in America: Coroner's, Medical Examiners, and the Pursuit of Medical Certainty* (Cambridge, MA: Harvard Medical Press, 2009), 82.
4. Alan R. Moritz, "Classical Mistakes in Forensic Pathology," *The American Journal Forensic Medicine and Pathology* 2, no. 4 (December 1981): 299–308.
5. Joseph H. Davis, "The Future of the Medical Examiner System," *The American Journal of Forensic Medicine and Pathology* 16, no. 4 (1995): 268.
6. Joseph H. Davis MD, "Mistakes and Failures in Forensic Pathology," *Academic Forensic Pathology: The Official Publication of the National Association of Medical Examiners* 1, no. 4 (2011): 382.
7. William R. Oliver, "Moritz Revisited: Modern Mistakes About How We Think About Forensic Pathology," *Academic Forensic Pathology: The Official Publication of the National Association of Medical Examiners* 5, no. 2 (2014): 187.
8. Thomas W. Young, *The Sherlock Effect: How Forensic Doctors and Investigators Disastrously Reason Like the Great Detective* (Boca Raton, FL: CRC Press, 2018), 19.
9. Thomas W. Young, *The Sherlock Effect: How Forensic Doctors and Investigators Disastrously Reason Like the Great Detective* (Boca Raton, FL: CRC Press, 2018), 21
10. Alan R. Moritz, "Classical Mistakes in Forensic Pathology," *The American Journal Forensic Medicine and Pathology* 2, no. 4 (December 1981): 303.
11. Alan R. Moritz, "Classical Mistakes in Forensic Pathology," *The American Journal Forensic Medicine and Pathology* 2, no. 4 (December 1981): 299.
12. Alan R. Moritz, "Classical Mistakes in Forensic Pathology," *The American Journal Forensic Medicine and Pathology* 2, no. 4 (December 1981): 299–308.

CHAPTER 17

JFK

Alan Moritz was an "honorary Texas citizen." It said so on a framed proclamation hanging in an upstairs bedroom where we grandchildren slept while visiting in the mid-1970s. The declaration was signed by Gov. John Connally and dated September 8, 1966.

As a teenager, I marveled at the proclamation because I knew that Gov. Connally was in President John F. Kennedy's car in Dallas on November 22, 1963, and was injured by the gunfire that killed the president. I didn't know then that my grandfather received his honorary citizenship for consulting work on another horrific shooting in Texas, the 1966 University of Texas Tower massacre at Austin, or that he had subsequently been called on by US Attorney General Ramsey Clark to review medical evidence in JFK's assassination.

I don't remember hearing my grandfather discuss the assassination, but the so-called Clark Panel affirmed the Warren Commission's official conclusion that assassin Lee Harvey Oswald acted alone. Thanks to never-ending public fascination, this tiny piece of Alan Moritz's career is responsible for most references to him on the internet—particularly since the panel inherited an autopsy that did not conform to my grandfather's standards.

A week after the assassination and 5 days after the suspected assassin had been shot to death by a local businessman, President Lyndon B. Johnson appointed the President's Commission on the Assassination of President Kennedy. It was known as the Warren Commission because it was chaired by Earl Warren, chief justice of the US Supreme Court. On September 24, 1964, the commission presented its report to President Johnson. The commission concluded that the shots that killed Kennedy and injured Connally were fired from behind the motorcade by Oswald, who was in a sixth-floor window on the southeast corner of the Texas School Book Depository.[1]

The Warren Commission's findings did not settle the rumors of a conspiracy, which began almost immediately after the assassination and the murder of Oswald by nightclub owner Jack Ruby. A second gunman fired at the presidential motorcade, some of the theories suggest. Or the

CIA was involved. Or the Mafia, or other foreign or domestic entities. To address some of the theories and suspicions, Attorney General Clark tapped Moritz, who was then a professor of pathology at Case Western Reserve University; Dr. William H. Carnes, professor of pathology at the University of Utah in Salt Lake City; Dr. Russell H. Morgan, professor of radiology at Johns Hopkins University in Baltimore; and Dr. Russell S. Fisher of Baltimore, chief medical examiner of the state of Maryland.[2] (Fisher had studied under Moritz as a Rockefeller Fellow at Harvard Medical School in the 1940s.)

The panel met secretly in February 1968 and spent 2 days in Washington, DC, looking at previously unseen X-rays, autopsy reports, photographs of Kennedy's wounds and the clothing the president was wearing. In January 1969, the panel released a report saying that the Warren Commission's conclusion was correct: Kennedy was killed by two bullets fired from above and behind as he rode in an open car through the streets of Dallas.[3]

While the four expert panelists didn't speak individually about their determination when their report was first released, the findings were widely reported in newspapers across the United States and beyond. "The panel said the autopsy reports, X-rays and photographs eliminated 'with reasonable certainty' any possibility that Kennedy was shot to death through the head from 'any direction other than from back to front,'" according to an article in the *Cleveland Press*.[4]

The following year, *Medical World News* published a long feature on Dr. Moritz and his career. It contains the only comments I have found by my grandfather about his participation in the Clark Panel. "The findings of the Warren Commission are not inconsistent with the facts as presented to us," Moritz said, according to the article.

But he also indicated that the autopsy was less thorough than he would have expected. "The President was rumored to have Addison's disease, but the report contained no mention of examination of the adrenals, for instance," Moritz said. "This information would probably have had no bearing on the assassination itself, but the fact that it was not reported indicates that the investigation as a whole was carried out with something less than professional exactitude."

Fellow panelist Russell Fisher, in the same article, said much of the suspicion surrounding Kennedy's death was fueled by the decision to move the body from Parkland Hospital in Dallas to the Bethesda Naval Hospital near Washington to complete the autopsy. That move violated Texas law, he said. And because the president's body was flown to Washington, the original X-rays and photographs taken at Parkland were not seen by those who conducted the autopsy in Washington, or even by the Warren Commission. The Clark Panel members were the first to review some of the evidence, Fisher said.

[S]kull fragments found on the street, which would have permitted a
more accurate reconstruction of the skull and hence a clearer notion
of the path of the bullet, were not seen by the Washington examiners;
for several hours the [Dallas] coroner was not told that a tracheotomy
had been performed at the place where one bullet emerged, and this
helped to cloud the issue of how many bullets had been fired and from
what directions.[5]

First Lady Jacqueline Kennedy made the decision to move her husband's
body to Bethesda for autopsy because Kennedy had been a naval officer and she wanted the Navy to take charge of his remains, according
to Jeffrey Jentzen's 2009 book *Death Investigation in America*. There
the autopsy was conducted by two US Navy pathologists, Cmdr. J.
Thornton Boswell and Lt. Cmdr. James J. Humes, neither of whom had
formal training or experience in performing autopsies in complex gunshot wound cases.[6]

Throughout the autopsy, "Humes and Boswell were harassed by
the FBI agents to hurry the examination because the first lady and
members of the Kennedy family were waiting in the hospital to receive
the body," Jentzen wrote. Ultimately, small mistakes and errors caused
by inexperience and outside pressures "added up to a situation of confusion and misinterpretation, violating the principles of good forensic
pathology practices Moritz had set forth just a few years earlier" in
"Classical Mistakes in Forensic Pathology." Among them: Not examining the body at the scene of the death, performing an incomplete
autopsy, and permitting the value of the findings to be jeopardized by
minor errors.[7]

Fisher said much of the confusion might have been avoided "if full
control of the investigation had been invested from the beginning in a
team of highly qualified pathologists." Neither he nor Dr. Moritz offered
opinions to *Medical World News* "on the nonmedical issues involved in
judging the Warren Report's veracity."[8]

CONSPIRACIES ABOUND

The Clark Panel didn't settle anything. A Google search finds hundreds
of articles, blogs and websites proclaiming that the original autopsy was
botched and the official conclusions were therefore wrong or, worse, part
of a deliberate coverup. Some skeptics to this day argue that Moritz's
vague comment in the 1970 *Medical World News* article and the failure of the Clark Panel to address "nonmedical issues" raise more questions and point to a possible conspiracy. They suggest that the panel's

statement was deliberately couched and phrased like a prosecutor rather than the way a fact-based researcher would. They also suggest the Clark Panel made its own errors.

Pat Speer, who has written extensive online criticism of both the Warren Commission and the Clark Panel and has published a book on the subject, suggests Moritz's words "revealed a deliberate caution, as if he knew people would someday realize the location of the entrance wound on Kennedy's head had migrated, and didn't want them to think he was unaware of how disturbing this was."

Speer goes on to deliver a backhanded compliment, saying Moritz "really knew how to conceal while appearing to reveal. Maybe he should have written a book telling doctors how to protect themselves at all costs, even if it means lying to their patients."

"It seems more than a coincidence that, in the aforementioned 1970 article in *Medical World News*, neither Dr. Fisher nor his fellow Clark panel member Dr. Moritz mentioned their re-appraisal of the head wound location," Speer wrote on his website, patspeer.com.[9]

Another skeptic website is historymatters.com, an archive for reports and investigations surrounding the 1963 assassination of Kennedy, but also a content aggregator for independent articles and research questioning the findings that Oswald acted alone. Many of the articles criticize the Clark Panel for interpreting Warren Commission's report and the autopsy findings rather than describing them.

"The Clark report is remarkable for its omission," Milicent Cranor wrote in an article for historymatters.com. The article suggests the Clark Panel mistakenly concluded that a bullet struck Kennedy from behind and exited through his throat.

> What is the requisite description of the quality of photos, and the distance from which they were taken? Where is the requisite list of details that distinguished this wound as an exit as opposed to an entrance? Where is the standard disclaimer making clear the fact that no definite conclusion could be based on such a paucity of materials?

Cranor then says that the Clark Panel "did not follow the principles as stated by the most prominent member of the Panel, Alan R. Moritz, M.D." in his article, "Classical Mistakes in Forensic Pathology."[10]

In 1978, Congress decided that yet another review of the Kennedy assassination, along with the 1968 assassination of Rev. Martin Luther King Jr., was needed. The House Select Committee on Assassinations was created. Dr. Michael Baden, who served as medical examiner for the state of New York for a time and would enjoy a measure of celebrity after forensic pathology became a staple of nonfiction television shows, chaired the Select Committee's Forensic Pathology Panel, which reviewed both the Warren Commission and the Clark Panel. [11]

In a 2018 interview for this biography, Baden said he supported the overall findings of the two reports. Baden, however, said he understands why conspiracy theories persist. "I think part of the reason for conspiracy theories is that right away there were some mistakes made by the doctors who did the autopsy who were not trained forensic pathologists," he said. The failure of many conspiracy theorists to understand forensic pathology, specifically gunshot wounds, and the belief that then-FBI director J. Edgar Hoover tried to cover up some of the Warren Commission's findings contribute to the continued suspicion.[12]

Dr. Cyril Wecht, another face familiar to fans of true-crime shows, also served on the congressional Forensic Pathology Panel. He alone disagreed with the findings, saying the original autopsy was poorly done and that subsequent reviews made liberal interpretations rather than basing their findings on facts. (Wecht, who died in May 2024 at age 93, was also acquainted with my grandfather. Moritz had inspected and certified the coroner's office in Pittsburgh when Wecht was medical examiner there in the 1970s.)[13]

THE TEXAS TOWER

Perhaps it was evidence of growing respect for the maturing field of forensic science that led to a new phenomenon in the 1960s: Official boards or committees appointed to review completed investigations of high-profile or politically sensitive crimes. A year before Moritz was appointed to the Clark Panel, he and more than 30 other medical and forensic experts were asked by Texas Gov. Connally to evaluate the autopsy, medical and psychiatric records of Charles J. Whitman, the Texas Tower sniper.[14]

On August 1, 1966, 25-year-old Whitman climbed to the top of a tower on the University of Texas campus in Austin lugging a footlocker containing seven firearms. In a shooting spree that lasted more than 90 minutes, he killed 15 and injured more than 30. The former US Marine marksman was eventually shot and killed by police. An autopsy discovered a tumor in Whitman's brain, and investigators learned he had seen a psychiatrist several months earlier.[15]

While the police investigation was straightforward, Connally asked the panel of experts to try to answer what police could not: Why did Whitman do it? The governor also wanted to know if there were any red flags in Whitman's behavior before the shooting that law enforcement, medical professionals or the public might have spotted and addressed before the horrible events of August 1.

Whitman's autopsy report and his medical and psychiatric records were provided to the panel, and Moritz served as an adviser on any medical and legal issues, according to the final report presented to the governor on September 8, 1966. Moritz was also the director of the study section regarding recommendations.

The committee concluded that Whitman's "highly malignant brain tumor" could have "contributed to his inability to control his emotions or actions," but all the expertise combined could not say for certain that the tumor caused his actions. The committee also said, among other things, that it could not make a formal psychiatric diagnosis on Whitman based on the evidence provided.

Among the committee's recommendations were additional mental health programs, including counseling, for students and employees on the university campus, and the creation of a statewide medical examiner system of the kind that Moritz had been championing for almost 40 years. Texas at that time relied on the coroner system.

Because of Whitman's military background, the panel also recommended that the military should consider doing more to help combat-trained personnel readjust to society. "It is believed possible for military personnel who have been trained to re-learn in such a way as to de-emphasize in their minds those hostile acts taught as laudatory in time of war," the report said.

Self-reflection by the media for its coverage of the shooting was also urged by the panel. "Acts of violence and tragedy are given prominence in all news media," the report said. The report recommended that "the communications media review their own role and attitude in obtaining and disseminating information concerning acts of violence and conduct research, with appropriate educational agencies, to determine means to best serve the public welfare in regard to these matters."[16]

When presenting the "Honorary Texas Citizen" proclamation, Connally included a personal letter expressing his appreciation for my grandfather's work on the Whitman case. "Not only was I impressed with your professional ability, but I watched with admiration as you articulated your views and opinions in a manner that laymen could understand," Connally wrote.[17]

ATTICA

About 5 years after serving on the Clark Panel, Moritz was again called into public service, this time as part of a review of the 5-day riot at New York's Attica Correctional Institution in September 1971. Moritz's assignment was to review the autopsies of 43 people who died when Gov. Nelson Rockefeller ordered armed officers to retake control of the prison. Moritz, in his report, reviewed the autopsy reports on 32 inmates and 11 guards and employees. Dr. Michael Baden, who was familiar with my grandfather from his work on the Clark Panel, was the deputy chief medical examiner of the city of New York at the time and conducted several of the autopsies that Moritz later reviewed. "I testified before him about my findings and the people who died at Attica," Baden recalled when interviewed for this biography on March 22, 2018.[18]

The Attica autopsies were particularly difficult, Baden said. "We had to make sure the bullets were recovered and who were the shooters," he said. Some of the bodies were so mangled that it was difficult to tell if they were guards or inmates. "There were so many things involved," he said.[19]

Moritz reviewed ballistic reports and photographs of each of the 43 riot deaths, as well as the autopsy reports. He concluded that none of the 32 inmates would have survived even if they had received medical attention sooner, according to the New York State Special Commission's official report on Attica. But he could not determine whether prompt medical attention could have prevented the "permanent crippling injuries" suffered by some surviving inmates.

The special commission's report said,

> What is clear is that wounded inmates immeasurably magnified the agony at Attica on September 13. Given the magnitude of the force to be used in the assault, and the apprehension of heavy casualties, there simply can be no excuse for the absence of advanced planning for medical care.[20]

NOTES

1. "Warren Commission Report and Hearings," *Gov.Org*, May 23, 2016, accessed August 8, 2024, https://www.govinfo.gov/features/warren-commission-report-and-hearings.
2. "Report of a special panel convened by the Attorney General of the United States on February 26 and 27, 1968 to re-examine the medical and other evidence relating to the fatal wounding of President Kennedy to determine the extent to which the findings do or do not confirm the conclusions found on pages 538 & 539 inclusively of the Warren Commission Report," (Path015 Alan R. Moritz, MD, Papers Stanley A. Ferguson Archives, University Hospitals of Cleveland).
3. Fred P. Graham, "Inquiry Upholds Warren Report: Finds Autopsy Photos Show 2 Shots Killed President," *New York Times*, January 17, 1969.

4. Merriman Smith, "Warren Findings on JFK Supported by More Doctors," *Cleveland Press*, January 17, 1969.

5. "Of Crimes and Change and the Doctor's Doctor," *Medical World News*, March 13, 1970, 33.

6. Jeffrey M. Jentzen, *Death Investigation in America: Coroners, Medical Examiners, and the Pursuit of Medical Certainty* (Cambridge, MA: Harvard University Press, 2009), 98.

7. Jeffrey M. Jentzen, *Death Investigation in America: Coroners, Medical Examiners, and the Pursuit of Medical Certainty* (Cambridge, MA: Harvard University Press, 2009), 99; Alan R. Moritz, "Classical Mistakes in Forensic Pathology," *The American Journal of Forensic Medicine and Pathology* 2, no. 4 (December 1981): 299–308.

8. "Of Crimes and Change and the Doctor's Doctor," *Medical World News*, March 13, 1970, 33.

9. Pat Speer, "Chapter 13: Solving the Great Wound Mystery," *patspeer.com*, accessed August 8, 2024, https://www.patspeer.com /chapter13solvingthegreatheadwoundmyster.

10. Milicent Cranor, "Trajectory of a Lie," *history-matters.com*, accessed August 8, 2024, https://history-matters.com/essays/jfk-med/TrajectoryOfaLie/TrajectoryOfaLie.htm.

11. "Dr. Michael Baden," *dr.michaelbaden.com*, accessed August 8, 2024, https://drmichaelbaden.com/bio.

12. Dr. Michael Baden, telephone interview by Rob Moritz, March 22, 2018.

13. Dr. Cyril Wecht, telephone interview by Rob Moritz, January 23, 2019.

14. "Report to the Governor, Medical Aspects, Charles J. Whitman Catastrophe," *Austin Texas*, September 8, 1966 (PATH 015 Alan R. Moritz, MD, Papers, Stanley A. Ferguson Archives, University Hospitals of Cleveland).

15. "Looking Back: 50 Years after the UT Tower Shooting," *Austin Public Library*, July 26–November 20, 2016, accessed July 9, 2024, https://library.austintexas.gov/ahc/looking-back-50-years-after-ut -tower-shooting.

16. "Report to the Governor, Medical Aspects, Charles J. Whitman Catastrophe," *Austin Texas*, September 8, 1966 (PATH 015 Alan R. Moritz, MD, Papers, Stanley A. Ferguson Archives, University Hospitals of Cleveland).

17. John Connally, letter to Alan R. Moritz, September 12, 1966 (Moritz Family Collection).

18. "Attica: The Official Report of the NYS Special Commission on Attica," digitized by the *New York State Library*, Albany, New York, in 2011, accessed July 13, 2024, https://nysl.ptfs.com/aw -server/rest/product/purl/NYSL/s/1d8e4c4c-dfd1-4de1-9ba3 -c5541ffb6506; Baden interview.

19. Dr. Michael Baden, telephone interview by Rob Moritz, March 22, 2018.

20. Alan R. Moritz, "Report by Alan R. Moritz, M.D., of an Investigation Undertaken by Him at the Request of the New York State Special Commission on Attica of the Fatal Injuries Sustained by 32 Prisoners and 11 Hostages Incident to the Rioting which Occurred at the Attica Prison on September 13, 1971," (Path015 Alan R. Moritz, MD, Papers, Stanley A. Ferguson Archives, University Hospitals of Cleveland).

CHAPTER **18**

The Moritz Formula

Dr. Moritz's research at Harvard on estimating how long a person had been dead was already showing up in pop culture in 1950. The mathematical calculation, which would be alternately known as Moritz's formula or the Moritz formula, was referenced in his friend Erle Stanley Gardner's *The Case of the Musical Cow.*

It was still showing up more than 40 years later. In "'I' is for Innocent," the 1992 installment in her best-selling series featuring detective Kinsey Millhone, mystery novelist Sue Grafton described the technique used at a murder scene to estimate how long the victim had been dead:

> Using the Moritz formula and adjusting for the temperature in the foyer, her body weight, clothing, and the temperature and conductivity of the marble floor of which she lay, the medical examiner placed the time of death roughly between 1 a.m. and 2 a.m.[1]

The use of the Moritz formula by a medical examiner is also mentioned by Tess Gerritsen in her novel *Girl Missing,* originally published in 1994 as *Peggy Sue Got Murdered*:

> She could make an educated guess about time of death. Livor mortis, the body's mottling after death, was unfixed, suggesting that death was less than eight hours old, and the body temperature, using Moritz's formula, suggested a time of death around midnight.[2]

Moritz, having been asked the time of death innumerable times by detectives and death investigators, was at Harvard when he developed a mathematical equation to estimate time of death—as long as the death had occurred within the past 24 hours. He wrote about the formula in his groundbreaking textbook *Pathology of Trauma*, as well as in *Handbook of Legal Medicine*. For the first time, law enforcement investigators could make an educated guess until a more accurate time of death could be established by an autopsy.[3]

    DOI: 10.4324/9781003539186-19

Handwritten notes found in Moritz's papers, archived at Harvard Medical School in Boston, show the formula as 98.6 (normal body temperature) minus the rectal temperature of the corpse, divided by 1.5, which is the rate of temperature change per hour if the environment where the body was found is above freezing.

"Beginning at the moment of death, a body undergoes a series of physical and chemical changes which continue until it is ultimately destroyed," Moritz wrote in *Handbook of Legal Medicine*. Each of the changes

> has a time factor. If each type of change began at a predictable time and continued at a predictable rate after death, it would be possible to estimate the duration of the postmortem interval with accuracy. However, because many unsuspected circumstances may modify the rate at which postmortem change occurs, deductions drawn from such evidence are susceptible to considerable error.[4]

Dr. Richard Ford, who succeeded Moritz as director of the Department of Legal Medicine at Harvard, said Moritz's mathematical formula, or "rate method," was useful but not accurate in all settings. "Less precise and requiring true expert appraisal is the rate method," Ford wrote, in a 1953 article for the *Journal of Criminal Law and Criminology*. "No man can encompass the necessary knowledge to evaluate all the postmortem phenomena in every case. The medicolegal pathologist can do the most." Body temperature after death, Ford wrote, falls slowly if the body "is in bed covered with blankets." If the body is "nude on ice in the winter wind the rate will be rapid like the quick freezing of food."[5]

In a study between July 2015 and August 2016, researchers in Bhopal tested the Moritz formula to determine how reliable it is in the tropical climate of central India. A total of 173 bodies were brought to a morgue at the Department of Forensic Medicine & Toxicology at Gandhi Medical College for autopsy. Bodies in which the time of death was known and documented were included in the research, and those in which the time of death was not known or the temperature at the time of death was either high or below normal were excluded.

After looking at the external appearance of the bodies, researchers removed the clothing and took the body's rectal temperature. At the same time, the temperature in the room where the body was located was taken, along with details about the deceased, such as age, gender, build, height and weight. The actual time of death and temperatures at the time of death were also noted from hospital or police documents.

The researchers then applied the original Moritz formula and a variation that halved the rate of temperature change to factor in the tropical weather of India. The results found that both methods were useful for determining the time of death in a 24-hour period, but the second method was a little more accurate, especially within 6 hours of death.[6]

BULLETS, GUNPOWDER AND CASINGS

While virtually all my grandfather's work was medical, he also contributed to forensic ballistics despite what he described as his "lack of enthusiasm for the inside of gun barrels."[7]

Moritz began dabbling in ballistics not long after he arrived in Glasgow in the fall of 1937. He told Harvard Medical School Dean Sidney Burwell in a letter that he had spent 3 days developing a technique to identify shells and cartridges fired from a variety of weapons. "I can actually identify the guilty gun in about 60 out of a possible 100," he wrote in December 1937. "I am not yet convinced that the other forty are possible." He went on to say that he could also "tell the difference between black and smokeless powder from a single microscopic grain which is not surprising but it did surprise me that there are about a dozen different kinds of nitro powders all of which have different microscopic characteristics."

In hindsight, this feels like a lost opportunity, as Moritz seems to have promptly moved on to a different ballistics research project. Six decades later, in 1998, the National Research Council recommended that a national gunpowder database be developed. The FBI had collected and cataloged about 100 powder samples, which were included in the Scientific Working Group for Fire and Explosions' Smokeless Powder Database when it ultimately launched in 2011.[8]

In 1938, Moritz published an article in *The Police Journal* about a technique he developed using red nail polish to analyze the markings left on fired bullets and shell casings. He presented his findings at a conference in Bonn, Germany, and his technique was also published in 1939 in the second edition of *Recent Advances in Forensic Medicine*.

His initial research used nail polish on a single strand of hair. He put the nail polish on the hair and let it dry. When he removed the individual hair, he could see under a microscope a detailed imprint of the hair in the dried polish. Using a similar process on a used bullet or shell casing allowed marks to be seen on the shell or casing with a microscope.

"It was felt that if transparent, flexible impressions, or casts of the surfaces under investigation, could be made, several difficulties inherent to direct examination would be reduced or obviated," he wrote in an article titled "A New Method for the Examination of Markings on Bullets, Shell Cases and Breech Faces."[9]

In a 1956 article for the *Journal of Criminal Law and Criminology*, Arthur A. Biasotti, who worked in the Pittsburgh and Allegheny County crime lab, discussed the development.

> The advantages cited by Moritz were that the flexible, translucent case produced by this method could be flattened and viewed by transillumination thus reducing or obviating the difficulties inherent in the direct observation of curved or inaccessible surfaces by reflected illumination.

Biasotti went on to say a "commercial adaptation of the technique described by Moritz" was being distributed under the name Faxfilm by The Brush Development Co. in Cleveland. While he had heard that Faxfilm was being used in law enforcement work, he wrote that he could not find any literature concerning its practical application.[10]

Seven years earlier, however, Faxfilm was mentioned in an article in the *Journal of Criminal Law and Criminology* titled "A Method of Comparison of Tool Marks." The article discussed what it described as "a new method for use in criminal investigations for the comparison of tool markings on metal or hard surfaces," but never mentions Dr. Moritz.[11]

NOTES

1. Sue Grafton, *"I" Is for Innocent* (New York: Henry Holt and Company, Inc., 1992), 10.
2. Tess Gerritsen, *Girl Missing* (New York: Ballantine Books, 2014), 13.
3. Alan R. Moritz, *Pathology of Trauma*, 2nd ed. (Philadelphia: Lea & Febiger, 1954), 396–404; Alan R. Moritz and R. Crawford Morris, *Handbook of Legal Medicine,* 4th ed. (St. Louis: The C.V. Mosby Company, 1975), 15–20.
4. Alan R. Moritz and R. Crawford Morris, *Handbook of Legal Medicine,* 4th ed. (St. Louis: The C.V. Mosby Company, 1975), 15
5. Richard Ford, "Critical Times in Murder Investigation (Time of Assault, Incapacitation and Death)," *Journal of Criminal Law and Criminology* 42, no. 5, Article 10 (1953): 676, accessed July 18, 2024, https://scholarlycommons.law.northwestern.edu/cgi/viewcontent.cgi?article=4073&context=jclc.
6. Jayanthi Yadav, Rajneesh Kumar Pandey, and Sujeet Kumar Samadder, "A Study to Estimate the Reliability of "Moritz Rule of Thumb - Method A and Method B,' Method of Estimation of Time Since Death in Tropical Climate of Central India," *Medico-Legal Update* 19, no. 1 (January–June 2019): 104–107.

7. Alan R. Moritz, letter to Sidney Burwell, December 7, 1937 (Center for the History of Medicine at Francis A. Countway Library, Harvard University).
8. Michael E. Sigman et al., "Smokeless Powder Reference Collection and SWGFEX Smokeless Powders Database Expansion," *Office of Justice Programs National Criminal Justice Reference Service*, July 2017, accessed August 10, 2024, https://www.ojp.gov/pdffiles1/nij/grants/250933.pdf.
9. Alan R. Moritz, "A New Method for the Examination of Markings on Bullets, Shell Cases and Breech Faces," *The Police Journal* 11, July-September (1938): 364–369.
10. Alfred A. Biasotti, "Plastic Replicas in Firearms and Took Mark Identifications," *The Criminology and Police Science* 47, no. 1 (1956): 110, accessed July 18, 2024, https://web.archive.org/web/20170922024718id_/http://scholarlycommons.law.northwestern.edu/cgi/viewcontent.cgi?article=4473&context=jclc.
11. David L. Cowles and James K. Dodge, "A Method for Comparison of Tool Marks," *Journal of Criminal Law and Criminology* 39, no. 2 (1948): 262, accessed July 18, 2024, https://www-jstor-org.ucark.idm.oclc.org/stable/pdf/1138170.pdf?refreqid=fastly-default%3A06e74c1a221bd7e07dda4f8a8ee16181&ab_segments=0%2Fbasic_search_gsv2%2Fcontrol&origin=&initiator=&acceptTC=1.

CHAPTER 19

Apartheid

James Lenkoe was a railway worker and black dissident who protested apartheid, the legal system that subjugated South Africa's black majority to the political will of the white minority. On March 5, 1969, South African security police arrested Lenkoe at his home, a two-room apartment in one of many long, barracks-like one-story buildings in Soweto, then a segregated black township on the outskirts of Johannesburg. Eight days later, Lenkoe's wife was told to collect his dead body, which had been found hanging in a prison cell in Pretoria, the capital city about 60 miles from Soweto.[1]

Three of Lenkoe's brothers soon sought help from Joel Carlson, a white South African attorney well known internationally for representing black dissidents against the repressive South African government. In his 1973 book, *No Neutral Ground*, Carlson recounted his work in the fight to end apartheid. He dedicated a chapter to the Lenkoe case.

"The story they told me of the death of their brother sounded much like the many cases of injustices I was now almost accustomed to hearing," Carlson wrote. "Indeed, because these had become so common, generally they were only of significance to the immediate circle of sufferers. Only once in a while would a cause break out of the circle and assume national and international significance." After discussing the incident with Lenkoe's brothers, Carlson agreed to meet with the widow.[2]

According to Carlson's account, Julie Lenkoe said she saw the police beat her husband before they took him away on March 5. When she tried to see him the next day in a Pretoria prison, she was told she would not be able to see him for 180 days. She was, however, told she should bring him clothes and food on Sunday, March 9. When she returned to the prison with his clothes and food as instructed, she was told her husband was not there. Four days later, on the 13th, she was informed that her husband had died on March 10. The police said a police surgeon had conducted an autopsy and concluded that he had hanged himself with his belt. During their first meeting, Mrs. Lenkoe handed Carlson her husband's only belt; he was not wearing it when he was taken by police.[3]

DOI: 10.4324/9781003539186-20

Carlson asked Dr. Jonathan Gluckman, a South African patholo-gist, to conduct an autopsy of Lenkoe's body. Gluckman found reasons to question the government's explanation that Lenkoe had hanged him-self. "If the fracture of the neck was made while Lenkoe was still alive, then there would have been a hemorrhage at the fracture site," Carlson wrote. "Their examination had revealed no trace of blood there—it was quite clean. This led them to ask whether the hanging could have taken place after death."

Dr. Gluckman also discovered "a curious mark on the second toe of the deceased's foot." It looked suspiciously like a burn he had seen in a medical journal some years earlier. He located the article at a library. It had been written by Dr. Alan R. Moritz and published in 1947 in the *Journal of American Pathology*.[4]

The article "dealt with different kinds of burns made under con-trolled experimental conditions," Moritz recalled in notes he typed in October 1977, perhaps for a speech or lecture. In his notes, he mis-spelled Lenkoe's last name. "It included burns caused by electricity. What [Gluckman] saw on Lencoe's skin under the microscope corresponded closely with a photomicrograph of a burn caused by electricity."[5]

Carlson had been in frequent contact with an American human rights group called the Lawyers' Committee for Civil Rights Under Law, which was created in 1963 at the request of President Kennedy to help champion the Civil Rights movement in the United States. After learn-ing from Gluckman that the "curious mark" found on Lenkoe's toe "showed a classic resemblance" to a series of slides in the article written by Moritz, Carlson sought the LCCRUL's help in tracking down the forensic pathologist he considered a "recognized world authority in his field."

Moritz, then 69 years old and living in Cleveland, was soon on the telephone with Gluckman. During their conversation, Moritz suggested further tests, including an atomic spectrographic test, which could deter-mine if the mark on Lenkoe's toe "was of an electrothermal nature," Carlson wrote. The test was conducted in South Africa and the photo-graphs were then sent to Moritz.[6]

"Under magnification of 60 x to 200 [Gluckman] was able to dem-onstrate the burn had been produced electrically," Moritz said in a 1970 article in *Medical World News*. The current "had passed through the skin in a scattered narrow column, producing discrete transepidermal injuries unlike those caused by the uniform conduction of heat from a hot object applied to the surface." Moritz added there was evidence of copper in the burned skin, indicating it had been caused by an electrical wire.[7]

In his book, Carlson said the photographs showed cysts just below the skin on Lenkoe's toe and the beginnings of a blister that had not yet fully developed. The belief was that the blister formation stopped

FIGURE 19.1   South African pathologist Dr. Jonathan Gluckman, left, and South African civil rights attorney Joel Carlson, center, with Dr. Moritz during his 10-day trip to South Africa in June 1969 to testify that anti-apartheid activist James Lenkoe had been tortured to death in police custody. The inscription says, "For Alan Moritz – A fine member of a fighting force –" (Moritz Family Collection)

when Lenkoe died. "This enabled us to fix the time of death as some-where within a period of two minutes and twelve hours" after the injury, Carlson wrote.

Carlson had sent Moritz the photographs taken at the scene.[8] In his 1977 notes, Moritz said the police surgeon's ruling on Lenkoe's cause of death was inconsistent with the photographic evidence. The surgeon had ruled that Lenkoe stood on the bottom of an upside-down bucket, "tied the end of the belt to the horizontal steel top of the door frame of his cell and stepped off to be suffocated by his own unsupported weight," Moritz wrote.

> An interesting feature of the picture was that the arms of the dead man were not at his sides, but were raised in front of him, with fingers extended and palms forward. Presumable rigor had developed in some position other than that shown in the photograph.[9]

In a letter, Moritz told Carlson that the condition in which Lenkoe's body was found reminded him of what he had seen three decades earlier in Nazi-controlled Germany and Austria. Moritz described "a common practice in some of the concentration camps, early in the Hitler period, to conceal homicide by suspending the body of the murdered prisoner so that the death could be officially reported as due to suicidal hanging."

Using the information provided by Moritz in the letter, Dr. van Praag-Koch, the state surgeon who ruled that Lenkoe had hanged himself, was asked during a preliminary hearing why the dead man, when found, had his arms raised in front of him and not at his sides. Van Praag-Koch said Lenkoe "had an instantaneous cadaveric spasm causing instant rigor mortis." Carlson said "such a spasm was an extremely rare occurrence, so rare that three of the four pathologists I consulted knew nothing about it."[10]

Not long after Moritz talked by phone with Carlson and Dr. Gluckman, Charles Mandelstam, a New York attorney with LCCRUL, telephoned and asked if he would be willing to fly to South Africa to serve as an expert witness in the Lenkoe case. Moritz agreed and applied for a visa to the Counsel General for the Republic of South Africa. "I told him the matter was urgent and he asked me why. I explained that I was to testify in the [Lenkoe] inquest which was now in session and due to be finished by next Friday." The Council General's office promptly told Moritz "it would take at least a fortnight to get the visa approved."

Mandelstam then referred Moritz to Charles Runyon, a lawyer in the US State Department who specialized in African affairs and human rights. Mandelstam said "the State Department was familiar with and interested in the [Lenkoe] affair" and that Runyon "could probably stimulate fast action on my visa." Moritz received his visa the following day and arrived in Pretoria a few days later.

The LCCRUL and the US State Department, according to Moritz, considered the Lenkoe case as a possible vehicle for gathering evidence on the human rights issues concerning apartheid, the practices of secret detention and torture used by Security Police, and to present that evidence to the South African Supreme Court. "If this could be done, there was a good possibility that the autonomy of the Security Police would be sharply curtailed. There had been several unsatisfactorily explained deaths of blacks under interrogation and maybe this would do the trick," Moritz said.[11]

When he finally arrived in South Africa—a 30-hour journey from Cleveland to New York to London to Pretoria[12]— Moritz was met by "an embarrassed and angry attorney Carlson," who said that the inquest had been recessed earlier that day and there was no indication when the magistrate would reconvene. Carlson told Moritz "it was clear that the magistrate did not want to hear my testimony and that the easy way to prevent it was to adjourn the inquest indefinitely."[13]

It would be a few days before the highest court in South Africa would order the magistrate to reconvene the inquest, and during that time Moritz was able to conduct his own autopsy of Lenkoe and develop more evidence to indicate the dissident had been tortured to death.

During 4 days of testimony, Moritz testified that chemical tests revealed that Lenkoe had suffered an electrical burn on his toe. Carlson said he "explained clearly how it was possible to determine Lenkoe had died within two minutes to twelve hours of receiving the injury to his toe. On all the evidence, he said, the only reasonable conclusion was an electrical burn."[14]

Moritz was also questioned by the magistrate, with many of the questions coming from the police commissioner, who sat to his right, and the medical adviser for the police on his left. At the end of his testimony, the attorney for the South African police requested and was granted a recess. "His reasons were that my English was so American and so difficult to understand that he would have to study the entire transcript to know what I had said and why," Moritz said. "He also needed time to consult his medical advisors."

When the inquest was reconvened 3 days later, the defense attorney for the police presented Moritz with "a dozen or so bound volumes of medical journals—all German—none of which I had read and all of which contained something on electrical injuries," according to Moritz, whose once-fluent German was rusty by the late 1960s.

Moritz spent that night reading each of the articles and "found only one that dealt with burns from currents such as were available in the prison—110 volt alternating." The article, Moritz continued, included descriptions of burns, along with photographs "that were qualitatively similar, although for the most part more severe, than the one on Lencoe's foot," he wrote, again misspelling the victim's last name. "Apparently neither the attorney nor his medical advisors had read this carefully enough to realize that it tended to confirm what I had been saying."[15]

Moritz's testimony at the inquest was also recounted in the 1998 book *No One to Blame*, by George Bizos, a human rights attorney who had emigrated to South Africa from Greece as a boy during World War

II.[16] During the hearing, Bizos wrote, Prosecutor C.G. Jordaan asked Moritz about the traces of copper found on Lenkoe's toe.

The prosecutor put it to Moritz that persons working with metal would have traces of the substance on their skin. When Moritz agreed, Jordaan pushed home his point: "Then you will agree that if the deceased had constantly come into contact with copper by reason of his work, then his skin would contain more copper?"

Calmly, Moritz agreed. "Yes, but can you tell me what work the deceased did involving the second toe of his right foot?"

Despite Moritz's testimony, the court ruled that Lenkoe committed suicide. "The two-month long inquest had been a complete farce," Bizos wrote.[17]

Carlson and Bizos both reported tension between South African prosecutors and Dr. Moritz. Carlson recounted a specific confrontation during a break for lunch during the inquest. The judge, at the request of prosecutors, forbade Carlson to speak to Moritz during the break. Moritz was about to leave the courthouse with Carlson's wife and the wife of Gluckman, the South African pathologist, when a security lieutenant walked up and asked Moritz to accompany him to a lunch that had been arranged by the government.

"Having made Dr. Moritz a state witness against his will, they now wished to convert him to their cause and make him a more friendly witness," Carlson wrote. "The doctor was reluctant to go with Lieutenant Richter but was too courteous to be rude and refuse outright." Carlson wrote that his wife quickly stepped in. She was hungry, Mrs. Carlson said, "and not interested in this nonsense." She pointed out that they had specifically invited Moritz to lunch and now he had to make up his mind about who he would lunch with. "Dr. Moritz grasped at this opportunity," Carlson wrote. "'I cannot be discourteous to the ladies,' he told the lieutenant as he left." Carlson said he saw the lieutenant "grit his teeth and as he noticed me watching, I thought he was going to spit at me." The prosecutor who was with the lieutenant "was white with rage." Carlson said he was informed later that restaurant employees were asked by government security to observe whether Moritz and the two women discussed the Lenkoe case during their lunch.

When Moritz returned to the courthouse after lunch, Carlson wrote, the lieutenant was waiting for his return. He took Moritz by the arm and led him up a set of stairs.

> I could not hear what they were saying but I did not trust the security police and I called up to Richter, "Look here, Lieutenant, I was ordered not to speak to Dr. Moritz or interfere with him and no doubt the order applies to you.'"

Carlson wrote that Richter "swung around as though about to strike me, his face distorted with rage. 'You go to hell,' he snarled, 'I'm taking the doctor to the toilet.'"

Before he left South Africa, my grandfather told Carlson that Richter had asked him to "tone down the evidence." Moritz also told Carlson that the trip was more difficult than he had expected. As Carlson recounted the conversation, Moritz

> expected simply to give evidence at an inquest but he felt as if he had gone through the mill of adversary proceedings. He's never had such a hectic, hard-working week. He warned me about living "too dangerously" and urged me to be careful. Then he was gone—back to America.[18]

Moritz's 10-day trip to South Africa, his testimony that Lenkoe was murdered by government police and the subsequent harassment of Carlson by state police were chronicled on the front page of the *Rand Daily Mail*, a Johannesburg newspaper known for its outspoken opposition to apartheid. Moritz's trip was also reported in numerous papers in the United States in 1969. "Dr. Moritz was of course of inestimable value in the Lenkoe inquest," Carlson said.

Moritz, in his notes recalling the trip, said Mandelstam met him at a New York airport after his trip from South Africa. That was when he learned that the inquest had ended and that Lenkoe's death had been ruled suicide.

> Mandelstam also said that throughout the inquest the most influential newspapers in South Africa had reported verbatim all of the testimony given by me at the inquest and that such editorials had appeared, particularly those published in the English language papers, took the position that the Magistrate's verdict was not in accord with the evidence presented.

Runyon, with the US Department of State, later sent several newspaper articles about the trial to Moritz.[19]

On June 25, 1969, more than two decades before apartheid was abolished in South Africa, Congressman Allard K. Lowenstein, a Democrat from New York, addressed his colleagues from the floor of the US House of Representatives about Lenkoe's death and the subsequent inquest.

In his speech, which was reproduced in the *Congressional Record*, Lowenstein discussed Moritz's trip to South Africa and his testimony. "The suspicion that Mr. Lenkoe was in fact electrocuted has grown with the odd behavior of the South African Government since the body was discovered," Lowenstein said. Allegations of torture in South African prisons "are, of course, not new, but the South African Government has always professed indignation at these allegations." Rep. Lowenstein said that after the Lenkoe inquest, the South African government seized Carlson's passport and began harassing him.[20]

The South African government's official actions were widely condemned. Under the headline "South African 'Justice'," a *New York Times* editorial criticized the South African Nationalist Government for dismissing the torture allegations and for legislation that protected its security police from transparency and public investigation. The editorial, published on June 17, 1969, noted Dr. Moritz's testimony "that beyond reasonable doubt an injury on Mr. Lenkoe's body was caused by electric shock."

The editorial went on to note that Carlson had his passport taken "because he was too skilled when he went up against monstrous laws and the apartheid system, in protecting the rights of Africans and exposing police barbarism." A subsequent news article in the *New York Times* on July 25, 1969, also reported on Lenkoe's death, the inquest and the court's decision.[21]

After returning to Cleveland, Moritz said he was not surprised by the court's decision nor by the harassment of Carlson, who "had been crusading for human rights and was regarded by the government as a public enemy." Despite the official loss, the Lenkoe case raised Carlson's profile and helped bring the injustices of apartheid to the conscience of America and the rest of the world. Carlson said he received "cables and messages of support" from the Lawyers' Committee for Civil Rights Under Law and its co-chairs, Arthur H. Dean and Louis F. Oberdorfer, and from Burke Marshall, then the assistant attorney general for the Civil Rights Division of the US Department of Justice.[22]

In his 1977 notes recalling the work he did in South Africa, Moritz also mentioned the recent high-profile murder of Stephen Biko, a black dissident and leader in the anti-apartheid movement, who was arrested and subsequently beaten to death by state police while in custody on September 12, 1977. Moritz wrote down his remembrances of his South Africa adventure about a month after hearing about Biko's death, and he wondered when or if the racial violence would end.

> It is clear from the press reports that a great change has occurred in the reaction of the black population of South Africa, even though the Security Police are still playing the role of the Nazi Gestapo. Certainly, a blood bath is in the making.[23]

The Lenkoe case promptly faded from memory in the United States, but it was not forgotten in South Africa. Nor was Alan Moritz. In 1996, the Truth & Reconciliation Commission, an official body created by the post-apartheid government of South Africa to acknowledge apartheid-era crimes and abuses, heard testimony from Lorraine Lenkoe, daughter of James Lenkoe. Just 11 months old when her father died, she said she had been told the story by her mother and grandmother. During her testimony she described her father's death and Carlson's unsuccessful efforts to hold the government accountable. And a decade after my grandfather's death, she told the commission about Dr. Moritz, who came from America and "discovered that my father was tortured before he died."[24]

NOTES

1. Joel Carlson, *No Neutral Ground* (New York: Thomas Y. Crowell Company, 1973); Alan R. Moritz, typed notes on 1969 trip to South Africa to help investigate death of James Lencoe, 1977 (Moritz Family Collection).
2. Joel Carlson, *No Neutral Ground* (New York: Thomas Y. Crowell Company, 1973), 218.
3. Joel Carlson, *No Neutral Ground* (New York: Thomas Y. Crowell Company, 1973), 219–223.
4. Joel Carlson, *No Neutral Ground* (New York: Thomas Y. Crowell Company, 1973), 226–227.
5. Alan R. Moritz, typed notes on 1969 trip to South Africa to help investigate death of James Lencoe, 1977 (Moritz Family Collection).
6. Joel Carlson, *No Neutral Ground* (New York: Thomas Y. Crowell Company, 1973), 226–228.
7. "Of Crime and Change and The Doctor's Doctor," *Medical World News*, March 13, 1970, 32–33
8. Joel Carlson, *No Neutral Ground* (New York: Thomas Y. Crowell Company, 1973), 228.
9. Alan R. Moritz, typed notes on 1969 trip to South Africa to help investigate death of James Lencoe, 1977 (Moritz Family Collection).
10. Joel Carlson, *No Neutral Ground* (New York: Thomas Y. Crowell Company, 1973), 231.
11. Alan R. Moritz, typed notes on 1969 trip to South Africa to help investigate death of James Lencoe, 1977 (Moritz Family Collection).
12. Joel Carlson, *No Neutral Ground* (New York: Thomas Y. Crowell Company, 1973), 238.
13. Alan R. Moritz, typed notes on 1969 trip to South Africa to help investigate death of James Lencoe, 1977 (Moritz Family Collection).
14. Joel Carlson, *No Neutral Ground* (New York: Thomas Y. Crowell Company, 1973), 242, 251.
15. Alan R. Moritz, typed notes on 1969 trip to South Africa to help investigate death of James Lencoe, 1977 (Moritz Family Collection).

16. George Bizos, *No One To Blame? In Pursuit of Justice in South Africa* (Cape Town: David Philip Publishers, 1998).

17. George Bizos, *No One To Blame? In Pursuit of Justice in South Africa* (Cape Town: David Philip Publishers, 1998), 17–18.

18. Joel Carlson, *No Neutral Ground* (New York: Thomas Y. Crowell Company, 1973), 251–253.

19. Alan R. Moritz, typed notes on 1969 trip to South Africa to help investigate death of James Lencoe, 1977 (Moritz Family Collection); "News Coverage of the Lenkoe Hearings," *Rand Daily Mail,* Johannesburg, South Africa, June 1969 (Moritz Family Collection); Joel Carlson, letter to Charles L. Mandelstam, August 6, 1969 (Moritz Family Collection).

20. Congressman Allard K. Lowenstein, "Allegations of Torture in South African Prisons, 91st Cong., 1st sess.," *Congressional Record* 115, no. 105 (June 25, 1969), 17353.

21. Editorial, "South African "Justice,'" *New York Times* June 17, 1969; "Lindsay's Brother and Briton in South Africa to Aid Lawyer," *New York Times,* July 25, 1969.

22. Joel Carlson, *No Neutral Ground* (New York: Thomas Y. Crowell Company, 1973), 256–257.

23. Alan R. Moritz, typed notes on 1969 trip to South Africa to help investigate death of James Lencoe, 1977 (Moritz Family Collection).

24. Lorraine Lenkoe, "Truth and Reconciliation Commission, Human Rights Violations, Submissions – Questions and Answers," April 29, 1996, accessed October 9, 2018, http://www.justice.gov.za/trc/hrvtrans%5Cmethodis/lenkoe.htm.

CHAPTER **20**

Of Myth and Legend

In the late 1960s, during a luncheon at Western Reserve University, Dr. Joseph T. Wearn, a retired dean of its medical school, recalled a highly publicized incident in which Alan Moritz got it wrong. Very, very wrong.

"I just happened to be in Boston on one occasion while Alan was still at Harvard and, picking up the morning paper, read that a mysterious leg had been sent to him by a medical examiner for identification," Wearn told the crowd. Moritz, he continued, consulted "orthopedic surgeons, anatomists and radiologists" before concluding the bones were probably from a human "and that the human from whom they came was deformed." According to Wearn, Moritz told the newspaper that "apparently the toes, the calcaneus and part of the head and neck of the femur were missing."

Wearn continued: "The next newspaper clipping I saw said something like this: 'Mysterious leg, said by Harvard expert to be human, turns out to be a bear's leg.'" The dog that found the first leg had later presented his master with a second leg, which still had the foot attached.

Wearn went on to praise Moritz for his professionalism and ability to remain unflappable in difficult situations.

> Those who have worked with Alan say that it is when under pressure that he is at his best. The stubbornness of his German ancestry comes out and he simply won't be pushed, so when someone tried to push him to admit that the bones were those of a bear he issued this statement: "Since the bones resemble those of a human and since there are more human bones than bear bones in New England, they should be regarded as human until proven otherwise."

Wearn said Moritz

> set up appropriate tests, rendered rabbits immune to muscle protein from a bear, and extracted the muscle tissue attached to the unknown bones and this gave a positive precipitin with the anti-bear muscle serums but did not react with controls including antihuman. He then issued this statement: "The aforesaid observations indicate that the

DOI: 10.4324/9781003539186-21

bones submitted for examination were those of a bear and not of human origin."[1]

Wearn's recitation seems to be liberally sprinkled with exaggeration, but he wasn't the first to use the erroneous identification of the bear's leg to embarrass my grandfather. In 1940, as the *Boston Globe* reported, a defense attorney forced Moritz to acknowledge his mistake during cross-examination. And Moritz himself would tell the story to a writer for *Roche Medical Image* in 1967—although he was careful to share the blame with an orthopedic specialist he consulted. The orthopedist told him the leg "must have belonged to a stocky, heavy-boned person who, because of a congenital deformity of the femur, had walked with a lumbering gait."[2]

Still, his reputation survived, and he became so well known in Boston and New England that a reporter told another tale of mistaken identity on the front page of the *Globe* on January 15, 1950.

In a first-person account, crime reporter Joseph F. Dinneen wrote that a friend helped him out by setting up an interview with Moritz at his apartment at 22 Prescott St., behind the Fogg Art Museum, for 3 p.m. Dinneen prepared for the interview by reviewing past articles about Moritz, noting in the last one that Moritz had left Harvard in September of the previous year to take a job at Western Reserve in Cleveland. The reporter said he wondered why Moritz was still living in Boston but "put his dossier in my pocket to read it closely on the way over in a cab." The reporter then prepared a list of questions to ask during the interview. When he got to the apartment building, he pressed the button labeled with Moritz's name.

The article continued:

> The door clicked. I walked up a flight. An apartment door was open for me and I went in. The professor was dismissing his stenographer and giving his final instructions, signing letters and clearing away his desk. He was wearing a sports jacket with suede patches at the elbows, an open neck sports shirt.

> "Sit down," he invited, nodding toward a deep easy chair by his desk. I did so. He sat back, relaxed, the tips of his fingers together, genial and friendly. "Now, where shall we begin?" he said.

> "I'm surprised to find you here," I said. "I understood you were being transferred to Western Reserve University."

> He stiffened in his chair. His eyes widened in utter surprise. "Me? Being transferred to Western Reserve? Me?"

> I nodded.

"Who says that?" he asked.

"It was printed in the *Globe*," I said, handing him the clipping.

As he read it, his face became pained. He put his hand to his forehead and said softly, "O, no, not again."

Then he turned to me patiently and said: "For years I have been receiving packages—entrails, carcasses, bones, parts of the human body, bullets, blunt instruments, sharp instruments, precision instruments, microscope slides and such.

"My name is Andre Morize. And while I have been receiving these things, Dr. Alan Moritz has been receiving the new books of French authors to review.

"I am a professor of romance languages. My specialty is French. Dr. Alan Moritz is the pathologist.

"The first time I met him—it was at a banquet—I looked him over and said, 'O, you're the man,' and he looked over at me and said 'O, you're the man.'

"We have had many a laugh over the confusion that has resulted because of this similarity of names; but at the same time it very often has been embarrassing and awkward and disconcerting."

Morize (1883–1957) turned out to be an interesting interview. He had been a captain in the French military and was wounded "two or three times" in World War I. In addition to being a professor at Harvard, he also was head of the French summer school at Middlebury College.

Dinneen concluded the article, saying: "Some day I hope to be in the neighborhood of Western Reserve University to get the interview I went after."[3]

(A couple of years later, Morize's divorce from Boston socialite Ruth Muzzy Conniston would result in many more column-inches of newspaper ink.)

EXONERATING THE INNOCENT

While some of Moritz's cases received national or international attention, most were only of local note. A 1946 article in the *New Bedford* (Massachusetts) *Standard-Times* recounted an early success of Harvard's Department of Legal Medicine. Moritz detailed a case in which the department helped the Village of Orleans on Cape Cod investigate a homicide and clear an innocent woman.

Police had been called to a home in the village and found the body of a man lying on the ground about 90 feet from his home. The man had been shot in the chest and the bullet had traveled through his heart. A recently fired revolver was found on a table in the living room of the man's home.

A woman who lived nearby admitted to police that she had been having a "clandestine romance" with the man and that she had been with him until 3 hours before his death. She was taken into custody.

The Department of Legal Medicine was asked to autopsy the dead man and found he "had a deformed chest which placed his heart slightly out of its normal position." The bullet had just "nicked one side of the heart, missing several vessels. Death would have taken a matter of minutes."

The dead man's fingerprints were also found on the gun. "After shooting himself, he laid the gun on the table and then started to walk to his father's home nearby," the article said. Moritz ruled the death a suicide.[4]

Moritz described three more cases in which initial suspicion of homicide was dispelled by forensic medicine to George W. Gray, a science writer who wrote monthly reports for the Rockefeller Foundation's trustees and staff.

In the first, an elderly woman was found dead in the bedroom of her country cottage about 10 a.m. one morning by the milkman who had entered the house to make his regular delivery. He followed a trail of blood from the kitchen to the bedroom, where the woman's bloody head was leaning against a wall. Her feet were on the floor and her clothing, according to both the milkman and the police, appeared to be "in a state of disarray."

The police originally theorized that the woman had been killed during a robbery. She was known to have kept money in the house and all the cupboard doors in the kitchen were open as if someone had been looking for the cash. The woman also had employed a neighbor's son as a "choreboy," and police said the boy was "not right in the head" and of "suspicious character." The boy had a record of juvenile delinquency for minor theft.

A doctor who was called to the scene said the woman's death was caused by a "blow on the head and that the woman had been carried from the kitchen, where the blow had been struck, to her bedroom." Police also learned that the choreboy had left his home, about a mile from the cottage, at 7 a.m. and that his whereabouts were not known until noon.

Moritz conducted an autopsy and discovered the woman's head wound was actually a "single superficial scalp laceration that had not caused death"and probably did not even cause her to lose consciousness. The head wound had occurred from "below upward so as to be consistent with the impact of the head against a hard object" during her fall. The autopsy also also discovered that the woman had been suffering from congestive heart failure for some time and that her death was caused by heart disease.

Moritz wrote, with his typical shortage of commas,

> Reconstruction of evidence made it seem likely that the woman had probably fallen in her kitchen incident to a heart attack striking her head on a stone ledge around the kitchen alcove and subsequently crawled to her bedroom where she lost consciousness and died of heart failure.

Moritz said the boy had a plausible explanation for his activities that morning, but he did not have "the kind of alibi that would have prevented further legal inquisition had it not been for the exonerating medical evidence." Moritz said the woman's money was later found in the house.

In the second case, a middle-aged woman was found dead by her mother early one afternoon. The dead woman's husband said she had been in good health when he left for work that morning, but for several months, the woman had been telling her mother that she thought her husband was trying to poison her. She even told local police officers of her suspicion, but the police concluded that she was "a little cracked,'' Moritz said.

With the husband now the prime suspect, an autopsy on the woman found she had "died of nicotine poisoning." However, the amount of nicotine in her stomach was "so great that it was perfectly apparent that it could not have been taken unknowingly." The woman, Moritz said, "had apparently died within a few minutes after the poison was ingested. The poison had not been taken with food and represented approximately 4 ounces of crude nicotine such as is used to spray plants." An inquest determined that the death was a suicide. "There was no hesitation on the part of the court to arrive at this decision when they were shown and permitted to smell a beaker of crude nicotine equivalent to the amount found in the stomach of the dead woman," Moritz wrote.

The last example was a young married woman who was found unconscious on the kitchen floor of her home. She was bleeding from the nose and had a recently blackened eye. Her husband admitted striking her after the two had argued and she had thrown dishes at him. Fragments of broken dishes were found on the kitchen and dining room floor, which seemed to confirm part of the husband's statement. An autopsy found intracranial hemorrhage, and the manner of death was found to be homicide. The husband was convicted of second-degree murder.

After the trial, it was discovered that the woman had preexisting health issues, including rheumatic heart disease. A judge authorized exhumation of the body and a second autopsy was performed by Moritz and fellows from Harvard Medical School's Department of Legal Medicine. The second autopsy "disclosed subacute bacterial endocarditis with evidence of very recent cerebral embolism," Moritz said. The original autopsy—"performed by an incompetent medical investigator," Moritz said—had "fortunately ... been so incomplete that it had not interfered with the embalming and it was apparent that the woman had not sustained any significant degree of traumatic injury."

Her husband was granted a pardon.[5]

CONVICTING THE GUILTY

On the other hand, many actual homicides go undetected, as Moritz told the California Academy of General Practice in a 1960 speech covered by the *San Francisco Chronicle*. To illustrate his point, he told of a car accident in which an independently wealthy woman was killed while her husband escaped unharmed.

Their car appeared to swerve to avoid an oncoming car and struck a telephone pole. The front passenger side of the car was heavily damaged, trapping the woman in the vehicle. The man, who was seen climbing from the driver's side of the vehicle, told a passerby who had stopped to help that his wife was unconscious. She later died and a witness told police it appeared to be a legitimate accident.

But during the autopsy, Moritz discovered on the woman's scalp "parallel bruises that did not fit any markings on the dashboard." He notified the police of his findings. Investigators then visited businesses along the road and found a waitress who remembered that the couple were in her coffee shop before the accident. She also "revealed a discrepancy in the husband's timetable of the evening. Forty-five minutes were missing."

Police searched "every inch" of the roadway between the coffee shop and the crash site and found "a tire iron, bloody and flecked with hair" that proved to be the woman's. They also found a glove that matched a glove that they had found in the wrecked car. The husband was convicted of murder.[6]

For a 1962 *Wall Street Journal* article about pathologists helping solve unexplained deaths, Moritz discussed a presumed hit-and-run case in which he "noticed an odd grayish dust on the forehead of a dead man."

Moritz put the dust under a microscope and found it "consisted of tiny red, blue and green glass spheres." He remembered that such material was used to coat movie screens. Armed with this information, police searched for home movie screens in the area near where the man was found dead on the side of the road. In a tavern, about 80 yards from the body, they found a movie screen.

Investigators questioned the bartender, who admitted the man had been killed in a brawl in the basement of the tavern the night before. During the fight, the man brushed against the movie screen. "Fearful of losing his license," the *Journal* reported, "the bartender and a customer dumped the body by the roadside."[7]

Moritz pounded home the continuing problem of untrained coroners in a 1970 interview with *World Medical News*. In one case, he said, the coroner ruled that the cause of death was heart disease, but the district attorney suspected foul play.

"I accepted the case because the coroner's report was virtually illiterate from a scientific point of view except for the description of the heart condition, which read like a textbook," Moritz said.

> At autopsy, I found that the coroner had gathered together the major heart vessels and tied them off with a string—for no reason that I could discern then or now—but that he had not opened the heart to inspect the valves. There was no evidence of heart disease. Instead there was a distinct crack in the skull and evidence of massive bleeding between skull and brain quite sufficient to have caused death.[8]

NOTES

1. Joseph Wearn, speech at luncheon honoring Alan R. Moritz, Case Western Reserve, late 1960s (Case Western Reserve Archives).
2. "Evidence Victim Fell Is Excluded in Blood Trial," *Boston Globe*, December 21, 1940, 5; "Focus on Alan R. Moritz, M.D.," *Roche Medical Image*, April 1967, 16.
3. Joseph F. Dinneen, "Globe Reporter Enjoys Case of Mistaken Identity," *Boston Globe*, January 15, 1950 (Center for the History of Medicine at Francis A. Countway Library, Harvard University).
4. Joseph D. Schwendeman, "Crack State Pathologist Always Set for Crime Call," *New Bedford Standard-Times*, August 4, 1946.
5. Alan R. Moritz, letter to George W. Gray, March 16, 1946 (Rockefeller Foundation Archives).

6. David Perlman, "Murder Easy To Hide, Doctors Told," *San Francisco Chronicle*, October 19, 1960, 3.
7. Donald A. Moffitt, "Medical Detectives: Pathologists Win Major Role in Finding Causes of Unexplained Deaths," *Wall Street Journal*, July 21, 1962.
8. "Of Crime and Change and the Doctors Doctor," *Medical World News*, March 13, 1970, 35.

CHAPTER 21

Legacy

A century has passed since the Rockefeller Foundation, the National Research Council, Frances Glessner Lee and Alan Moritz began blowing the whistle, yet incompetent coroners are still in the headlines. In one of the most sensational cases of the 2020s, a newly elected Idaho coroner with minimal training initially ruled the death of 49-year-old Tammy Daybell as a natural death. She agreed not to order an autopsy despite the fact that Tammy was already cold and stiff when her husband, "doomsday" novelist and self-proclaimed prophet Chad Daybell, said she rolled out of the bed they shared.

Two months would pass—during which Chad Daybell would marry a woman, Lori Vallow, whose two children were missing—before Tammy's body was exhumed and autopsied by credentialed medical examiners. Her cause of death was determined to be asphyxiation. Chad Daybell was ultimately convicted of his first wife's murder, and Lori Vallow Daybell was convicted of conspiracy to commit the murder. They were both convicted of murdering her children, whose bodies were discovered months later.[1]

It's clear that fixing the coroner system is not my grandfather's legacy, no matter how hard he tried. So what is?

Dr. Jeffery Jentzen, in "Death Investigation in America," and Thomas Young, in "The Sherlock Effect," make a good case that Alan Moritz's greatest contribution to forensic science was his enumeration of the "Classical Mistakes." Dr. Moritz thought his research on burns at Harvard would be his legacy, and Dr. Cancio of the US Army Institute of Surgical Research Burn Center would probably agree.

But years of research for this book have persuaded me that Alan Moritz's greatest contribution was his influence on his students and future generations of pathologists, forensic pathologists and death investigators. They are his legacy.

Dr. Kathryn H. Haden-Pinneri with the American Academy of Forensic Sciences wrote in 2014 that nearly "half of all American forensic pathologists can be traced back to Dr. Moritz." In her article, "Celebrating the Forensic Science Family Pathology/Biology: Honoring

Our Mentors and Remembering Our Roots," Haden-Pinneri noted Moritz's groundbreaking work organizing the Department of Legal Medicine at Harvard, "training future forensic scientists" as well as homicide detectives and forensic pathologists. "Thus, he forms not only one of the deepest roots of our tree but also part of the thick, solid trunk. Descendants of Dr. Moritz have gone to other countries and undoubtedly helped educate forensic scientists all over the world." (Moritz was president of the AAFS in 1956–1957.)

Haden-Pinneri illustrates Moritz's impact on future generations of forensic scientists by singling out Dr. Russell Fisher, a "world-renowned forensic pathologist" who also had "a large part of the trunk of our forensic family tree." Fisher was an early fellow in the Department of Legal Medicine at Harvard in the 1940s, when Moritz was its first director, and from 1949 to 1981 was medical examiner for the state of Maryland. Fisher is also credited with mentoring and training a number of accomplished medical examiners over the years, including Dr. Cyril Wecht, one of the most famous coroners and death investigators in the country.[2]

Wecht was coroner of Allegheny County in Pennsylvania for more than 20 years and consulted on a number of high-profile death investigations, including the 1968 assassination of US Sen. Robert F. Kennedy and the 1976 outbreak of Legionnaires' Disease in Philadelphia. Before his death, Wecht told me that my grandfather and Fisher were early titans of forensic pathology and that he credits them "when I give my I talks and describe to people how modern-day forensic pathology began to evolve, leading to the creation of the sub-specialty board examination in forensic pathology under the aegis of the American Board of Pathology in 1959."

Wecht was well known for his criticism of the Warren Commission that investigated the Kennedy assassination, while Moritz and Fisher were members of the panel appointed by US Attorney General Ramsey Clark in 1968 that ultimately supported the commission's findings.

Wecht recalled a visit from Moritz in the early 1970s when he was trying to get the Allegheny County coroner's office accredited by the American Board of Pathology for a residency fellowship in forensic pathology. Moritz "spent a better part of a day, we talked, and he approved us and got us accredited," Wecht said. "He was a marvelous gentleman. He looked like a gentleman, he talked like a gentleman and acted like one. He was a distinguished, non-pompous, gracious individual and deeply devoted to the field of forensic pathology."

I asked Wecht if he and Dr. Moritz ever discussed their differences of opinion on the Warren Commission's findings. He said they did not. "He was there to review us … I don't know whether he would have talked about it or not."[3]

Dr. Michael Baden, who hosted the HBO show "Autopsy," said Moritz was a proctor when he took the exam to be board-certified in forensic pathology in the mid-1960s. Later, he would disagree with Moritz on the findings of the Clark Panel, and the two would work together in the aftermath of the Attica prison riot.

"Of course, he was known for that iconic paper on things forensic medical pathologists should not do, and that is still, as I understand it, widely read," Baden told me. "I wasn't that close [to Moritz] ... I certainly admired him, and he was one of the icons of forensic pathology when I was starting out."[4]

Moritz's impact on students and faculty was praised by Dr. Joseph T. Wearn, dean of the Western Reserve School of Medicine from 1949 to 1959, in the same 1965 speech in which he dredged up the mistaken identification of a bear's leg. Wearn noted the variety of collaborators who worked with Moritz on research projects.

He said,

> Surgeons, orthopedic, general, G.U. (genitourinary), gynecologists, practically all of my residents, dermatologists ... and he even published one paper with one of the superintendents of the administrative staff. I watched all this with great interest and finally I thought, what the hell, so I applied and Alan and I went to work together and to me, it is a happy memory.

> "The point I am making is that Alan attracted the young members of the whole institution to work with him, and they welcomed the chance to collaborate with him as I did."[5]

Moritz's championing of the medical examiner system and the impact he had on leaders of the National Association of Medical Examiners can be seen in an online history of NAME and its leadership.

Dr. James Luke, who served four terms on the NAME board and as a trustee from 2007 to 2015, studied cardiovascular pathology under Moritz at Western Reserve and called him a mentor. "He gave a number of the course lectures on cardiovascular pathology. He participated regularly in clinical pathology conferences and medical and surgical grand rounds, particularly those related to cases involving sudden cardiac death and trauma," Luke said in a 2013 history of NAME. During his career, Luke served as chief medical examiner of Oklahoma, the District of Columbia and Connecticut.

"Dr. Moritz was an advocate for medical examiner systems nationally," Luke said. He quoted Dr. Lester Adelson, who said Moritz's "most important contribution to our specialty is to have given it academic respectability."

"It was not by chance that a seemingly disproportionate number of students and pathology residents at Western Reserve"—who studied under Moritz—"chose forensic pathology as a career," Luke said.[6]

Dr. Joseph Davis, chief medical examiner of Dade County in Florida for 40 years and president of NAME from 1975–1976, participated in the NAME's history project in 2011. In his contribution, he illustrated Moritz's direct line of influence: When Davis joined the pathology faculty at Louisiana State University in 1954, he worked on autopsies with Dr. Stan Durlacher of the Orleans Parish coroner's office. Durlacher, Davis said, had been recruited because of his affiliation with Dr. Russell Fisher, and "Fisher was one of the early pioneers who trained with Alan Moritz at the Harvard Department of Legal Medicine. Accordingly, his thinking was along the lines of Moritz—pretty good mentoring if any of you have recently re-read Moritz's 1956 article, 'Classical Mistakes in Forensic Pathology.'"

Davis concluded his history with this sentence: "I wish Alan Moritz could come back for a look-see."[7]

So do I.

NOTES

1. Garona Mejia, "Tammy Daybell Investigation; Idaho Allowed Her Burial Without an Autopsy," *KSL-TV*, June 23, 2020, https://www.eastidahonews.com/2020/06/tammy-daybell-investigation-idaho-law-allowed-her-burial-without-an-autopsy; *East Idaho News*, "Full Testimony: Fremont County Coroner Brenda Dye Testifies at Chad Daybell Trial," YouTube Video, 1:37: 21, April 25, 2024, https://www.youtube.com/watch?v=KJn77aCKAJs.
2. Kathryn H. Haden-Pinneri, "Celebrating The Science Family Pathology/Biology: Honoring Our Mentors and Remembering Our Roots," *Academy News*, May 2014, https://www.scribd.com/document/238530549/Forensic-Science-News-May-2014.
3. Dr. Cyril Wecht, telephone interview by Rob Moritz, January 23, 2019.
4. Dr. Michael Baden, telephone interview by Rob Moritz, March 22, 2018.
5. Joseph T. Wearn, speech at luncheon honoring Alan R. Moritz, Case Western Reserve University, late 1960s (Case Western Reserve Archives).
6. "The History of the NAME: National Association of Medical Examiners Past Presidents History eBook 2013 Edition," *National Association of Medical Examiners*, 2013, https://www.thename.org/assets/docs/NAME_eBook_2013.pdf.
7. "The History of the NAME: National Association of Medical Examiners Past Presidents History eBook 2012 Edition," *National Association of Medical Examiners*, 2012.

Appendix 1

Dr. Alan R. Moritz

POSITIONS HELD

Intern, Lakeside Hospital, Cleveland, 1923–1924.
Hanna Research Fellow (Pathology), Western Reserve University, 1924–1925.
Instructor in Pathology, Western Reserve University, 1925–1926.
Extern in Pathology, City Hospital in Vienna, Austria, 1926–1927.
Pathologist, Lake Hospital, Cleveland, 1927–1931.
Pathologist-in-Charge, University Hospitals of Cleveland, 1931–1937.
Senior Instructor, Western Reserve University, Cleveland, Ohio, 1929–1930.
Assistant Professor, Western Reserve University, 1930–1932.
Associate Professor of Pathology, Western Reserve University, 1932–1937.
George Burgess McGrath Professor of Legal Medicine, Harvard Medical School, Boston, Massachusetts, 1937–1949.
Rockefeller Foundation Traveling Fellow, 1937–1939.
Pathologist to the Department of Safety of the Commonwealth of Massachusetts, 1939–1949.
Lecturer in Legal Medicine, Boston University School of Medicine, 1941–1949.
Lecturer in Legal Medicine, Tufts College Medical School, Boston, 1941–1949.
Pathologist-in Chief, Peter Bent Brigham Hospital, Boston, 1947–1949.
Consulting Pathologist, Department of Mental Health, Commonwealth of Massachusetts, 1941–1949.
Associate Medical Examiner, Suffolk County (Mass.), 1942–1949.
Director, Institute of Pathology, Western Reserve University, 1949–1965.
Professor of Pathology, Western Reserve University, 1949–1967.

Vice President, Western Reserve University, 1964–1965.

Provost, Western Reserve University, 1965–1967.

Provost, Case Western Reserve University, 1967–1969.

Provost Emeritus, Case Western Reserve University, 1969.

Director of Professional Affairs, University Hospitals of Cleveland, 1969–1970.

Chief of Staff, University Hospitals of Cleveland, 1970–1971.

President and Chairman of Board of Trustees of Hillcrest Hospital, 1971–1979.

GOVERNMENTAL AGENCY ACTIVITIES

Consultant and Official Investigator (1941–1945), National Defense Research Committee, Office of Scientific Research and Development of the National Research Council, 1941–1945.

Official Investigator for the Committee on Medical Research of the United States Navy, 1942–1945.

Consultant, Army Medical Museum (later named Armed Forces Institute of Pathology), 1943–1944.

Member, Study Section on Pathology of the National Institutes of Health, 1949–1953 and 1955–1960.

Consultant to the US Air Force, 1955–1960.

Member, Scientific Advisory Board of the Armed Forces Institute of Pathology, 1959–1970.

Member, Training Grant Committee on Pathology of the National Institute of Health, 1961–1964.

AWARDS AND HONORS

Ward Burdick Award of the American Association of Clinical Pathology, 1958.

Scientific Products Foundation Award of the College of American Pathologists, 1964.

Distinguished Membership Award of the Academy of Medicine of Cleveland, 1967.

Honorary Life Trustee of the American Board of Pathologists, 1970.

Honorary Life Member of the Scientific Advisory Board of the Armed Forces Institute of Pathology, 1970.

Gold Headed Cane Award of the American Association of Pathologists and Bacteriologists, 1970.

SCIENTIFIC SOCIETIES

Academy of Medicine Board of Directors, 1951–1954; Chairman Program Committee, 1951–1952; Expert Medical Testimony Committee, Chairman, 1957–1964; Joint Committee on Medical Testimony, Chairman, 1961–1962.
Aesculapian Club, Harvard University.
Alpha Omega Alpha, 1923.
American Academy of Arts and Sciences.
American Academy of Forensic Sciences; President, 1955–1956.
American Association for the Advancement of Science.
American Association of Pathologists and Bacteriologists; President 1959.
American Board of Pathology; Trustee, 1956–1969; President, 1958.
American Cancer Society, Cuyahoga Unit, Ohio; President, 1958.
American Medical Association; Chairman of Committee on Legal Medicine, 1941–1960.
American Society of Clinical Pathology.
British Association for Clinical Pathology.
College of American Pathologists; Governor, 1954–1960.
International Academy of Pathology.
Intersociety Committee on the Research Potential of Pathology; Chairman, 1956–1961.
Medico-Legal Society of Belgium.
Medico-Legal Society of Paris.
National Research Council Committee on Pathology, 1952–1965.
New England Pathology Society; President, 1944.
Pasteur Club of Cleveland, Ohio.
Sigma Xi, 1921.
Society of Experimental Pathology.

Appendix 2

Books

Moritz, Alan R. *The Pathology of Trauma*. Philadelphia: Lea & Febiger Publisher, 1942.

Moritz, Alan R. *The Pathology of Trauma*. 2nd ed. Philadelphia: Lea & Febiger Publisher, 1954.

Moritz, Alan R., M.D., and David S. Helberg, J.D., eds. *Trauma and Disease*. New York: Central Book Co., Brooklyn, 1959.

Regan, Louis J., and Alan R. Moritz. *Handbook of Legal Medicine*. St Louis: The C.V. Mosby Co., 1956.

Stetler, Joseph C., and Alan R. Moritz. *Doctor and Patient and the Law*. 4th ed. St. Louis: The C.V. Mosby Co., 1962.

Morris, Crawford R., Alan R. Moritz, Joseph Stetler, and Louis J. Regan. *Doctor and Patient and the Law*. 5th ed. St. Louis: The CV Mosby Co., 1971.

Moritz, Alan R., and R. Crawford Morris. *Handbook of Legal Medicine*. 3rd ed. St. Louis: The C.V. Mosby Co., 1970.

Moritz, Alan R., and R. Crawford Morris. *Handbook of Legal Medicine*. 4th ed. St. Louis: The C.V. Mosby Co., 1975.

Hirsch, Charles S., R. Crawford Morris, and Alan R. Moritz. *Handbook of Legal Medicine*. fifth ed. St. Louis: C.V. Mosby Co., 1979.

Moritz, Alan R., and C. Joseph Stetler. *Handbook of Legal Medicine*. 2nd ed. St. Louis: The C.V. Mosby Co., 1964.

Appendix 3

JOURNALS AND PUBLICATIONS

1. Poynter, C. W. M., and A. R. Moritz. "The Effects of Ultraviolet Light on Pond Snails (Linnaeus)." *The Journal of Experimental Zoology* 37, no. (1923): 1–13.
2. Goldblatt, H., and A. R. Moritz. "Experimental Rickets in Rabbits." *Journal of Experimental Medicine* 41, no. 4 (1925): 499–506.
3. Moritz, A. R. "The Effect of Ultraviolet Irradiation on the State of Serum Calcium." *Journal of Biological Chemistry* 54 (1925): 81–89.
4. Moritz, A. R. "The State of Serum Calcium in Experimental Hypo- and Hypercalcemia." *Journal of Biological Chemistry* 56, no. 2 (1925): 343.
5. Moritz, A. R., and H. Goldblatt. "Studies on the State of the Serum Calcium." *Proceedings of the Society for Experimental Biology and Medicine* 22, no. 2 (1925): 111.
6. Goldblatt, H., and A. R. Moritz. "On the Growth-Promoting Property of Irradiated Fat in the Diet, of Direct Irradiation, and of Cod Liver Oil." *Journal of Biological Chemistry* 71 (1926): 127.
7. Goldblatt, H., and A. R. Moritz. "The Effect of Heat and Oxidation on the Nutritive Value of a Protein." *Journal of Biological Chemistry* 72 (1927): 321.
8. Moritz, A. R. "Tabische Arthopathie." *Virchows Archiv für pathologische Anatomie und Physiologie und für klinische Medizin* 267, no. 3 (1928): 746–855.
9. Moritz, A. R., and M. Douglass. "A Study of Uterine and Tubal Decidual Reaction in Tubal Pregnancy." *Surgery, Gynecology and Obstetrics* 47 (1928): 785–790.
10. Moritz, A. R. "Effect of Cholesterol Activated by Ultraviolet Irradiation on Growth of Tubercle Bacilli In Vitro." *Proceedings of the Society for Experimental Biology and Medicine* 25 (1928): 43.

11. Joelson, J. J., C. S. Beck, and A. R. Moritz. "Renal Counterbalance." *The Archives of Surgery* 19 (1929): 673.

12. Cutler, E. C., A. R. Moritz, and R. M. Zollinger. "A Histological Study of Tumors of the Central Nervous System." *Ohio State Medical Journal* (April 1929), 269-277.

13. Harbin, M., and A. R. Moritz. "Autogenous Free Cartilage Transplanted into Joints." *The Archives of Surgery* 20, no. 6 (1930): 885.

14. Moritz, A .R., and C. Krenz. "The Relation of the Fat-Soluble Vitamins A and D to the Development of Experimental Rickets in Rabbits." *The Journal of Nutrition* 2 (1930): 257.

15. Moritz, A. R., and E. Walker. "A Tumor Record." *The Bulletin of the American College of Surgeons* 14 (1930): 3.

16. Moritz, A. R. "Interacinar Epithelium of the Thyroid Gland." *The American Journal of Pathology* 7, no. 1 (1931): 37–46.

17. Moritz, A. R., and F. Bayless. "Papilliferous Tumors of the Thyroid Gland and the Aberrant Thyroid Tissue." *The American Journal of Pathology* 7 (1931): 675.

18. Moritz, A. R., and J. D. Morley. "The Schwartzman Phenomenon in the Knee Joints of Rabbits." *Proceedings of the Society for Experimental Biology and Medicine* 29 (1931): 321.

19. Moritz, A. R., and F. Bayless. "Lateral Cervical Tumors of Aberrant Thyroid Tissue." *The Archives of Surgery* 24 (1932): 1028.

20. Moritz, A. R. "Syphilitic Coronary Arthritis." *The Archives of Pathology* 11 (1931): 44.

21. Moritz, A. R., C. L. Hudson, and E. W. Orgain. "Augmentation of the Extracardiac Anastomoses of the Coronary Arteries through Pericardial Adhesions." *Journal of Experimental Medicine* 56 (1932): 927.

22. Moritz, A. R. "Mesenterium Commune with Intestinal Obstruction." *The American Journal of Pathology* 8 (1932): 735.

23. Moritz, A. R. "Medionecrosis Aortae Idiopathica Cystica." *The American Journal of Pathology* 8 (1932): 717.

24. Zollinger, R., and A. R. Moritz. "Effects of Necrobiotic Agents on the Walls of Cysts Experimentally Produced in the Brains for Dogs." *Archives of Neurology and Psychiatry* 28 (1932): 1046.

25. Hudson, C. L., A. R. Moritz, and J. T. Wearn. "The Extracardiac Anastomoses of the Coronary Arteries." *Journal of Experimental Medicine* 56 (1932): 919.

26. Gammel, J. A., and A. R. Moritz. "Experimental Monosporosis." *Archives of Dermatology & Syphilology* 27 (1933): 100

27. Moritz, A. R. "Developmental Anomalies Causing or Predisposing to Intestinal Obstruction." *Ohio State Medical Journal* (July 1934), 429-433.

28. Moritz, A. R., and J. M. Andy Hayman. "The Disappearance of Glomeruli in Chronic Kidney Disease." *The American Journal of Pathology* 10 (1934): 505.

29. Karsner, H. T., and A. R. Moritz. "Pathologic Histology of the Schwartzman Phenomenon with Interpretative Comments." *Journal of Experimental Medicine* 60 (1934): 37.

30. Reichle, H. S., and A. R. Moritz. "Subacute Peribronchiolar Pneumonia." *American Journal of Diseases of Children* 48 (1934): 1001.

31. Moritz, A. R. "The Pathogenesis of Sudden Death." *Transactions of the American Therapeutic Society* 34 (1934): 1.

32. Beck, C., S. V. L. Itchy, and A. R. Moritz. "Production of Collateral Circulation of the Heart." *Proceedings of the Society for Experimental Biology and Medicine* 32 (1935): 759.

33. Moritz, A. R. "Repair of the Body after Autopsy." *Report of Com. on Necropsies of American Hospital Association* 12: 78 (June) (1938).

34. Wearn, J. T et al., "The Incidence and Significance of Blood Vessels in Normal and Abnormal Heart Valves." *The American Heart Journal* 13 (1937): 7.

35. Moritz, A. R., and D. Weir. "Unilateral Inhibitions of the Renal Schwartzman Phenomenon Following Injection of Bacterial Filtrate into the Renal Artery." *Journal of Experimental Medicine* 66 (1937): 755.

36. Moritz, A. R. "The Relation of Altered Local Tissue Reactivity (Schwartzman Phenomenon) to Infection and Inflammation." *Journal of Experimental Medicine* 66 (1937): 603.

37. Moritz, A. R., and C. S. Beck. "The Production of a Collateral Circulation to the 38 Heart." *The American Heart Journal* 10 (1935): 26.

38. Moritz, A. R., and M. R. Oldt. "Arteriolar Sclerosis in Hypertensive and Non-Hypertensive Individuals." *The American Journal of Pathology* 13 (1937): 679.

39. Moritz, A. R., and J. P. Atkins. "Cardiac Contusion." *Archives of Pathology* 25 (1938): 445.

40. Moritz, A. R., and W. B. Wartman. "Post-Traumatic Internal Hydrocephalus." *The American Journal of the Medical Sciences* 195 (1938): 65.

41. Moritz, A. R. "A New Method for the Examination of Markings on Bullets, Shell Cases and Breech Faces." *Police Journal* 11, no. 3 (1938): 364–369

42. Moritz, A. R. "Medical Science and the Administration of Justice." *Proceedings of the Institute of Medicine of Chicago* 13 (1940): 54.

43. Moritz, A. R. "Sudden Death." *The New England Journal of Medicine* 223 (1940): 798.

44. Moritz, A. R. "Impression Method for Matching Bullets." In *Recent Advances in Forensic Medicine,* edited by Sidney Smith and John Glaister, 2nd ed. Philadelphia: Blakiston Son & Co., Inc., 1939.

45. Moritz, A. R. "The Cuticular Scales of Hair." In *Recent Advances in Forensic Medicine,* edited by Sidney Smith and John Glaister, 2nd ed., Philadelphia: Blakiston Son & Co., Inc., 1939.

46. Moritz, A. R. "Legal Medicine in the United States." In *Forensic Medicine,* edited by Sidney Smith, 6th ed., Boston: Little-Brown Co., 1939, xvii.

47. Moritz, A. R. "The Need for Forensic Pathology for Academic Sponsorship." *Archives of Pathology* 33 (1942): 382.

48. Moritz, A. R., and W. W. Jetter. "Antemortem and Postmortem Diffusion of Alcohol through the Bladder Mucosa." *Archives of Pathology* 33 (1942): 939.

49. Moritz, A. R. "The Medical Examiner System in Rhode Island." *Rhode Island Medical Journal* 25 (1942): 205.

50. Moritz, A. R. "The Office of County Coroner in Virginia." *Virginia Medical Monthly* 70 (1943): 164.

51. Moritz, A. R. "The Medico-Legal Autopsy." *American Journal Clinical Pathology* 13 (1943): 132.

52. Jetter, W. W., and A. R. Moritz. "Changes in the Magnesium and Chloride Contents of Blood from Drowning in Fresh and Sea Water." *Archives of Pathology* 35 (1943): 601.

53. Moritz, A. R. "Mechanisms of Head Injury." *Annals of Surgery* 117 (1943): 562.

54. Moritz, A. R. "Investigation of Deaths in the Interest of Public Safety." *Connecticut State Medical Journal* 7 (1943): 310.

55. Moritz, A. R. "A Digest of Laws Pertaining to the Practice of Medicine in Massachusetts." *Transactions of the Massachusetts Medical Legal Society* 10 (1942): 93.

56. Moritz, A. R. "Chemical Methods for the Determination of Death by Drowning." *Physiological Reviews* 24 (1944): 70.

57. Moritz, A. R., and F. R. Dutra. "Scientific Evidence in Cases of Injury by Gunfire." *Archives of Pathology* 37 (1944): 1.

58. Moritz, A. R., E. R. Cunniffe, J. W. Hollowa, and H. Martland. "Report of the Committee of the American Medical Association

to Study the Relationship of Medicine and Law." *Journal of the American Medical Association* 125 (1944): 577.

59. Moritz, A. R., F. C. Henriques jr., and R. McLean. "The Effects of Inhaled Heat on the Air Passages and Lungs." *American Journal of Pathology* 21 (1945): 311.

60. Moritz, A. R., and J. R. Weisiger. "Effects of Cold Air on the Air Passages and Lungs." *Archives of Internal Medicine* 75 (1945): 233.

61. Moritz, A. R., and N. Zamcheck. "Sudden and Unexpected Death of Young Soldiers." *Archives of Pathology* 42 (1946): 459.

62. Henriques, F. C. jr., and A. R. Moritz. "Studies of Thermal Injury. I. The Conduction of Heat to and through Skin and the Temperatures Attained therein. A Theoretical and an Experimental Investigation." *American Journal of Pathology* 23 (1947): 531.

63. Moritz, A. R., and F. C. Henriques jr. "Studies of Thermal Injury. II. The Relative Importance of Time and Surface Temperature in the Causation of Cutaneous Burns. An Experimental Study." *American Journal of Pathology* 23 (1947): 915.

64. Moritz, A. R. "Studies of Thermal Injury. III. The Pathology and Pathogenesis of Cutaneous Burns. An Experimental Study." *American Journal of Pathology* 23 (1947): 915.

65. Moritz, A. R., F. C. Henriques jr., F. R. Dutra, and J. R. Weisiger. "Studies of Thermal Injury. IV. An Exploration of the Casualty-Producing Attributes of Conflagrations; Local and Systemic Effects of Teneral Cutaneous Exposure to Excessive Circumambient (Air) and Circumradiant Heat of Varying Duration and Intensity." *Archives of Pathology* 43 (1947): 466.

66. (noted only for completion of references on above studies): Henriques, F.C. jr. "Study of Thermal Injury. V. The Predictability and the Significance of Thermally Induces Rate Processes Leading to Irreversible Epidermal Injury." *Archives of Pathology* 43 (1947): 489.

67. McLean, R., A. R. Moritz, and A. Roos. "Studies of Thermal Injury. VI. Hyperpotassemia Caused by Cutaneous Exposure to Excessive Heat." *Journal of Clinical Investigation* 26 (1947): 497.

68. Roos, A., J. R. Weisiger, and A. R. Moritz. "Studies of Thermal Injury, VII. Physiological Mechanisms Responsible for Death During Cutaneous Exposure to Excessive Heat." *Journal of Clinical Investigation* 26 (1947): 505.

69. Moritz, A. R. "Is the Coroner System Passe?" *Southern Funeral Director* 56 (1947): 18.

70. Moritz, A. R. "Official Medical Investigation of Deaths in Behalf of Public Welfare." *California Medical* 67 (1947): 33.

71. Moritz, A. R. "Medical Investigation of Obscure and Suspicious Deaths in the Interest of Public Safety." *Northwest Medical* 47 (1947): 851.

72. Moritz, A. R. "Medical Science and the Administration of Justice." *Journal of the American Medical Association* 138 (1948): 751.

73. Moritz, A. R. "Physical Agents in the Causation of Injury and Disease." In *Pathology*, edited by W. A. D. Anderson, chapter 6. St. Louis: Mosby, 1948, 116-139.

74. Moritz, A. R. "Unexpected Deaths of Apparently Health Adults from Natural Causes," Northwest Med., 47 (1948), 500-502.

75. Moritz, A. R. "Medical Science and the Administration of Justice," J.A.M.A., 138 (1948), 751-752.

76. Silverman, L., and A. R. Moritz. "An Experimental Study of Tissue Reaction to Fused and Unfused Quartz." *Journal of Industrial Hygiene and Toxicology* 1 (1950): 499.

77. Moritz, A. R. *Monograph: Symposium on the Relation of Law and Medicine.* Arranged by Academy of Medicine. Chicago and Philadelphia: Lea and Febiger.

78. Moritz, A. R. "Death due to Conflagration." *The New England Journal of Medicine* 240 (1949): 901.

79. Peirce, E. C. II et al., "Transplantation of Aortic Segments Fixed in 4% Neutral Formalin. Report of Experiments in Dogs." *American Journal of Surgery* 78 (1949): 314.

80. Moritz, A. R. "Pathology in Forensic Medicine." *American Journal of Pathology* 25 (1949): 779.

81. Moritz, A. R. "Unexpected Death of Apparently Healthy Adults from Natural Causes." *Northwest Medical* 47 (1948): 500.

82. Moritz, A. R. "The Pathologist's Approach to Pulmonary Neoplasms." *Radiology* 55 (1950): 712.

83. Moritz, A. R. "Trauma and Heart Disease." Report to Association of Life Insurance Medical Directors of America. October 1952.

84. Moritz, A. R. "Sudden Death." *Cyclopedia of Medicine, Surgery, and Specialties* 4 (1952): 373.

85. Moritz, A. R., and Frank Dutra. "The Medio-Legal Autopsy." *Cyclopedia of Medicine, Surgery, and Specialties* 8 (1952): 141.

86. Moritz, A. R., and F. W. Henriques jr. "Effect of Beta Rays on the Skin as a Function of the Energy, Intensity and Duration of Radiation." *Laboratory Investigation* 1, no. 2 (Summer 1952): 167–185.

87. Moritz, A .R. "Scientific Evidence in Establishing Time of Death." *Annals of Western Medicine and Surgery* 6 (1952): 302.

88. Moritz, A. R. "Injuries of the Heart and Pericardium by Physical Violence." In *Pathology of the Heart*, edited by S. E. Gould. Chapter XI. Springfield, IL: Charles Thomas, 1953.

89. Moritz, A. R., R. W. Scott, H. B. Sprague, J. McGuire, and C. S. Keefer. "Clinical Pathological Conference." *Annals. of Internal Medicine* 38 (1953): 878.

90. Moritz, A. R. "Pathology of Epidemic Typhus." *Archives of Pathology* 56 (1953): 512.

91. Moritz, A. R. "Trauma, Stress and Coronary Thrombosis." *Journal of the American Medical Association* 156 (1954): 1306.

92. Moritz, A. R. Sudden and unexpected death due to disease, G. P., 10:35, 1954.

93. Moritz, A. R., C. Walker, L. Wurz, L. Todd, L. Pillemer, and O. A. Ross. "Role of Properdin System in Whole Body Irradiation." *Federation Proceedings* 14 (1955), 496.

94. Moritz, A. R. "Scientific Medicolegal Investigation in the Undergraduate Medical Curriculum." *Journal of the American Medical Association* 158 (1955): 243.

95. Moritz, A. R. "Classical Mistakes in Forensic Pathology (Ward Burdick Award Address)." *American Journal of Clinical Pathology* 26 (December 1956): 1383.

96. Moritz, A. R. "To Get Somewhere Else." *Journal of Forensic Sciences* 3 (1958): 1.

97. Ross, O. A., P. Keep, and A. R. Moritz. "The Cancerigenic Potential of Thermal Injury in the Skin of Whole-Body Irradiated Rats." *Archives of Pathology* 67 (1959): 211.

98. Moritz, A. R. "The Institute of Pathology of Western Reserve University." *Laboratory Investigation*, 7 (1958): 287.

99. Brown, K. L., and A. R. Moritz. "Myositis, Fasciitis, Fibrositis, Myofasciitis, Medical or Legal." *Journal of Trauma* 1 (September 1961): 509.

100. Moritz, A. R. *Should You Be a Pathologist?* New York: New York Life Insurance Co., 1962.

101. Moritz, A. R. et al., "Seminar on Forensic Pathology." Proceedings – Twenty-Seventh Seminar of the American Society of Clinical Pathologists, Seattle, Washington, October 6, 1961.

102. Moritz, A. R. "The Expanding View of Pathology." *Laboratory Investigation* 13 (June 1964): 597.

103. Brown, Kent L., and A. R. Moritz. "Electrical Injuries." *Journal of Trauma* 4 (September 1964): 608.

Index

Adventures of Superman (TV series), 110–112
American Academy of Forensic Sciences, 122, 127
American Board of Pathology for residency fellowship, 164
American Journal of Forensic Medicine and Pathology (Davis), 127
The American Journal of Pathology (Moritz), 23
American society and the legal system, 88
Animal doping, 75–76
Anti-Semitism, 47
Archives of Pathology (Moritz), 74
Army Institute of Pathology, 72

Bad Day at Black Rock (Sturges), 102
Baden, M., 164–165
Barnum & Bailey Circus, 81
Bennett, B., 102
Berkshire Eagle (Moritz), 87
Berry, G. P., 99
Bessolo, H., 110
Biasotti, A. A., 143
Bizos, G., 149
Boardman, V., 24, 25
Boston Daily Record, 89
Boston Globe (Benzaquin), 40, 55, 79, 80, 85, 87, 156
Boy Scouts of America, 8
The Brush Development Co. in Cleveland, 143
Burn studies, 70–76
and inhalation injury, 71
Burwell, C., 122
Burwell, S., 72

California Academy of General Practice, 160
Cancio, L., 71
Carlson, J., 145–147
Carter, J., 119
Case Institute of Technology, 119
The Case of the Cautious Coquette (Mason), 104
The Case of the Musical Cow (Gardner), 140
Categorical intuitive deduction, 128
Certification system for medical examiners, 3
Chautauqua Institution, adult education movement, 8–9
Chicago Sun-Times (Kleckner), 126
Chicago Symphony Orchestra, 58
Civil Rights Division of US Department of Justice, 152
Civil Rights movement in United States, 146
Clark Panel, 133–137
Classical Mistakes, 126–129, 163, 166
Cleveland, F., 110
The *Cleveland News*, 109–110, 115
Cleveland Press, 109
Cocoanut Grove nightclub, 79–82
Conant, J., 62
visit to Ipswich, 64–66
A Concise History of Euthanasia: Life, Death, God and Medicine, 89
Congressional Record, 151
Considine, B., 110
Coroner system, 31–32, 63, 163
Cranor, M., 134
Crile (George Washington), 19–23
surgical service, 19

Crime and mystery stories, 102
Criminal investigation, 117
Cutler, E., 70

Daniel, R., 4, 5
Davis, J., 127, 166
Daybell, C., 163
Death Investigation in America
(Jentzen), 133
Delvecchio, 104
Dental project, 81
Department of Forensic Medicine &
Toxicology, 141
Department of General Pathology, 92
Department of Legal Medicine, 33,
34, 55, 56, 61, 62, 76, 82,
92, 97, 99
Department of Pathology, 98
Dyke Business School in Cleveland,
122

Eastern Racing Association, 76
Edward, R., 4, 5
Erdheim, J., 24, 26, 27
European Society of Pathology, 28
Experimental Rickets in Rabbits, 21

Fisher, R., 132, 133
Flamethrowers, 71–75
The Flying Nun (TV comedy), 104
Fonda, H., 15, 17
Ford, R., 98
Forensic medicine, 1, 34, 36, 38, 41,
92, 126, 158
Forensic pathology, 34, 42, 46, 92,
103, 118, 126, 127, 133,
135, 164
The Fugitive (1963–1967), 109

Gardner, E. S., 2, 104–106, 108
Gerber, S. R., 115, 116
German Consulate in Cleveland, 46
Gerritsen, T., 140
Gidget, 104
Glaister, J. L. Jr., 36
Glessner, F., 81
Glessner, G., 32
Gluckman, J., 146, 147

Goldfarb, B., 60
18 Tiny Deaths, 103
Google search, 133
Grafton, S., 140
The Great Escape (Sturges), 102
Gregg, A., 52, 53, 55, 56, 61, 81, 93,
95–97
Griswold, E., 95

Haden-Pinneri, K. H., 163, 164
Handbook of Legal Medicine
(Moritz), 140
Hard-fought movement, 3
Harvard Associates in Police Science
(HAPS), 63
Harvard Medical School, 96
Harvard President Conant of Moritz's
concerns, 93
Harvard's Center for the History of
Medicine, 99
Harvard's law school, 94
"Honorary Texas Citizen"
proclamation, 136
Hoover, C. F., 19
Hopper, H., 104
The House Select Committee on
Assassinations (Baden), 134

Identification methods, 80
Inhalation injury, 71
Institute of Pathology, 115,
118–119
Iroquois Theater in Chicago, 81

Jamaica Plain neighborhood of
Boston, 41–42
Jentzen, J., 126
John F. K. (JFK), 131–137
Johnson, L., 74
Journalism, three-decade career, 2
Journal of American Pathology
(Moritz), 3, 146
*Journal of Criminal Law and
Criminology* (Ford), 141, 143

Karsner, H., 96
Kettering Laboratories in Cincinnati,
110

Lakeside Hospital in Cleveland,
        19–23, 29
Law enforcement agencies, 110
Law-Medicine Center, 117
    seminars, 118
Lawyers' Committee for Civil Rights
        Under Law, 146
LCCRUL, 146, 148
Leary, T., 37, 80
Lee, F. G., 41, 42, 59, 93, 103, 163
    crime scene models, 63
    *Nutshell Studies of Unexplained
        Death*, 60
    publicity for the new department,
        56
Legal Medicine and Pathology, 92
Legal medicine programs, 41
    at Duke University in North
        Carolina, 94
Lenkoe case, 152, 153
Lenkoe, J., 145–148, 152, 153
Los Angeles Times, 102–103
Lowenstein, A. K., 151, 152

The Magnificent Seven, 102
Magrath, G. B., 31
Massachusetts' coroner system,
        84–85
Massasoit Greyhound Association, 76
Mass-casualty investigations, 81
McAdoo, 102, 103
McGrath Library of Legal Medicine,
        41
Medical World News, 54, 132–134,
        146
Medico-legal issues, 94
Melody Lounge, 79
Mercy killing, 88, 89
Morales, P., 103
Moritz, A.
    academic program, 51
    animal doping, 75–76
    ballistics, 142
    burn studies, 70–76
    Classical Mistakes, 126–129
    Cocoanut Grove nightclub, 79–82
    college and medical school, 10–13
    conversations with Schroeder, 116

death investigation seminar, 82
    experimental observations, 12
    expert in death investigations,
        110–112
    family curse, 124–125
    family mystery, 122–125
    at Harvard Medical School, 53, 66
    history, 4–7
    honorary Texas citizen, 131
    Institute of Pathology, 118–119
    medical education, 13
    military service for college, 11
    Noxon case, 84, 85
    resignation, 96–99
    thermal trauma, 70
    wartime research, 70
Moritz, A. B., 123
Moritz, G. R., 4, 6–7
Moritz, V., 38, 39, 108
Moritz formula, 140–143
Morize, A., 157
The Murders in the Rue Morgue
        (Poe), 102
Mystery Street (Metro-Goldwyn-
        Mayer feature film), 102,
        103

National Association of Medical
        Examiners, 127, 165
National Defense Research
        Committee, 72
National Research Council (NRC),
        31, 70, 73, 163
Nazi Party, Germany, 46–50
Nazi persecution of Austrian Jews,
        48
Neff, J., 109
New Bedford (Massachusetts)
        Standard-Times (Moritz),
        157
New England Journal of Medicine
        (Moritz), 22
New Hampshire Medical Referees,
        57
"A New Method for the Examination
        of Markings on Bullets,
        Shell Cases and Breech
        Faces" (Moritz), 142

New York City World's Fair, 1939–
    1940, 56
New York's Attica Correctional
    Institution, 136
New York Times, 84, 104
No One to Blame, 149
Noxon, J. F. Jr., 84–89
Noxon, L., 84–89
NSMR, 73
*Nutshell Studies of Unexplained
    Death* (Lee), 60

The Ohio Story (Waldrop), 117
Omaha riot, 15

Pathology of Trauma (Moritz), 42,
    81, 117
Perry Mason, 104–108
Pinanki, A. E., 87
Poe, E. A., 102
The Police Journal (Moritz), 142
Prater, 25, 27
Public enlightenment, 62
Pusey, N. M., 99

Quick friendships, 19

Racing Commission, 76
Rand Daily Mail (Johannesburg
    newspaper), 151
*Recent Advances in Forensic
    Medicine* (Moritz), 142
Red Summer, 1919, 15–18
Reeves, G., 110, 111
Renwick Gallery of the Smithsonian
    American Art Museum, 64
Revere Racing Association, 76
Ringling Brothers, 81

Rockefeller, N., 136–137
Rockefeller Foundation, 31, 32, 34,
    35, 52, 63, 93, 163

Schallert, E., 103
Schroeder, O., 29
Scientific crime detection, 33
Sheppard, S., 109–110
Sherlock Holmes of forensic
    medicine, 1
Smith, E. P., 16
Suffolk County, 52

Taunton Greyhound Association, 76
Three-decade career in journalism, 2
18 Tiny Deaths (Goldfarb), 103
*Transactions of the American
    Therapeutic Society*
    (Moritz), 74

US Army Institute of Surgical
    Research Burn Center, 74
US Army Medical Corps, 70
US Chemical Warfare Service, 71
US National Archives & Records
    Administration's *Prologue*
    magazine, 75

Vienna, 24–28

Western Reserve University, 61, 104,
    115
    Institute of Pathology, 23, 30, 34,
    73, 96
Westwood Memorial Cemetery
    mausoleum, 111
Wolbach, S. B., 40
The Wrong Man (Neff), 109